Dear Reader:

The book you are  St. Martin's True Crime Library, what *Publishers Weekly* calls "the leader in true crime." Each month we offer you fascinating accounts of the latest, most sensational crimes that have captured the national attention. St. Martin's is the publisher of John Glatt's riveting and horrifying SECRETS IN THE CELLAR, which shines a light on the man who shocked the world when it was revealed that he had kept his daughter locked in his hidden basement for 24 years. In the Edgar-nominated WRITTEN IN BLOOD, Diane Fanning looks at Michael Petersen, a Marine-turned-novelist found guilty of beating his wife to death and pushing her down the stairs of their home—only to reveal another similar death from his past. In the book you now hold, KILLING FOR YOU, Keith Elliot Greenberg documents the case of an actor who thought he had performed the perfect murder.

St. Martin's True Crime Library gives you the stories behind the headlines. Our authors take you right to the scene of the crime and into the minds of the most notorious murderers to show you what really makes them tick. St. Martin's True Crime Library paperbacks are better than the most terrifying thriller, because it's all true! The next time you want a crackling good read, make sure it's got the St. Martin's True Crime Library logo on the spine—you'll be up all night!

Charles E. Spicer, Jr.
Executive Editor, St. Martin's True Crime Library

KILLING
for
YOU

**A Brave Soldier,
a Beautiful Dancer, and a
Shocking Double Murder**

KEITH ELLIOT GREENBERG

St. Martin's Paperbacks

ACKNOWLEDGMENTS

Writing a true crime book is always challenging, since the details are so painful and the questions often intrusive. Steve and Raquel Herr never wanted to become public figures. Nor could they have imagined that the son they cherished would lose his life in such a shocking manner—particularly after he survived the war in Afghanistan. As they struggled to make sense of the tragedy and navigate the justice system, their privacy was invaded on many levels. Yet, their innate goodness allowed them to welcome me into their home and treat me as a friend, even when I was forced to bring up topics that should have been confined to the family. I'm gratified not only by their cooperation, but their camaraderie. Despite everything they suffered, they were still able to be hospitable, generous, and fun. I hope I've treated them with kindness and respect, and that we can still enjoy Mexican food and tell stories when I visit California.

I am also grateful to the Costa Mesa Police Department. Even when they were not at liberty to discuss the fine points of the case, investigators never misled me. Ultimately, they painted the picture I needed to appreciate the efforts made to secure justice for both the Herr and Kibuishi families. In particular, I'd like to thank Lieutenant Ed Everett for his insights and assistance.

When I started researching this book, no one had any idea that we would have to wait more than five years for the case of Daniel Wozniak to come to trial. At times, I worried that this project might never be completed. However, my family—Jennifer, Dylan, and Summer—encouraged me, and I hope the dignity I've tried to convey to the victims makes them proud.

The long waiting period between the crime and the trial created a good deal of anxiety for the staff at St. Martin's Press, and I appreciate them remaining committed to the project. Special thanks goes to executive editor Charles Spicer, associate editor April Osborn, managing editor John Rounds, copy editor Barbara Wild, text designer Meghan Day Healey, jacket designer Jeremy Fink, marketing manager Martin Quinn, marketing team leader Paul Hochman and publicist Justin Velella.

After meeting the Hathcock family, owners of the ill-fated Liberty Theater, I came away admiring their dedication to creating a family atmosphere around the dramatic arts, and sympathizing with the way these crimes blackened that dream. And I'm indebted to Chelsea Smith—who I met in New York when she was doing a reading for a play my friend, Mike Sheehan, wrote about his crazy uncles—for reaching into her own past in Orange County and putting me in contact with friends who danced with and loved Juri Kibuishi.

It's not a nice thing to do. People wouldn't understand. . . . What I mean is, well, this is developing into a very bad habit.

—Mortimer Brewster, lead character
in *Arsenic and Old Lace*

PROLOGUE

If the police were going to arrest Dan Wozniak, they could have waited. Waited until after the wedding and the honeymoon. The strapping actor was in the midst of the busiest week of his life, and sitting in an interview room at the Costa Mesa Police Department was a serious inconvenience.

But, really, Dan had no choice but to go along with the police after they'd barged into his bachelor party and made a whole dramatic scene by placing him in handcuffs in front of his friends. As bachelor parties went, it had been a pretty tame gathering, just a bunch of guys hanging out at a suburban Japanese restaurant, eating sushi and drinking saki. Dan had been a lumbering presence in his Hawaiian shirt and khakis, telling stories the way he always did and chortling loudly. But the other patrons hadn't minded. With his trimmed, brown beard and large, blue eyes, Dan was pleasant to behold, genial, if not a bit affected and stagy. Certainly, no one would have taken him for the person whose face would stare out at the public from newspaper covers and television shows, described alternately as a conniving sociopath and callous predator.

Certainly the detectives flanking Dan weren't treating him like a criminal. While Dan enunciated his sentences, and spoke in a solemn timbre that suggested that all he wanted to do was help them, the investigators smiled and nodded at the suspect, fetching him water and acting as if they related to his predicament.

"Before we can actually talk to you," Dan was told, "I have to read you your rights."

Wozniak didn't seem worried. "I'll tell you anything you want to know."

Although he had never made the quest some forty miles north to ply his trade in Hollywood, Dan appeared contented in his accomplishments on the stages of Orange County. He and his fiancée had recently completed a run of the play *Nine* at the Hunger Artists Theatre Company in the town of Fullerton. Daniel had received glowing reviews for his virtuosity in the lead role, while his girlfriend, Rachel Mae Buffett, played one of his innumerable love interests.

Rachel was a cute, button-nosed blonde who looked every bit like the homeschooled Christian girl she'd been. She'd even found work in Disneyland, playing a storybook princess to the squeals of young visitors. The problem was that there were a lot of girls in Southern California who looked like Disney princesses. And, as much as local theater audiences appreciated Dan Wozniak, the couple couldn't really pay their bills. Recently, investigators would learn, Rachel had been perusing the Internet in search of topless dancer jobs that might yield some crumpled tens and twenties. It was the same night that she and Dan had appeared in a rendition of *Nine*—the night that a body was found in the apartment downstairs.

That was the reason that police had come into the Japanese restaurant, waving their badges and patting down the guest of honor. There was the suspicion that the affable actor might know something about the dead girl in his neighbor's apartment.

In the interview room, Dan insisted that he hadn't had any dealings with a corpse. But, since they were being completely frank with one another, there were a few details, he admitted, that he'd neglected to tell the police.

"Now, I have a quick question," he started. "If I disclose to you something that was wrong, to my standing, can you use that against me?"

The detectives seated closest to Dan drew a breath.

"Not related to what happened," Dan added quickly, sweeping a hand to the side for emphasis.

"Are you talking about lying to us?"

"No, this is something completely—An illegal act, an idea, the whole thing started because of an illegal act"—Dan shook his head from side to side—"that I . . ." He breathed in and considered his next word.

"Well, why don't you just tell us?" the detective urged in a warm, empathetic tone. "Just tell us. I can't tell you until you actually tell—"

Dan spoke over the investigator, holding up his palms and shaking his fingers. "You know. I don't care." He folded his hands and leaned into them, then separated his fingers. "Here it is."

What followed was a long, convoluted tale about not the dead body, but a scheme that he claimed to have launched to procure some desperately needed funds.

His partner, he said, was a resident of his building, the same downstairs neighbor in whose apartment the cadaver had been located. Interestingly, the neighbor had also been missing since shortly before the discovery of the dead girl. Detectives patiently listened as Dan assured them that the purpose of the plot had never been to perpetrate violence but to generate cash. It was a relatively harmless endeavor, Wozniak said, and, when it was over, he was excited that he'd finally raised enough revenue to pay off his debts.

"I said . . . , 'Everything's set,'" Dan stated at the conclusion of the yarn. "'All squared. We got away with murder.'"

Catching himself, he quickly shut his eyes and brought his fingers up to his face, moving his head from side to side. "Sorry," he muttered. "Bad pun." He coughed out a short laugh. "Bad, *bad* pun."

Within days, police would find the severed head of the missing neighbor in a nearby nature center. But, right now, detectives had yet to learn anything about that. All they knew was that they hardly believed anything that Wozniak was telling them.

CHAPTER ONE

On the fifth anniversary of the day his son was murdered, Steve Herr did what he normally does, taking a brisk, sloping, one-mile walk past the housing developments and shade trees in Anaheim Hills, a planned community some fifteen miles from Disneyland. Since the crime, Steve's hair had whitened. But it might have anyway, and there were few other outward signs that betrayed what he'd endured.

Fit and tan, the former Marine was spirited and fun, his gray-blue eyes sparkling when he told a story or sent a friend a goofy video on YouTube. In his home, he invited visitors to use his exercise equipment and try his food. The graciousness came naturally. But the support network that had been built around Steve and his Argentinean-born wife, Raquel, enabled him to maintain it. Almost daily, the couple received messages from the guys and girls who'd served with their son, Samuel Eliezer Herr, in Afghanistan and partied with him near their base in Germany.

In the Army, Sammy had nicknames for a number of

his friends. Five years after Sam's death, Steve affectionately referred to the group as "the knuckleheads."

Sam's teen years had been a struggle. He'd drifted from his parents and had issues with the law. But he'd learned from his mistakes, and the military had instilled the young man with confidence, maturity, and purpose. At the time of his death—a week before his twenty-seventh birthday— Sam and his father were best friends. They each had tattoos commemorating their service to their country and regularly worked out together. The pair lived less than a half hour away from each other, with Sammy residing in a palm tree–laden apartment complex in the town of Costa Mesa, where he swam, hung out in the hot tub, and made new friends. He was more focused than ever before, talking about marrying Katharina, the girl he'd met while stationed in Germany with the 173rd Airborne, and attending classes at Orange Coast College in case he decided to reenlist as an officer.

After his walk, Steve rewarded himself with a cookie, a small indulgence considering what he intended to do next. With Raquel indoors nursing a cold, he cut through the muggy air, stepped into his car, and cranked up the airconditioning. Then, he drove east on California 91 toward Riverside Cemetery, a 921-acre sanctuary dedicated to the interment of U.S. military personnel and their spouses.

It was a ritual that the Herrs tried to repeat every week. But this day carried a special burden. As he stepped onto the grounds and approached the gravesite, Steve stared at the dates etched into the stone and felt a mixture of melancholy and anger, knowing that he and Raquel would be returning in eight days to mark their son's thirty-second birthday.

With Memorial Day coming, Steve made sure to bring a few flags to the grave, along with flowers. He noted that other Jewish people generally avoided the floral garnishment, placing a simple stone on their relatives' graves. Flowers withered and died, the logic went, while stones were eternal. But there was a joylessness in the custom that Steve didn't like. Sammy *deserved* flowers. Plus, with the grave embedded in the lawn, the lawn mowers would eventually kick the stones away.

It was only when the flowers were in place that Steve was able to relax. He'd honored his son, and thought of the happy times and the love that they had shared for each other. It felt good, knowing how close they'd truly been. Just being there, with Sam's remains, created a sense of peace. Before returning to the car, Steve removed his phone and snapped a photo to show his wife.

Later, the two went out for lunch at El Cholo, a Mexican restaurant in the entranceway of an Anaheim shopping plaza. To aid in the recuperation from her illness, Raquel ordered a hot bowl of Albondigas soup, a combination of meatballs, vegetables, and herbs, while joking merrily with Fausto, the waiter, in Spanish. Even Steve threw in a word or two, amusing his wife and Fausto with pronunciations that divulged a childhood spent not in Buenos Aires or Tierra del Fuego but an industrial section of New Jersey.

When the order was completed, Fausto walked away, never reading the pain that his customers carried. Reaching into his pocket, Steve showed his wife the photo he'd taken at the cemetery: a plaque flanked by American flags and flowers, with the words "Samuel Eliezer Herr, PFC Afghanistan, May 29, 1983–May 21, 2010. 'Til We Meet Again, Our Precious Sam."

Raquel stared at the image on the small screen and appeared to grow content. "I believe my son is alive in heaven," she said. "I really know that, and I know I'm going to meet him again."

Steve's lips curled. "We have a whole different perspective, obviously."

While the tragedy had turned Raquel more spiritual, Steve viewed himself as a realist whose mission it was to bring Sammy justice. It was a daunting and aggravating task. In the five years since their only child had been lured to a theater, shot, and beheaded, the man whom the authorities held responsible, thirty-one-year-old Daniel Patrick Wozniak—a local actor who charmed acquaintances, sang karaoke, and taught theater classes to children—had yet to go to trial. "It's a travesty," Steve said, the skin tightening around his face. "It's shocking. It's ludicrous. I have literally been to court more than one hundred times." By his estimation, he'd attended seventy hearings for Wozniak, and at least thirty for others associated with the case. "They put our family through this, and every time it's postponement, postponement, postponement."

During each session, Steve made it a point to look straight at Wozniak. Invariably, the grieving father received a nod and, from time to time, the actor's thousand-watt smile. Steve never believed that the defendant was mocking him. After five years, the pair had seen each other so much that they enjoyed a dysfunctional familiarity. This despite the assertion that, after he'd killed Sam and hidden the body in the attic of the theater, Wozniak had murdered another member of their social network, Juri "Julie" Kibuishi, scrawled vile messages on her body, and tried to imply that the still-missing veteran was responsible for the crime.

It was all very confusing, and, in an effort to understand the precise circumstances of Sam's demise, Steve had even visited Wozniak in jail. Viewing each other through the Plexiglas, they chatted guardedly but with a surprising degree of decorum. Still, Wozniak and his defense team knew that Steve Herr was never going to feel compassion or sympathy for the accused. In interview after interview,

Steve declared that he would settle for nothing less than Wozniak's execution.

"I get so angry about what happened," said Leah Sussman, Sammy's first cousin who viewed him as a brother. "It's more than just what happened. It's the absence of family. [Wozniak] . . . took away somebody who my daughter loved, who I was looking forward to being in my daughter's life and my life."

The fact that Wozniak hadn't been tried, much less sentenced, filled Steve with fury. Another man might have fallen. Fortunately for the Herrs, there were loving relatives and friends from Sam's Dark Horse military unit around to catch them.

Back at home, Steve and Raquel took solace in the posts on a Facebook page called "Sam's Buddies." Sitting at a laptop, the two were surrounded by signs of Sam's accomplishments in the military: a National Defense Service Medal, Afghanistan Campaign Medal with two campaign stars, Army Service Ribbon, Overseas Service Ribbon, Parachutist Badge, Combat Action Badge, NATO Medal, and other awards. One friend, Adam Zierer, posted a photo of the large tattoo on his arm dedicated to Sam. Nathan Ray, who'd chosen Samuel as his son's middle name, simply wrote: "Miss you, brother." George Clouse remembered, "You were fearless on the battlefield, a great friend to many people and touched many lives. Your memory lives on through your Airborne brothers."

Larry "Gonzo" Gonzales offered a photo of himself and Sam in Germany, holding plates of the Turkish *döner* kebabs sold near the base, describing his late friend as "not a brother by blood, but . . . a brother by Dark Horse comraderie. . . . Sammy, you asked me to never leave and disappear like a lot of people do when they get out. I'm still here, brother, still sharing the stories. . . . This is a special honor for me, and I'd like to introduce Samuel Herr into my family Hall of Fame."

Commented one mutual associate: "I still remember all the food binges and hard workouts like it was yesterday. RIP, brother."

Said another, "Thanks, Gonzo. Now, I miss Sam AND *doners*."

The reminiscences heartened Steve and Raquel, and they read them repeatedly, secure in the reputation that Sam had left behind. But there was another post on the page—the first one, in fact—tempering the pleasant thoughts with the harsh pragmatism of the current situation.

It had been written by Steve himself, at 10:30 the previous night:

"It's been five years since Sam and Julie were brutally murdered. Shame on the California justice system. Shame on Scott Sanders, the murderer's defense lawyer. Dan Wozniak, rot in hell."

CHAPTER TWO

Saturday, May 22, 2010

When Steve hadn't heard from his son for more than twenty-four hours he got in his car and drove.

Sammy always stayed in touch. Even in the Army, even in the war zone, Sammy managed to send messages to his family. He might not provide coordinates or specify the type of danger his unit faced, but Sam never vanished for long. Regardless of his circumstances, he made sure that his parents knew that he cared about them and he was okay.

The disappearance was even more confusing because Sam was supposed to have come to his parents' home for the weekend. Steve couldn't understand why his son had neglected to show up. Sam could be a wild guy if he was out in a club with his friends, but he wouldn't blow people off—especially his parents.

It was dark when Steve pulled into the Camden Martinique apartments and found a spot in the parking lot abutting 2855 Pinecreek Drive. Sam didn't turn off his phone. If he had lost the device, Steve knew, he'd borrow a friend's. He'd text or e-mail. He wouldn't evaporate. As

Steve climbed the stairs toward Apartment D110, he wondered if he'd walk in to discover a perspiring Sam in bed, wrapped in sheets, fighting off a cold. But even then, he would have called to say that he was too sick to talk and they'd speak again when the illness passed.

Steve stuck the spare key he carried into the door and let himself into the apartment. The lights were on, and Steve had the sense that someone was there.

"Sammy?"

And that's when he realized that something really bad had occurred. As he entered the bedroom, he saw a slim young woman with long jet-black hair kneeling, her torso on the bed, her knees bent on the carpeted floor. Her jeans were ripped from the rear and pulled down to just above her knees. Her top was still on, and something was scrawled across her back in black marker:

FUCK YOU

Bewildered as well as frightened, Steve noticed that there was blood in the room, too. And, even more horrifying, on the side of the woman's head Steve detected what he knew was a gunshot wound.

As he cautiously leaned forward to examine the woman's face, Steve's heart skipped. It was Juri Kibuishi, the cheerful twenty-three-year-old Japanese-American student who'd been tutoring Sam in anthropology. The two attended Orange Coast College together, about a mile away. Sam and most of their mutual friends generally referred to Juri by her Americanized name, Julie. A talented dancer, Julie was a bit of a character who accessorized herself with colorful eye shadow and told comical stories about her mistakes and misadventures. Steve himself had spent time with her and immediately picked up on her innate kindness and positive energy. But what was she doing in Sam's apartment? And why was her body exposed like that? Steve took pride in the fact that his son told him virtually everything. And he knew that Julie was Sammy's good friend and nothing more.

Sammy?

Where was Sammy? Steve searched the apartment, called his son's name, but, deep down, understood that Sam couldn't possibly be there. Not with Julie in that kind of position. Maybe he'd gone after the person who did it. Maybe he'd left to find help. Both father and son viewed themselves as men who could take charge of virtually any situation. But not this one. A young woman was dead, and Sam was nowhere to be found.

Just after 9:00 P.M., Steve called 911. "There's a body in my son's apartment . . . a dead body," he said frantically.

The operator asked if Sam could identify the victim.

"He's not here," Steve replied, his voice rising and anxious.

Before officers could arrive, another person appeared. Like Steve, Jake Swett, a fellow resident of the Camden Martinique apartments, said that he'd been unable to contact Sam. They'd had plans earlier in the day and, when Jake hadn't heard anything, he walked over to the apartment several times and knocked. Now he spotted the door slightly ajar and entered, he said, expecting to find Sam. Instead, he was met by Steve.

Immediately Steve noticed that Jake had alcohol on his breath and didn't want him entering the bedroom—to protect both Julie's dignity and the integrity of the crime scene. There was a moment of uncertainty. Steve didn't know Swett and wondered if he had something to do with the murder. And it took Jake a few minutes to realize that Steve was Sam's father and not an intruder.

Ushering Jake into the hallway, Steve decided to wait for the police alone. The initial responders arrived at 9:20.

As soon as they realized what had occurred, they called for backup and alerted the Costa Mesa Police Department to apply for a warrant to search the apartment. Det. Jose Morales was designated the lead investigator.

Morales had been at a communion party that day with two of his children. "We were out there with a clown and were doing the cake thing and all the kid stuff," he said. He'd just put his children to sleep and was ready to go to bed himself when the phone rang.

"We need you to come in. We have a homicide."

It was close to midnight when he entered Sam's building. The apartment was cordoned off with yellow tape, and an officer was stationed at the scene, keeping a log of those coming and going. Juri's purse was still on the dinner table bench. Morales surmised that she'd innocently placed it there upon entering the apartment, oblivious to how the visit would end.

In the bedroom, her body had yet to be moved. Morales moved in close to the cadaver and made his own observations. "We are looking at the back of her sweater," he'd later testify. "There is a tear in the sweater. It is a long-sleeve sweater, and the words 'ALL YOURS, FUCK YOU' written on the back of it in what appeared to be to us in black marker."

There was still no sign of Sam. Steve claimed he didn't know the whereabouts of his son, and neither did any of the neighbors.

Judging the scene at face value, investigators concluded that Sam Herr was their primary suspect.

CHAPTER THREE

Steve Herr told police the same thing that he told every-one else: he knew Sammy was innocent of the crime. He was sure of it because he and his son were as close as brothers.

"We were the best of buddies," Steve said. "Sam and I confided in each other about everything. *Everything.* Up until the day he was murdered, we worked out at least once a week together. I worked twelve miles from where he lived, so after work, I'd go over there, and then, we'd go to Twenty-Four Hour Fitness, go out to dinner, and just hang out together."

The relationship was starkly different from the one Steve had with his father. He was born in the Bronx, the son of a clothes cutter in New York's Garment Center.

"My dad loved me," Steve said. "I knew that. But he never shared much with me, and he died at a young age, so I didn't get to know him further. And I remember swearing—making a note to myself—that my son would know me backwards and forwards."

Although Steve's parents had both been born in the United States, their home had an immigrant flavor. All four of Steve's grandparents were Yiddish-speaking immigrants—from Ukraine on his mother's side and Austria-Hungary on the Herr side of the family. When the adults wanted to exclude the children from the conversation, they'd switch to Yiddish.

"If it was in Yiddish," he'd recount, "it usually wasn't good."

By the time Steve was a teenager, the family had relocated to Freehold, New Jersey, close to the oldest racetrack in the United States. There was a familiarity in the way everyone's father struggled to support his family, and Steve remembers the blue-collar spirit bonding the students at Freehold High School. Of everyone he knew, though, the one person who expressed the mood best was a fellow pupil named Bruce Springsteen.

"He was a year behind me in school," Steve said. "I knew him well."

Sometimes, Bruce was among the group of kids who cut school with Steve. Other times, Steve watched Bruce perform with his band, the Castiles, alongside other friends such as George Theiss, Vince Manniello, and Bart Haynes, who'd later be killed by mortar fire near Quang Tri in South Vietnam.

Reportedly, Haynes hated the scenes of horror he'd witnessed in Vietnam. But Steve was excited when he joined the Marines in 1967; he attributes his enthusiasm to "John Wayne syndrome." Unlike Sam, Steve never saw active combat but gained a great deal from the valuable life experience of being around the other servicemen.

"I wasn't as screwed up as I thought I was," he said. "When you're out of your hometown, and you meet guys from all over the country, you realize you're not as bad as you thought you were, that you have more potential to accomplish things in your life. It was an epiphany for me."

Upon his release in 1970, he took advantage of the GI Bill and attended college, first Brookdale Community College in Lincroft, New Jersey, then Monmouth College in West Long Branch. While in the Marines, he'd experienced the West Coast while stationed at Camp Pendleton and Twentynine Palms in California and become fond of its slower pace. After initially teaching in New Jersey, he relocated to the LA area and began a junior high school career that lasted a quarter century.

It was at Olive Vista Junior High School in Sylmar that he met a Spanish teacher named Raquel.

The two shared a similar background. Raquel's parents were Jewish refugees from Germany who'd charted the rise of Adolf Hitler and tried gaining admission to the United States. When Argentina accepted them instead, they moved to South America.

In 1960, Raquel picked up a newspaper and examined a photo on page 1. It featured Adolf Eichmann, the SS lieutenant colonel charged with being one of the chief engineers of Hitler's "Final Solution"—the total extermination of European Jewry. Israel's intelligence agency, the Mossad, had recently found him in a Buenos Aires suburb and smuggled him back to Jerusalem, where he was eventually tried and hung.

Raquel studied Eichmann's benign smile, long nose, and large ears and instantly recognized him. In Buenos Aires, he'd painted her house. Eichmann always claimed that he never had a personal issue with Jews and was simply following orders. Certainly, no one in Raquel's family sensed that, had they remained in Germany, the polite housepainter would have shipped every member of the clan to the death camps.

Like many Argentinean Jews, Raquel studied in Israel. But after a year or so in the Holy Land, she opted to immigrate to the United States rather than return to South America.

In 1979, eleven months after their first conversation, Steve and Raquel married. It was the second marriage for both.

Sam was born on May 29, 1983. Raquel was thirty-five at the time, and both teachers were established in their careers. Very quickly the two decided that Sam would be an only child. "She said her childbirth was miserable, and she literally screamed, 'No más. No más.'" It was the same phrase boxer Roberto Durán had shouted at the conclusion of his rematch with Sugar Ray Leonard three years earlier. "If you're a boxing fan, you'll understand what I'm talking about."

From the beginning, Steve felt an unconditional commitment to his son. "I could never understand how fathers, after they get divorced, can ever leave their children and not be part of their lives," he said. "To me, that is the lowest kind of person, the lowest kind of man."

Although Sam lacked siblings, there were close relatives willing to fill the void. His cousin Leah Sussman, the daughter of Steve's sister, was eleven and a half years older and had grown to view the Herrs as a second set of parents. But that was the way the family was structured. Steve and his two sisters talked twice a day. And Raquel and her twin sister, Miriam, spoke even more.

Every other weekend, Leah and her brother spent time with her uncle Steve and the aunt she called Raqi, sometimes hiking in Newhall, a vast rustic area on the northern edges of Los Angeles County. "I can't even explain the importance of my uncle Steve in my life," she said. "He was the coach of my T-ball teams. He was the coach of my football teams.

"When Sammy came into the picture, I was, of course, a little jealous. But I was grateful to have a little cousin. He was always 'Sammy' to me, never 'Sam.' And as he got a little older, I could see that he was a lot like my uncle Steve, a very friendly, very silly, very macho but kind of a big teddy-bear type of guy. I think that's why he joined the military, as well. Both of them have a sense of duty to family, to country."

While he was stationed in Afghanistan, Sam and Leah remained close. Every morning when she woke up, there was usually an e-mail from her cousin. When he couldn't communicate that way, he'd tell his German fiancée to send Leah a message on Facebook. "That's just how he was," Leah said.

At home, Steve encouraged Raquel to teach their son Spanish. But after instructing a room full of unruly pupils all day, Raquel had little patience to begin yet another Spanish lesson. Plus—despite Raquel's ability to also converse in German and Hebrew—the family communicated in English, except when she had something private to convey to Steve.

"I guess I understood enough Spanish to get the gist of what Raqi was trying to say," he recollects. In some ways, Spanish was used the way Yiddish had been employed in Steve's childhood home.

Because of his background as a coach, Steve tried introducing Sam to a number of team sports. Although the boy liked roller hockey, his favorite competitions involved contests in which he could thrive independently: track, jiu-jitsu, and weight training.

"He was very sort of macho, even as a child," Leah said. "We'd wrestle and he'd *like* when I'd beat him up. He'd *ask* me to beat him up. But when the day came when he was clearly able to beat *me* up, he never really did. He knew he was stronger, but he would just tickle me and stuff."

At that point, Sam would occasionally ask his cousin to intercede with his parents when they appeared to be intractable on a particular issue. "I remember he wanted a Stone Temple Pilots tape," Leah said, "and he asked if I'd talk to my aunt Raqi, and see if I could persuade her. She's a bit conservative, and she didn't like the vulgar language. He'd always come to me because he knew how close I was with her. But his parents' rules were his parents' rules and I told him, 'Nope. There's no persuading her.'"

By and large, Sam followed his parents' directives. At school, though, he bristled when confronted by authority. "Most of us guys, we become teenagers, our horns sprout out, our fangs grow," Steve said. "We tend to break off. When he got to be sixteen, he didn't want much to do with us."

Despite the affection that they had for one another, the Herrs faced the same challenges as any family. According to a psychological report later introduced in court, Sam had been treated for bulimia and obsessive-compulsive disorder since age twelve but stopped both his medication and psychiatric treatment at sixteen years old.

At five foot ten and a muscular two hundred pounds, Sam was not someone who backed down from physical altercations. Although he was never in a gang himself, he had friends with gang affiliations. One was reportedly Byron Benito, a Guatemalan immigrant with a reputation as a street fighter. In January 2002, after an apparent rival of Benito's was shot to death, authorities said that Sam helped lure the nineteen-year-old to a deserted business park on Soledad Canyon Road on the eastern edge of Santa Clarita. There, police said, he was set upon by a mob that beat and punched him. The assault was so vicious that court records said that some of the attackers accidentally knifed each other.

Benito was also hit with a crowbar, prosecutors said,

and stabbed thirty-three times. He died of a stab wound to the lung.

Authorities called it the bloodiest gang fight ever in Santa Clarita, home to the Six Flags Magic Mountain amusement park, some thirty-five miles northwest of downtown Los Angeles. As it turned out, there was no evidence linking Benito to the earlier killing.

Eighteen people, including five juveniles, were accused of participating in the murder. Sam was eighteen at the time. He was close to Benito, police said, and knew his family. Along with another friend, Sam was accused of persuading the victim to come to the crime scene, under the pretense of smoking marijuana. Sam never struck Benito, a witness told prosecutors, but attempted to deceive him about setting up the ambush by pretending to fight with someone else.

When Los Angeles County Sheriff's Department deputies heard that Sam was the one who drove Benito to the industrial park, they began staking out his home. Sam drove by but didn't stop. He was followed by deputies, who reported that he was driving 37 miles per hour in a 25-mile-per-hour zone and failed to signal before he made a left turn. He was immediately pulled over and taken in for questioning.

His attorney later claimed that, during the twelve-hour interrogation, Sam's request for legal assistance was ignored while Steve and a lawyer were deliberately stalled outside the station. Furthermore, Sam should have never been pulled over, the attorney stated, because he'd been "driving prudently." A judge eventually agreed, ruling that the fingerprints, fibers, and other contents taken from Sam's car—as well as the statements that he made in police custody—should be excluded from the jury trial.

He was acquitted and cleared of any wrongdoing in the case.

But in between, he sat in a jail cell for the better part of a year, waiting for the wheels of justice to turn. About six months after his arrest, he was interviewed by Dr. Kaushal K. Sharma, a psychiatrist specializing in diagnosing criminal defendants. Sharma wrote that Sam was wearing a suicide prevention suit and spoke about thoughts of harming his parents—even though he professed to love them. To the psychiatrist, Sam appeared to be "mentally ill and in need of continued medication and treatment."

But was the assessment really accurate? Sam was a teenager from a loving family who was now locked up in jail, isolated from his parents, relatives, and other positive influences. That he felt hopeless should not have surprised anybody. Because of some bad choices, he'd reached his lowest point and shared his pessimistic sentiments with a mental health counselor—never imagining that the information would later be made public.

This was the one aspect of their son's life that Steve and Raquel were most hesitant to discuss. "We're kind of hedging between the two of us because it's a sore point," Steve said. "He was acquitted, totally acquitted. You've done your research on this. You know the past."

Yet Steve admitted thinking about the case later when he'd enter court for a hearing involving the man accused of murdering his son. "I've done both sides of this. You know what I'm saying? Sam was implicated with a gang, and got acquitted of that. We all knew he was innocent. And now, I'm sitting on the other side, so it's tough. No parent should have to go through that."

CHAPTER FOUR

"I never want to go back to jail again."

After his trial ended, Sam rekindled the closeness with his family that had been lacking during his later teens. "We always loved each other," Steve said. "That had never been the problem. But now, we both appreciated each other, and became real buddies—not father and son buddies, but men buddies."

Sam's devotion to his parents was reflected in a tattoo across his chest: the words "Mom and Dad" in a heart surrounded by roses. But the fidelity extended to other close relatives. "If you were a family member, that was it," said his cousin Leah. "You were automatically with him. And whatever your flaws were, he never saw them. You were his blood, and that was good enough for him."

After his acquittal, Sam worked for a delivery service; security company; and pet store, cleaning and grooming dogs. But he didn't see a career in any of those jobs. He'd grown up hearing his father and an uncle discuss the camaraderie they felt in the military, and a number of friends had enlisted and told Sam about the travel opportunities.

Over a two-year period, he gradually decided that the Army would be the best place for him.

"I'd love to say that he was motivated by patriotism," Steve said. "That was part of it. But it was also the allure of travel and adventure. He wanted something new."

Given his arrest record, though, he wasn't automatically welcomed. For several months, he made weekly visits to a recruiter, who monitored Sam's progress back in society, eventually determining that he possessed the type of character that the Army wanted.

Sam started basic combat training at Fort Jackson in South Carolina, followed by advanced training at the Aberdeen Proving Ground in Maryland, and jump school in Fort Benning, Georgia, gaining a new level of self-awareness with each step.

Prior to boot camp, Steve made his son a bet. If Sam could graduate, his father would do whatever the young man requested. Up until this point, Steve had never been tattooed, because his wife was not a particular fan of body art. But the first time that Sam came home on leave after finishing up at Fort Jackson, he took his father to a tattoo parlor and told Steve that it was time to get inked.

Steve chose a tattoo dedicated to his time as a U.S. Marine.

Raquel was the one member of the family who expressed caution about Sam's entry into military service. "You're an only child," she said. "Do you think if you tell them that, they won't send you to fight somewhere?"

Sam shook his head. "There's no way, Mom. I'm not going to do that. We're at war. I knew the consequences going in."

Assigned to the 173rd Airborne Brigade Combat Team, Sam spent a week at its base in Vicenza, Italy before being sent to Germany for four months of war training. One morning at the Conn Barracks, located in Schweinfurt—

German for "pig ford"—in Bavaria's Lower Franconia region, fellow soldier Theresa Glowicki was sitting in the backseat of a vehicle headed toward PT formation—a physical-training exercise—when Sam entered and introduced himself. He was wearing jeans and a sleeveless white T-shirt under a leather jacket. "He was so new," she recalled, "that he didn't have a uniform yet."

Theresa had been raised in Auburn, Michigan, a farming town with a population of just over two thousand. Like Sam, she joined the Army to travel, but she also hoped to earn money for her education. While Sam was learning generator repair, Theresa was a truck driver. Both knew that they were going to be deployed to Afghanistan and accepted that warfare came with the job. But Theresa was struggling in Germany. "Some units had like thirty or forty females," she said. "But I got stuck in this one unit with five. That was really hard for me. I grew up with all these females, and then I was thrown in with all these men, and they were all trying to get with me. I cried every night."

As soon as Sam learned about her situation, he vowed to make her time in Schweinfurt easier. He made her peanut butter and jelly sandwiches and accompanied Theresa and her roommate, Helen, to their door each night, his mere presence sending a message that the two young women were to be left alone. Then, he'd stand outside and watch them enter, not leaving until he knew that they were safe inside. "He looked out for me like I was his little sister," she said.

It would not be the last time that Sam would display this kind of courtesy to a fellow soldier. Remembered one Army friend, "Sam was the type of man who would give you the shirt off his back, and throw in his pants to lighten your mood."

In 2007, Sam and Theresa were sent to Afghanistan. Stationed at Camp Keating, a remote outpost near the border with Pakistan, Sam was part of a team that included Americans and Afghans. Sam would often be dispatched to mountaintop observation posts, sometimes for as long as six weeks at a time, to watch for infiltrations by the Taliban, as well as maintain the generators in the wilderness. Because of the rugged terrain, supplies had to arrive by helicopter.

Time after time, Sam volunteered for the most dangerous assignments. "He did not like sitting there on the [base] . . . and not doing enough," Theresa said. "He wanted to do the most he could while he was there. That's how he looked at it."

"He loved being in those dangerous situations," said his close friend and squad leader, Larry "Gonzo" Gonzales. "He felt as though he had a purpose being out in combat and was real comfortable with it."

His troop commander remembered Sam as a true warrior. Despite the harsh conditions, the commander noted, Sam thrived, operating independently while preserving a sense of humor and raising the standards of those serving alongside him.

At the same time, he maintained the suspicion of authority he'd exhibited in his teens. "He was pretty complicated," said Miles Foltz, a friend from Camp Keating, who joined the Army after watching the Twin Towers fall on television in his English class at Butte College in Oroville, California. "He was opinionated and didn't really get along with the upper chain of command. But he was very close to the lower enlisted guys, really loyal and dedicated. His guys, he'd do anything for them."

Said one fellow soldier, "He had the heart of a lion and the soul of a saint."

Located at the base of two steep mountains, Camp Keating was vulnerable to .50-caliber machine-gun and other heavy-gun fire. In the course of a typical day, Sam's unit was subject to mortar and rocket attacks, as well as random "potshots" from smaller weapons. "When you're in that kind of situation, getting attacked so often, it definitely brings everyone closer," Miles said. "You learn to trust one another. I mean, everyone just knew that it was a shitty situation. There was no other way around it. There's nothing we can do. We're going to get shot at."

Yet there were unexpected moments of repose. "We'd set up above the camp, a kilometer up the mountain," Miles said. "And basically, we'd be scanning the mountain ranges as much as we could, trying to stop the enemy from attacking us. But when you're up there together, away from everyone else, there's also a relaxing kind of downtime."

Supplies were transported by Russian pilots contracted by the U.S. military, who had no objection to delivering a bottle of vodka for a few extra dollars. One night, after Sam had been drinking and his instincts were not as sharp as usual, a mortar sailed directly toward him.

"Sam told me Miles pulled him down," Steve said. "Sam always said Miles saved his life."

At times, Miles, a cavalry scout, also helped Sam fix the generators. "My dad's a contractor, so I know a little bit about that. We had these shitty generators that were leftover stock from Vietnam. That's when I'd see Sam's temper. He'd get pretty frustrated working on those generators."

Even then, Miles frequently found an agitated Sam as entertaining as the guy who told jokes and good-naturedly teased his friends. "He was a big ox, basically Arnold Schwarzenegger without the accent. As his dad would call him, 'a big, dumb galoot.'"

Insulated from the opposite sex, Sam wrote home and asked Steve to send him magazines "with pictures of girls." Remembering the humor of his own time in the Marines, Steve instead mailed a Disney princess calendar.

Amidst the loneliness and the peril, Sam was developing a true sense of resolve. He posed for photos with his allies in the Afghan National Army, convinced that he was liberating them from an enemy who was keeping them mired in the primitive past. He handed out pens to children, believing that, as a member of the U.S. military, he was a vehicle toward helping them receive a modern education. "He was never as proud of what he was doing as when he was in that war zone," Steve said. "He talked about really accomplishing something. As a parent, we're always worried about our children. But I liked how the Army made him feel."

Finally, Sam could relate to the pride that his father experienced when he wore the uniform. "We all have our love of country, especially after 9/11," Steve said. "But now, he really understood what the concept meant. He never felt more like he was doing something than when he was in Afghanistan. And that's when he really came to appreciate the military."

But the U.S. Army could only counterbalance the Taliban for so long. In October 2009, insurgents attacked Camp Keating, killing eight American soldiers and wounding twenty-four. Although the Americans estimated that as many of one hundred of their enemies also died in the battle, momentum was on the side of the Taliban. The camp's generator had been hit, forcing the Americans to battle at night in darkness. Strong winds fanned fires throughout the base until every building in the camp was engulfed, except one. As the fighting continued over the next several days, the Army abandoned the base. Whatever remained of the outpost was deliberately destroyed in order to prevent it from falling into Taliban hands.

But this was one fight that Sam missed. By that point, he'd been gone from the Afghan highlands for more than a year, forsaking the mud-caked houses, pothole-rutted roads and stalls selling grapes, pomegranates, and apricots for the strip malls, planned communities, and apparent safety of Orange County, California.

CHAPTER FIVE

In total, Sam served in Afghanistan for fifteen months. When his tour was complete, he was sent back to Germany for his final eleven months in the military and finally had the opportunity to enjoy the travel he had envisioned when he signed up. Whenever he had a few days off, he and his friends would fly around Europe—to France, Spain, Italy, Holland, and the Czech Republic, among other locations.

"We'd be out in a bar together, and one of us would just name a city—Paris or Ibiza," said Miles Foltz. "And it was like, 'Fuck it. Let's go.'"

Sam had several cousins in Israel, and he and Miles traveled there. The journey lasted eleven days. It was 2009, and the Israeli government was battling guerillas from Hamas, a militarized group opposed to the occupation of Palestinian lands by the Jewish state. At one stage, Sam and Miles were driving outside of Tel Aviv when they heard the familiar sound of rocket fire. They tore down the highway, laughing hysterically.

"Look at this," Miles pointed out. "We're just out of a war zone, we're on vacation, and we're still getting rocketed."

Back in Germany, Sam's friends made frequent observations about his voracious appetite, particularly in the commissary. Squad leader Larry "Gonzo" Gonzales noted that the Army withdrew $250 every month from each soldier's paycheck, but Sam earned his money back in food. At night, he'd sometimes stack three trays on top of one another and cart them to his room.

Off-base, Sam became fixated with *döners*, Mediterranean-accented dishes featuring rotisserie-cooked lamb. Because of the large influx of Turkish immigrants to Germany, there were *döner* shops everywhere, and Sam wanted to try them all. Gonzo recalled Sam finishing his meal quickly—he was the only U.S. serviceman known to devour three *döners* in a row—then staring hungrily as his friend consumed his. Occasionally, Sam beseeched the proprietor to open a franchise in Orange County.

Even when Gonzo was working late, Sam could always convince him to go out to a club on Friday night. Sam generally bought the first few rounds of drinks and encouraged Gonzo to do the funky chicken or other ridiculous dances. When Gonzo complied, Sam seemed happier than he'd ever been.

For all the male bonding, Sam also developed a serious relationship with a German girl who lived close to the base. After he returned to the States in May 2009, he arranged for Katharina to join him and immediately introduced her to his parents. Although Raquel spoke German, Katharina addressed her in fluent English. Like Sam, Katharina was plain-spoken and fun. She seemed to enjoy herself in California but missed her family in Germany. Still, she'd visit Sam for weeks, and sometimes months, at a time.

Sam referred to her as his fiancée. They were in the process of figuring out where they'd ultimately live when Sam's life was cut short.

Because of all the time he'd spent at war, Sam had accumulated some sixty-two thousand dollars in combat pay and hoped to eventually purchase a house. In the interim, he didn't feel a great deal of financial pressure as he transitioned back to civilian life. He still missed the Army, as well as his friends who continued to serve. For the time being, though, he was staying put in Orange County.

Like many veterans, Sam struggled with night terrors, flashbacks to the war that occurred while he was sleeping. Yet he learned to cope with the condition and expected it to ease over time. The Army had taught Sam to rely on his own strength. Both physically and psychologically, he believed that he could handle anything.

Socializing had never been a problem for Sam. But he'd come back from his overseas tours with leadership qualities that drew even more people around him. Men considered him a "guy's guy." Women found him magnetic, witty, and chivalrous.

He was particularly proud of his attitude about gays in the military. He told his cousin Leah, who had come out as a lesbian, that—although the U.S. armed services still had a "don't ask, don't tell" policy while he was serving—he considered it his duty to look out for gay soldiers who might feel uncomfortable. Not long after Sam's return, he and Leah were walking with her small daughter, Sonia. After so much time abroad, Sam was enjoying his time with the relative he viewed as an older sister. Leah and her wife, Tanya, had named Sonia after the cousins' great-grandmother, and Sam was gratified by the link to the family's past. As they wandered down a pier overlooking the Pacific Ocean, the group spotted a homeless man approaching an attractive female. They couldn't hear the dialogue, but it was obvious that the vagrant wanted something. When the woman tried to walk away, the man became more demanding, blocking her path.

Sam didn't even hesitate before he intervened. "Man, listen," he said authoritatively as he stepped between the two. "You need to stand back."

The homeless man surveyed Sam for a moment and concluded that this was one confrontation that he didn't want. Sam nodded reassuringly at the woman as she walked away quickly.

"He handled it with grace," Leah said. "He was big and strong, and he used his size to make others feel safe."

By this point, Sam had moved into the Camden Martinique apartments in Costa Mesa, a series of stucco terraced buildings with adobe roofs, indistinguishable from hundreds of other apartment complexes in Southern California. There was a swimming pool and gymnasium, along with Jacuzzis and strategically placed laundry rooms. Given the proximity to Orange Coast College, there was a youthful feel to the development. "It was almost like a *Melrose Place* kind of thing," said one prosecutor, comparing the Camden Martinique apartments to the 1990s prime-time soap opera, "kind of a vibrant social scene."

"It's such a nice community," Daniel Wozniak said in an interview with police. "Everyone's friends."

On the surface, the verdant landscaping and generally sunny climate created an idyllic flavor. But all was not how it seemed. Every month, the assistant property manager would testify, residents of between seventy-five and one hundred apartments in the 714-unit complex received delinquency notices, warning them to make good on their late rent or risk eviction.

"Aesthetically, it looks nice," one resident complained to an author circulating on the grounds. "But last month, I had my motorcycle stolen. And now, I'm walking around trying to find the guy who got on my balcony and took my surfboard."

Having survived Camp Keating, Sam wasn't frightened of running into a surfboard thief. The Camden Martinique apartments were perfect for the lifestyle he was living. It was close to his parents and other relatives and even closer to Orange Coast College, where he was developing a fondness for political science. Once he earned his four-year degree, he'd be in an ideal position to reenter the military as an officer.

"You get more pay," Steve said, "and, obviously, more respect."

Very quickly Sam began befriending his neighbors, learning little snippets of their life stories. On the surface, Daniel Patrick Wozniak seemed to have some of the same outgoing qualities as Sam.

He was born one year after Sam, on March 23, 1984, and had lived in Orange County his entire life. Allyson Hathcock remembered meeting Dan at Los Alamitos High School, where he was one grade ahead of her. Both were in the choir, as well as the theater department. She recalled a tall, handsome, grinning student with a wardrobe consisting of a variety of Hawaiian shirts. "Real personable," she said. "Life of the party. He played the jester, but he was also very helpful."

The two appeared together in the musical comedy *Once upon a Mattress,* an adaption of the Hans Christian Andersen fairy tale "The Princess and the Pea." Dan was a junior, but he went out of his way to assist freshmen who were in the show and make them feel welcome. "Everybody knew him," she said. "Everybody liked him."

Because of their mutual interests, the two attended a number of the same parties, but, after graduation, Allyson lost touch with Dan until she'd graduated from college and he auditioned for a play at the theater her parents, Jeff and

Nancy, had opened on the Joint Forces Training Base, a military installation in Los Alamitos.

Despite the fact that Hollywood was so close by, Dan had remained local, attending California State University in Long Beach and majoring in drama. He'd been intrigued by the acting profession since childhood, characterizing himself in his MySpace description as a "nerd" who loved science-fiction and fantasy films. But he had wide-ranging tastes when it came to movies, and many of the cinematic choices he listed seemed to reflect his lighthearted public persona: *Willy Wonka and the Chocolate Factory, Ace Ventura: Pet Detective, Bill and Ted's Excellent Adventure, Airplane, Groundhog Day, Weekend at Bernie's, Animal House, Tommy Boy,* and *The Wedding Singer.*

His favorite books included the Bible, *The Da Vinci Code, The Hitchhiker's Guide to the Galaxy,* and—given the events that later transpired—two titles that appeared to provide insight into the way he thought and operated: *The Strange Case of Dr. Jekyll and Mr. Hyde* and *How to Win Friends and Influence People.*

Certainly, a stranger viewing his social media preferences would come away with the sense that, for all his quirks, Dan was an upstanding young man. He described his heroes as "God, my parents, the men and women in the military, and any single person in this world who is willing to take a stand and fight for what is right!"

Yet, in another entry, he wrote: "I'm a pretty easy going guy" with a penchant for getting "into some kind of trouble." He joked that his best friends would describe him as "deceitful, dishonest, egotistical and untrustworthy." He ranted about "how quickly the world can turn against you . . . Come on, face it, life will screw you over one way or another. My best advice to everyone is this: live each day of your life to the fullest as if it were your last!"

*   *   *

Sam didn't confine his new friendships to the apartment complex. Ruben Menacho met Sam on the first day of classes at Orange Coast College. Unlike Wozniak, Ruben and Sam seemed to have an unspoken understanding of each other.

Ruben had been born in Bolivia, and his family bounced back and forth between the United States and his home country throughout his childhood. Like Sam, he struggled to stay focused during his late teens. He attempted to attend college in Bolivia but spent more time drinking than studying. Returning to the United States, he realized that he needed discipline and joined the Marine Corps.

The two veterans were seated on opposite sides in their communications class when the teacher asked the students to describe their lives. Sam stood up and spoke about his experiences in the Army. Then, Ruben went.

"My name is Ruben Menacho," he began. "I'm a United States Marine."

Sam patiently listened to the impromptu speech before rising, crossing the room, and taking a seat at the desk adjoining Ruben's.

"From now on, you're stuck with me, buddy," Sam announced. "You're my friend now."

He wasn't joking. From that point forward, the two saw each other almost daily. Sam introduced Ruben to other friends, as well as Steve.

Ruben was impressed by the way Steve would show up at his son's apartment and just hang out, watching television and exchanging anecdotes with Sam's other friends. It seemed so natural. Sam's behavior didn't change around his father. Whatever Sam thought just came out of his mouth. And Steve was equally honest.

One day, when father and son were alone, the pair

launched into a discussion about death. "You're our only boy, our only child," Steve said. "The only thing I ask is that, when I'm gone, you take care of your mom."

"Why are you talking like that?" Sam replied. "You're one of the healthiest guys I know. Nothing's going to happen to you."

Steve nodded. "I know. I know. But listen, it's something to think about. You're a young man. I'm going to be going first."

Sam acknowledged his father's words. After the challenges of Sam's late teens and his encounters in the war zone, he was looking forward to a long, satisfying life.

CHAPTER SIX

The one friend of Sam's who could relate to the way he interacted with his family was Juri "Julie" Kibuishi. Although her Japanese-born parents seemed to be more proper than the free-spirited Juri, she clearly cherished them. When the family was together—Juri was the third of four siblings, and the first girl—her laugh infected everyone. While the elder Kibuishis might have questioned some of her unconventional decisions, they'd always encouraged her artistic impulses. Like Sam, she had a habit of checking in with her family and reminding her parents that she loved them.

Friends remembered dropping in at the Kibuishi home and seeing Juri and her mother on the couch raptly watching *Tabatha's Salon Takeover*, a reality show featuring salon owner Tabatha Coffey swooping in and saving failing beauty shops. And Juri was close with the rest of the family, as well. In fact, the last communication that she had before she died was with her brother Taka.

Steve and Raquel first met Juri when they stopped by their son's apartment and found her there, helping him study. Sam explained that Juri—a fashion student at Orange Coast College—was tutoring him in anthropology and he needed her help for an upcoming test.

Once the books were closed, the Herrs invited Juri to join the rest of the family for dinner. She was animated and drew people out. As with his friend Theresa in the Army, Sam, the only child, treated Juri like a sister. She had an open invitation to crash on his couch whenever she didn't feel like making the fifteen-minute drive back to her home in Irvine. To the Herrs, it was obvious that the relationship was strictly platonic. Regardless, Steve and Raquel were completely charmed.

"Julie and Sam—I didn't see much difference between the two of them," said Ruben Menacho. "They both talked to everybody. They had a lot of friends."

Juri's posts on MySpace, which had recently been overtaken by Facebook as the world's largest social media destination, provided a window into her personality. She listed her tastes as comedy and romance movies, poetry by Emily Dickinson and Pablo Neruda, the television shows *LA Ink, Project Runway,* and *Dancing with the Stars,* and music ranging from country, to jazz, to trance, house, and hard rock. There was also a tribute to the late King of Pop, Michael Jackson.

As carefree as she appeared, she also spoke about showing strength, despite adverse predicaments. "What doesn't kill you," she wrote, "only makes you stronger."

Her recommendations to online friends: "For beautiful eyes, look for the good in others. For beautiful lips, speak only words of kindness. And for poise, walk with the knowledge that you are never alone."

In her personal history, Juri emphasized the fact that she'd been born in Newport Beach on Valentine's Day, a coincidence that seemed to suit her world view. "She was a hopeless romantic," remembered her friend Natalie

Jameson Sommer. Having witnessed her parents' long marriage, Juri also hoped to find the perfect mate and raise a family.

In fact, she described her mood on MySpace as "in love." "I'm laid back, dorky, sweet, loving," she wrote.

Five years after the murder, childhood friend Jessica Wolf grinned at the memory of Juri's vigorous laugh. "I can still hear it," Jessica said. "It was kind of a cartoony, funny laugh. I can't even mimic it. It was a 'just explode' kind of laugh. She was kind of a goofy person—in the best way. I think of Julie and it makes me giggle.

"I don't have any bad memories about her. I can't think of any time when she made me feel anything bad. Nothing she did bothered me. And you can't say that about everyone. I could find twenty things about me I don't like. But she was just this good person."

When Jessica and Natalie decided to share their memories about Juri, they arranged a meeting at the Disneyland Hotel during the regional Showstopper competition, featuring performers from dance academies all over Orange County. It was a place where Juri would have felt at home. She met Jessica in the fifth grade at the Irvine Dance Academy, later the FOCUS Dance Center for the Performing Arts. Every year, the girls participated in the Showstopper regionals. At five foot three, Juri—a standout softball player as a child—was known as an athletic, creative dancer, hardworking and quick on her feet, particularly in tap.

"We spent a big portion of our lives growing up in the Disneyland Hotel," Jessica said as contestants simultaneously competed nearby in three separate ballrooms, each containing a trio of stages.

It was noisy in the lobby, so Jessica and Natalie led a visitor to an escalator. At the top, they instinctively turned a corner, then another, before settling in a quiet collection of couches just outside the Magic Kingdom Ballroom.

"We know all the nooks and crannies," Jessica explained.

"This is where we go and hide out," Natalie concurred.

For Juri and her friends, dance was not a hobby but a lifestyle. Some students began going to the studio at age three and continued through high school. "You train five to seven days a week with your teammates at a dance studio," Jessica said. "It's hard to describe to someone who isn't part of it."

"You go until eighteen, and then you go to college," Natalie said. "Most of us become a dance instructor or a professional dancer. I definitely went the teacher route, but Jessica did some dancing professionally."

During Disneyland's fiftieth-anniversary commemorations, Jessica appeared in the Parade of Dreams, performing on the theme park's Main Street. She also danced with Beyoncé in her "Run the World" music video. "Watch it on YouTube," Jessica suggested. "You'll see me. I'm the only blonde. I rep it for the white girls."

Removing her phone, Jessica displayed a photo of her, Juri, and a group of other girls at around twelve or thirteen, posing outside their dance studio. "I remember there was so much drama because we'd already been dancing all day and now we had to put on our costumes again and go up on this hill. And we were being yelled at to go up on this hill, and everyone was in a bad mood." She pointed at another female in the picture. "That's Julie's cousin, Cathy. She danced with us and Julie's little sister danced for a company called Jet. I remember seeing her sister dance a solo a couple of times." She stared at the photo. "We all danced together forever."

As an adult, Jessica would tell her students that their

dance friends would be the ones who'd end up in their wedding parties and babysitting their children. "You're just connected. In high school, you start to migrate to other studios, but you always know what everyone is doing. I'm way closer to my dance friends than any of my school friends.

"You live together. You're in rehearsals for hours, sweaty and running out after midnight to get food. It becomes such a family in a dance setting."

What makes the Orange County dance world distinct is the presence of Disneyland as a backdrop to virtually everything. Even outside the fences, children sit on their fathers' shoulders, watching the amusement park's fireworks display lighting up the night sky, some fantasizing about playing a character one day in a Disney movie. It's this dream that may have enticed Dan Wozniak to try out for high school musicals—and Juri to go to a specialized school to study dance.

Both Natalie and Juri attended the Orange County School of the Arts, then catering to high school students interested in the performing, visual, literary, and culinary arts. In order to gain acceptance to the dance department, both were required to pass an audition.

"She was beautiful; she was graceful; she was strong; she was emotional," Juri's high school jazz instructor, Cindy Peca-Dolan, would tell ABC News. "Julie's kindness was really immeasurable. . . . She was very warm and talented and compassionate . . . very fun to watch onstage."

A year apart in school, Natalie and Juri lost touch after Juri graduated. But when they saw each other again at Orange Coast College their friendship became stronger than it had ever been.

As a fashion major, Juri hoped to find an internship at an Orange County action-sports company, like Quicksilver, which specialized in surfwear, among other items. But she continued to take dance seriously. In between classes, she and Natalie would chat and joke together outside the dance room. Occasionally, Juri invited Natalie for frozen yogurt or to her home, driving there in a green Toyota Corolla with an iPod dock in the glove compartment. Among their other music preferences, each liked specific Orange County metal bands. Natalie listened to Atreyu, while Juri regularly played Avenged Sevenfold.

Twice a week, they attended ballet class at college. "I remember watching Julie and thinking, 'You're so good, I hate you,'" Natalie joked. "She had flexibility, really nice feet, beautiful turnout. She was just such a natural. It was hard to take class with her because we'd be at the barre together and I was like, 'You make me look really bad.'"

Yet, despite her composure, Juri never took herself too seriously and invariably found a way to make everyone laugh. During one phase, she wore her dance pants unusually high. "They were flare-bottom yoga pants," Natalie said. "She practically wore them up to here." She pointed at the area just below her breasts. "She would roll them like a hundred times, where they were really low and you could see her undershorts. We'd be standing, but then we'd have to move, and your butt would stick out, so we'd wear tight shorts underneath."

Jessica had similar memories: "We'd make her unroll them. I'd say, 'Julie, just unroll it two rolls and we'll be perfect.'"

While other dancers would wipe the makeup from their faces before class, Juri stood at the barre in full eyeliner and flourescent green eye shadow. "She was brave with her eye shadow," Jessica said. "She'd wear bright colors, and looked beautiful with it. And her skin was perfect. I don't think I ever saw her with a pimple."

To further accessorize herself, Juri accentuated her hair

with a flower, like a pinup girl. "Everything matched," Jessica said. "She was the pinup girl with the rolled-up pants."

In a photo from the era, Juri and a group of friends are going to the Orange County Fair. As the others smile, Juri scrunches up her face, sticks her tongue out of the side of her mouth, and gestures at Natalie with a long, colorful fingernail.

For a period, Juri was dating someone who worked at the Irvine Spectrum, an outdoor shopping center featuring a Ferris wheel, carousel, and twenty-one-screen movie complex, and she had his three initials tattooed on the back of her neck. When they broke up, she and Natalie went to a tattoo shop in Newport Beach, where Juri had the etching covered up with a black cross.

"She x-ed it out," Natalie said. "When people would ask about the cross, she'd say, 'I don't know. It's a religious thing.' I don't even remember if she was Christian."

Like her eye makeup and long fingernails, body art was a way Juri asserted her individuality. She had a total of six piercings and seven tattoos and intended to get more, like one of her fashion heroes, model, musician, tattoo artist, and TV personality Kat Von D. "She liked Kat Von D's 'just, like, whatever' attitude," Natalie said. "I know she tried to hide her tattoos from her parents, but as far as everyone else went, she'd say, 'I'm going to do whatever I want to do, and not worry about what other people think of me.'"

One day, Juri walked up to Natalie, pointed at her wrist, and declared, "Look what I got."

It was a new tattoo of two intertwined hearts—the same tattoo Natalie had to formalize her relationship with the man who'd become her husband.

Once again, Juri had managed to make Natalie burst out in laughter. "She never even told me about it beforehand. She just got the same tattoo I had. She was impulsive in a fun way. But the hearts meant something to her because she believed in love."

In 2010, she excitedly told friends about an online relationship with Mark Johnson, a Marine corporal stationed in Okinawa. She branded herself "Cpl. Johnson's Sweetheart" on MySpace and posted a photo of Johnson in uniform. "I'm proud to say that he is [one of] the few and the proud," she wrote, paraphrasing the Marine motto, "and truly knows how to make me laugh, smile and [be] happy. He comes back to the States in June."

But by the time the corporal returned to the mainland, the high-spirited, lovable fashion student was already dead.

CHAPTER SEVEN

Not long after Juri's body was found, her brother Kazu
Kibuishi, a graphic-novel author and illustrator, posted a
message on his Twitter feed. "My sister was murdered &
we need help finding the suspect," he wrote. "Please contact the detectives if you have any info."

In an effort to make sense of the case, investigators were
probing the red Samsung phone that Juri had left in Sam's
apartment, examining the log of recorded messages, along
with the texts.

"Can you come over tonight at midnight alone?" began
a text from Sam's cell phone. "Going out for a bit. Very
upset. Need to talk."

"Yeah," Juri answered. "About what?"

"Please don't tell anyone. Please."

"I won't, Sam. I don't talk to anyone from the Camden's
anymore because I am so busy talking to Mark," she said,
referring to her online boyfriend.

"Please, no sex. I need to talk to someone."

The request seemed preposterous to Juri. "LOL, you,
Sam, we are like brother and sis. No sex."

"Jesus, I really just want to talk. I can't talk about it. I need someone I trust."

"You can trust me. I promise. I am not going to say anything. I promise. Pinkie promise."

"I'm hurting w some bad fam crap. I can't be alone. No sex. Please. I am begging as a brother."

"Yeah, that's fine. Sam, I am here for you like family."

"Thank you. Be here at midnight. I will be back around then."

"Okay. I can't spend the night though."

"That's cool. You are saving my life." This was followed by another text from Sam's phone: "Okay. Thank you so much again. I feel I have no one I can share this with. You sure you won't let me down?"

"I never let my friends down when they need me there. . . . No problem."

"Thank you. You are an angel."

Later, Juri received another text from Sam's phone in an anxious tone: "Where are you? Just about back. Can you come by? I don't want to be up late."

"Yeah, I will leave now. I am in Long Beach at my brother's."

"Getting off the freeway. Feel like talking a bit. Don't want to make it a late night."

Juri was asked how soon she thought she'd be able to arrive at Sam's apartment.

"30 mins."

"Cool. . . . Please don't bring anyone. I really don't want anyone else to know what's going on."

The next message from Juri: "Hey, buddy, I am here. I am walking to your place."

It was cold outside, and the texts revealed that Juri was also communicating with her brother Taka. She'd visited with him and his fiancée at a Thai restaurant near his Long Beach home earlier in the evening. Then, the group continued to Taka's residence. Along the way, Taka had handed Juri the tiara that she'd be wearing at his wedding. True to form, she gleefully put it on.

When the texts from Sam's phone began coming in, Juri told her brother about the odd messages. "Sam's like a big brother," she explained as she rose to leave for Sam's apartment. "You'd like him."

Once she entered Sam's floor, shortly after midnight, she wrote, she heard an unsettling sound from the other side of a door. "Huh-oh," Juri messaged her sibling. "Sam is crying. It's not good."

On the surface, it appeared that Sam had lured Juri to her death. Because of his military background and his youthful encounter with the justice system, police were warned that the veteran could be "armed and dangerous." But Det. Sgt. Ed Everett knew not to take anything at face value.

Like the others assigned to the case, Everett had grown up in Orange County, specifically in the bedroom community of Orange, where he attended El Modena High School before taking classes at Fullerton College and opening a bicycle shop. The hours were long and, from Ed's standpoint, the rewards limited. When he met a group of police officers, he found himself drawn to their line of work.

"I knew there was always going to be job security," he said, "and I looked forward to putting bad guys in jail."

In California, many officers "self-sponsor" their police training. Everett went to a police academy at Rio Hondo College in Whittier, paid for his own equipment and uniform—he was prohibited from sewing any patches from actual departments to the fabric—and applied to agencies all over the region. In 1995, the town of Tustin hired him as a reserve, or part-time, officer.

"Once you start training, you're taught to be more vigilant, more aware of your surroundings," he said. "You learn to scan the streets sidewalk to sidewalk, and just look for signs of trouble."

His first true police experience occurred when someone called the station and reported a robbery at a sporting-goods store. Everett rushed to the location, heart pumping. By the time he arrived, the suspects had fled. But as he surveyed the scene he felt a mixture of excitement and satisfaction.

"This is it," he told himself. "You're a police officer now."

A few months later, in an unrelated incident, he pulled up at a home and saw a body squirming in the driveway. He soon learned that the wound was self-inflicted. The victim was a parolee who'd violated the terms of his probation by acquiring a tattoo associated with one of the Hispanic gangs in neighboring Santa Ana. Distressed about being sent back to prison, the man shoved a flare gun into his mouth and fired. "He was just laying there, screaming, with a burned tongue and smoke coming out of his mouth," Everett said. "We conducted a small investigation. We recovered the flare gun. We spoke to the parole officer. We weren't able to get a statement from the victim because he couldn't speak."

The incident provided a lesson on the human condition. The awful episode could have been avoided if the person simply followed the rules of his parole and refrained from getting the tattoo. But it was an impulse that he couldn't control, and Everett would see dozens, if not hundreds, of others find trouble because of similar circumstances.

"Someone's told not to do something, and they continue to do it," he said. "You have a court order to not contact someone, but you call someone you shouldn't call. Gang members are ordered to stay away from other gang

members, but they don't. It's mind-boggling that someone would lose their liberties over a simple commonsense
thing."

After a year in Tustin, Everett learned about a full-time
job in Costa Mesa and was hired. Compared to other
departments in the area, Costa Mesa seemed to be one of
the better ones. "We were one of the first agencies with
computers in the car," he said. "We had a helicopter program. It was a good agency."

While not nearly as busy as nearby municipalities like
Anaheim or Long Beach, Costa Mesa was an active city
for police officers. Consumers from all over the area
poured into South Coast Plaza, a luxury shopping center
whose sales of $1.5 billion annually rated it as one of the
highest-grossing malls in the United States. Others stopped
by the bars and restaurants while coming or going from
Newport Beach. "We do have a large transient population,"
Everett said. "I'm still trying to figure out what the draw
is to Costa Mesa."

Costa Mesa police work independently in one-man cars,
and—after going through additional instruction at the
Orange County Sheriff's Regional Training Academy—
Everett was dispatched into every corner of the city.

In 1997, he responded to a report of a woman not breathing in her second-floor apartment. When he arrived at the
home of Sunny Sudweeks, a twenty-six-year-old photography student at Orange Coast College, it was clear that
she'd been strangled in her bedroom. Investigators would
discover that she'd also been raped. Sunny lived with her
boyfriend and another roommate. Each had alibis; they
were taxi drivers and didn't discover the body until they'd
completed their shifts. Sunny's mother theorized that the
attacker had watched her from afar and deliberately struck
when she was alone.

Everett helped set up a perimeter around the building

and spoke to some of the neighbors. When he'd run into detectives working on the case, he'd ask about progress. But as of this writing, the murder of Sunny Sudweeks remains unsolved.

The dead ends frustrated Everett, even though he'd played a minor role in the case. Although he was expected to maintain a level of detached professionalism, he was still a human being and would find himself wrestling with his emotions throughout his career—particularly after meeting families like the Herrs and Kibuishis.

After three years at the Costa Mesa Police Department, Everett was asked to work investigations. At first, he hesitated; he was relatively new to the department and still believed that he had a lot to learn. But his supervisor explained that the opportunity might not arise again, and Everett decided to take advantage of it.

As in other departments, Costa Mesa divided its detectives into units for Crimes Against Property (thefts, burglaries, credit card scams, identity fraud) and Crimes Against Persons (homicide, rape, domestic violence, armed robberies, and other violent felonies). After six months in the Crimes Against Property section, he filled an opening in the Crimes Against Persons division.

Within an eight-year period, Everett investigated twenty-three murders. By the time Juri was killed, Everett had been a detective sergeant for three years. Because of the scrawl on Juri's back, the motive appeared to be emotional. Detectives suspected some type of love triangle and were baffled over Sam's absence.

"They kept asking me if Sam owned a gun and things like that," Steve Herr said. "And I kept vehemently denying that Sam did this."

Yet even Steve realized that, under the present circumstances, there was no way that any investigator could dismiss Sam as a suspect. When police questioned Raquel, she offered her own theories. "I knew something was wrong," she told the *Los Angeles Times.* "I thought maybe he was being held hostage, but was still alive."

Meanwhile, the other people who loved Sam were experiencing their own tortured emotions. Leah Sussman couldn't conceive how a dead body would end up in her younger cousin's apartment. And she wondered where Sam had gone. But she knew that he was 100 percent innocent. "I understood how much he respected women, how he protected them," Leah said. "If he was capable of any sort of violence, it would never be against a woman. And then, to see the media showing his face and naming him as the suspect was very, very upsetting."

Like Raquel, Leah wondered whether Sam had been kidnapped at gunpoint by the people who killed Juri. Otherwise, he would have found a way to send a message to his family. "Some people thought, 'Well, he's a young guy with a life of his own. He's not going to call his parents right away,'" Leah said. "But they didn't understand that Steve and Sammy were best friends. When we didn't hear from Sammy, I started to get really scared that the worst had happened. And I was worried about my aunt and uncle. This was their only child. I didn't know if they could even survive this."

Miles Foltz had seen Sam in life-and-death situations in Afghanistan, as well as alcohol-fueled altercations in the military, and believed that he understood his fellow veteran's triggers. "First of all, I knew how much Sam liked Julie and would never hurt her," Miles said. "Yes, he did have a temper, but he was a guy who'd use his fists. And the only reason he would ever hurt somebody is if they were threatening him and he had to defend himself. He didn't start fights, and he wouldn't pick on someone weaker than him, especially a really great girl who he treated like a sister. The whole thing didn't make sense."

The situation was so confusing that Miles wondered whether the person responsible for Sam's disappearance might target Steve and Raquel next. Anxious to protect his friend's parents, Miles volunteered to sleep on their couch, his gun at his side, to protect them.

Sam's classmate and fellow veteran Ruben Menacho learned about Juri's death before it was ever reported in the media. He'd been eating at a LongHorn Steakhouse with his wife when Sam's neighbor Jake Swett phoned. What followed was a bizarre tale about walking up to Sam's apartment, finding Steve inside, and being questioned by the police about a murder there.

"We have to go," Ruben told his wife, signaling the waiter for the check.

As the two drove toward the Camden Martinique apartments, Ruben repeated the fragmented information he had but couldn't come up with a coherent supposition of what might have occurred. Outside Sam's building, Ruben saw a large police presence and Steve and Jake with detectives. Stepping forward, Ruben told police that he was willing to assist them in any way possible.

He was instructed to drive to the Costa Mesa Police Department and provide a timeline of his recent communications with Sam. Ruben knew that detectives were investigating Sam, and repeatedly told them that his friend was not a murderer. "There are a lot of people who go in and out of that apartment," Ruben emphasized.

Perhaps Sam had walked in on the murder, Ruben thought, seen the weapons, and fled. Maybe he'd gotten himself involved in something that he hadn't confided to Ruben. "I was actually expecting a phone call from him from Mexico," Ruben said. " 'I'm here. This happened. Come and get me.' "

Theresa Glowicki was still in the Army, deployed in Altimur, Afghanistan, when someone in her platoon told her that Sam had gone missing in California. On the base, she went over the Army MWR—for Morale, Welfare, and Recreation—tent, found a desktop computer soldiers used to communicate with loved ones back home, and Googled her friend's name. Immediately a photo came up with a caption describing Sam as the number one suspect in Juri's murder.

Incredulous, Theresa dialed Sam's cell phone, but no one answered. Then, she realized that she had the number for Sam's fiancée, Katharina, in Germany. Katharina picked up but was as confused as everybody else. "I couldn't get ahold of anyone with any answers," Katharina said.

Independent of the detectives, Steve decided to search for his own answers. In the event of an emergency Sam had given his father access to financial information and passwords, and on Monday, May 24—three days after Juri was killed—Steve began monitoring his son's banking activities. Someone was withdrawing money from Sam's account. Given the fact that so many people were currently looking for Sam, Steve concluded that his son would have been spotted by now had he been the one coming and going from the bank or ATM.

Steve also noticed that Sam's credit card had been used at a place called Ecco's Pizza in Long Beach. On Monday evening, Steve first drove to a Chase Manhattan Bank where some money had been withdrawn, then sat down at Ecco's and watched the clientele closely. If someone drove up in Sam's car, Steve intended to latch himself on to the person until police could arrive.

On the television, the Orlando Magic and Boston Celtics were competing in the NBA play-offs, and Steve noticed many of the customers raptly watching and studied each face in case he came across the person later. Over at the bar, he spotted one man pacing back and forth, agitated, speaking animatedly into a cell phone. Maybe the guy had money on the game or was having a fight with his wife. For all Steve knew, the man's car was in the shop and the mechanic had quoted an exorbitant price. After making a mental note of the patron's face, Steve stared out the window into the parking lot. None of the cars even resembled Sammy's.

Looking down at his phone, Steve checked to see if any of Sam's associates were calling him back. Since Saturday, he'd been contacting Sam's friends, questioning them about other acquaintances who might have seen Sammy or heard rumors about his whereabouts. Whenever he heard a new name, Steve immediately asked for the person's number.

Eventually, Steve was directed to a fellow resident of 2855 Pinecreek Drive, who'd been spending a good deal of time with Sam and their other associates. Dave Barnhart—the roommate of Jake Swett, the man Steve encountered shortly after finding Juri—said that, on the day he was last seen, Sam was with an actor who lived in the complex. From what Dave remembered, Sam and the man planned to travel to a theater at any Army post and set up backdrops for a play.

On Tuesday morning, Steve called and spoke to the actor, Daniel Patrick Wozniak.

As with the police later on, Dan seemed only too happy to help.

CHAPTER EIGHT

Steve was so preoccupied with his son's disappearance that he visited a doctor and received medical clearance to stay home from work in order to conduct the investigation. As he chatted with Dan, he had the sinking feeling that the actor had more information than he was willing to reveal. "He said Sam told him he had women problems and family problems," Steve said. "Immediately, I knew Dan was lying."

At that stage of his life, Sam didn't have family issues; anyone who'd seen him with Steve knew that. Nor did he have "women problems." Yes, Katharina was uncertain over whether she wanted to leave her family in Germany and get married, but Sam was letting his life play out. For all he knew, he might be an officer in a few short years, stationed in Turkey or Guam or South Korea. As much as he cared about his girlfriend, he wasn't plagued by the ambiguity of the relationship.

And even if Sam was consumed by these topics, he wouldn't confide to Dan Wozniak, not when he had friends such as Ruben and Miles and Gonzo. Sam and Dan were neighbors who lived three floors apart from each other.

Despite the fact that they hung out together from time to time, Dan was more of an acquaintance than a real friend.

So why was he making up this story? Although Steve couldn't prove anything, he sensed that Dan was involved in Juri's death and might be able to lead police to Sam. As a result, Steve listened with relative passivity—he didn't want to challenge Dan and scare him into silence—hoping to learn more about the events of the previous week, and Dan himself.

There was nothing particularly menacing about the actor. Few who knew Dan perceived him as dangerous or even angry. He imbibed copiously at social gatherings—Jack Daniel's and rum, usually mixed with Coke—and was generally a jolly drunk. Allyson Hathcock, the high school associate whose parents owned the theater where Dan later performed, remembered him as a harmless type, who sometimes tried too hard to impress acquaintances. "I would take him out and, even if he didn't know the people that well, he'd pick up the tab," she said. "He'd buy drinks for everybody. He'd buy everybody dinner. Sometimes, the check would run two hundred or three hundred bucks. He would pick it up."

Occasionally, Dan would slur his words while making a point or annoy another guest by hanging all over the person. But most of Dan's regular companions just wanted a night of fun and had the same notions about partying as their garrulous friend. "The group he ran around with, that he was buddy-buddy with, every Saturday night, their ritual was to take pictures of everybody passed out and throwing up," Allyson said. "Then, you'd go on Facebook and see a picture of someone's head in the toilet."

To support himself, Dan worked in sales and training positions, but admitted, "I haven't always been great at it."

Associates recall him working at a Sprint store and Verizon shop. However, the jobs never seemed to last. "He kept getting fired," Allyson said. "And it would be because he was accused of stealing something here or funds were missing there. He would always blame it on somebody else. But I never understood why he always had money to pay for things, when he was constantly getting fired." No charges were ever brought.

For close to two years, Dan worked in Daniel Halkyard's home appraisal business. Halkyard had known Wozniak since he was in high school. In fact, Dan had dated Halkyard's daughter and contemplated marrying her. To Halkyard, Dan possessed the respectful, responsible qualities the older man sought in both an employee and a son-in-law. "He was like a son to me," Halkyard told the *Orange County Register.* "He was always coming over the house, staying the night. He was just the nicest kid."

Even when he was unemployed, Dan continued performing with local theater troupes and was a known commodity in the so-called storefront theater movement. The first storefront theaters had opened in Orange County in 1996. The venues—among them the Monkey Wrench Collective and Maverick Theater in Fullerton, Chance Theater and STAGEStheatre in Anaheim, and Breath of Fire Latina Theater Ensemble in Santa Ana—were far smaller than professional theaters in the area. Actors were in it for the love of their craft, rather than any financial reward. Unlike community theater companies, the fare was more varied and exciting than the popular musicals and mainstream productions favored by senior citizens and Orange County's traditional, suburbanized audiences.

While some of the storefront plays were recognizable— *The Rocky Horror Picture Show, Hedwig and the Angry Itch, Cabaret*—the material tended to be more subversive and a disproportionate number of the actors young and exuberant. If someone on the circuit took the time to write an original play, there was a very real possibility that one of the storefront theater companies would perform it. At times, the results were disappointing, but more frequently there were flashes of brilliance in the writing, composing, and acting. And since the prices were palatable, the small crowds tended to be forgiving.

"In any community that's so conservative, there is a counterweight to that," said Joel Beers, theater columnist for the *OC Weekly* and a playwright himself. "Especially in a college town like Fullerton, you'll find younger, anti-conformist people who support storefront theaters. Some of them are either in college or right out of college. The best and brightest actors eventually seem to go away to LA or New York, and they either make it or they don't and come back. So you have an interesting dichotomy of people in the theater community here.

"These actors might get paid ten, twenty, thirty bucks a run, sometimes a little bit more, but they're doing it with passion. At the same time, they're building up their résumés, making contacts, and always dreaming that the right person will see their show."

The Orange County Children's Theatre was different from the storefront showcases around the county. Founded in 1969, the theater was the region's oldest continuously running institution created particularly for young people. Children could audition at age five, and the theater sought out actors of all economic backgrounds. The goal—in addition to teaching the dramatic arts—was building self-esteem and a sense of belonging.

Halkyard, Dan's boss at the home appraisal business, directed Dan in *The Sound of Music* there. "He played Captain von Trapp," Halkyard said. "He was wonderful with the children. He did a fabulous job. He threw himself into the role."

Among his friends in the acting community, Dan was perceived as a performer who'd travel virtually anywhere to appear in a play. Some of the venues were as far away as Ventura County, a distance of more than two hours from his home.

The Liberty Theater at the Los Alamitos base, however, was practically walking distance from the place where Dan grew up. It was housed in a building opened in 1942 to provide briefings, host USO shows, and show movies and newsreels to American servicemen about to be shipped abroad. Because of its proximity to Hollywood, the base was also used in feature films about the U.S. military. In 1977, it became a National Guard post.

In the mid-1970s, Jeff Hathcock—the son of Richard Hathcock, the *Los Angeles Examiner* crime reporter who covered the Bugsy Siegel, Black Dahlia, and Manson Family murder cases, among others–was studying theater at the school Dan Wozniak would later attend, California State University, Long Beach, when he met his wife, Nancy. She'd also been raised in Southern California and was performing in and doing her thesis on the musical *The Apple Tree*. While others went on to more practical professions after graduation, the pair stayed rooted in local theater. Jeff started a theater guild in 1994, and in 2002 the couple purchased the Liberty Theater.

Clearly, whoever designed the building never foresaw the stage shows that the Hathcocks hoped to present. There was an old, yellowing movie screen at the front of the shoebox-shaped room, and the walls, according to Jeff's description, were a dismal pea green. But the Hathcocks believed in the venue's potential and invested ten thousand dollars of their own money into the theater.

The stage was widened eight feet until it was thirty-eight feet long by thirty-eight feet wide. "We put in new seats, new curtains," Jeff said, "new lighting, and a sound system." A Cal State Long Beach student painted two large murals on the walls as part of her master's thesis.

At times, the Hathcocks and their daughter, Allyson, worked side by side in the large room, refining their improvements. Still, Jeff insisted, the family was never truly alone in the building. "It was loaded with ghosts." Some, he was certain, had come from a morgue that once stood on the base. But there were so many phantoms in the theater, Jeff said, that he came to recognize many of them.

"When I first got here, one of the sergeants said to me, 'If you see the nurse, it's nothing.' I said, 'What nurse?' He said, 'Oh, Edna. Edna Alcorn. She was the nurse here from '43 to '48, and people still see her in the building.' Well, I saw her."

Apparitions aside, under the Hathcocks' stewardship the Liberty Theater quickly became a welcoming place. In addition to established plays, both Jeff and Allyson wrote shows with the sensibilities of the audience in mind. "Because we were on a military base and, really, because of the type of people we are, we weren't the type of theater that would put on a show like *Hair*," Nancy said. "We wanted to do something that everyone would enjoy. Kids were our specialty. We wanted you to bring your kids."

Not only did Dan perform on the Liberty Theater stage, but his cousins, Justin and Rachel Brown, also appeared in the group's plays. "They were very nice," Jeff said. "Different personalities than Dan, didn't look like him at all. Dan had dark hair, and theirs was kind of reddish. Rachel's roommate was also in some of our shows."

It was exactly the kind of atmosphere that the Hathcocks wanted to create: a family running a theater featuring another group of relatives acting alongside a close friend—for an audience consisting of parents and kids.

At the time, Dan was living at home with his family. His parents, Daryl and Mary Anne, were observant Catholics who seemed to be much older than Dan and his two brothers. His father, in particular, was overweight, with circulation problems in his legs, and once fell over in one of the rocking theater seats—feet thrust into the air—as Dan was acting onstage. But both parents continued coming to the theater and remained extremely supportive.

Their names appeared on donor lists at various theaters in the area, including the Huntington Beach Playhouse and Musical Theatre West, a Long Beach location that claimed to "bring the best of Broadway to your backyard." "If Dan was in thirty performances of a show, they were at every single one," Allyson said.

"He was an ideal son," Daryl would tell the *Daily Mail*. "He went out of his way to help everybody."

The affirmation that Dan received at home added to his confidence, a quality that he was able to use to make other people feel better. "When I first met the guy, I thought, 'This is a young man who's going someplace,' " Jeff said. "He had everything going for him—good looks, charisma. He just seemed great. He was one of those people you'd look at and go, 'This guy's marked for success.' "

By Dan Wozniak's estimation, the Liberty was the "Mayberry of theaters," a reference to the fictional small town that was the setting for the 1960s TV program *The Andy Griffith Show*.

"So homey, so folksy," Nancy remembered. "He'd say it with a smirk, but we would laugh it off because we were happy with what we did."

Once, when they were talking about the concept of family, Jeff asked Dan if he was related to computer pioneer Steve Wozniak.

"No," Dan answered with his ever-present sparkle. "I wish I was. I wouldn't mind some of his money. But I'm not."

Onstage, though, Dan seemed as dedicated to his vocation as the man who developed the first Apple computer. "It was weird the way Dan would take on a role and live the part," Allyson said.

One character he particularly relished was Harold Hill, who materializes in a small Iowa town in *The Music Man*, selling musical instruments and band uniforms while pledging to form a children's marching band. But Hill is neither a musician nor a bandleader. He's a flimflam artist who intends to leave town with the ill-gotten funds.

It would be years before Nancy saw the irony in Dan's portrayal. "Harold Hill is a con artist," she said. "But Dan was like, 'Whoopie, this is the role for me.'"

During *The Music Man*'s run at the Liberty Theater, Dan began using an e-mail address beginning with Music-ManDan. Every week, he'd lead his cousins and other friends to Mr. B's Sports Bar and Grill or the Starting Gate in Los Alamitos for karaoke sessions. When it was Dan's turn to sing, he invariably requested Broadway show tunes, particularly *The Music Man*'s signature song, "Seventy-Six Trombones."

"He *became* Harold Hill," Allyson said. "He'd get carried away, and have everybody up, singing 'Seventy-Six Trombones.' He was a blast. He just totally got into it."

Sometimes, Jeff wondered if Dan was enjoying himself as much as his companions were. "He always had to be the center of attention," Jeff said. "Whatever group he was in or whatever the occasion, Dan had to be in the middle of everything. He was always one of the tallest people in the room, and because of his loudness, his joking, his smile, he'd make sure everyone was focusing on him. And his laugh wasn't just '*ha, ha, ha.*' It was '*aha! aha! aha! aha!*' The sweat would pour off, and there'd be very big movements. That's how he operated. He'd move from place to place, drink in hand, telling a joke, slapping people on the back."

While Dan was playing Harold Hill, an impressionable teenager named Wesley Freilich portrayed Winthrop, the introverted, self-conscious boy whom the Music Man is able to draw out. Like Winthrop, Wesley had his challenges. He was being raised by a single mother, a schoolteacher who relied on her parents to assist with his upbringing. The Hathcocks considered Wesley a gifted young actor. But it was Dan Wozniak who instilled a new self-assurance in him.

"My impression of Wesley?" Allyson said. "Honestly, I thought he was a good kid who was looking for a father figure."

Dan had experience teaching drama to children and knew how to step into that position. For extra money, he'd occasionally babysit for people associated with the theater, and the parents felt fortunate to have Dan in their children's lives. Occasionally, Dan invited Wesley to activities away from the *Music Man* setting, and the teen's mother seemed both relieved and grateful. "She thought of Dan as a mentor," Nancy said.

When Allyson had a birthday party with a murder mystery theme, Dan came with both Wesley and his mother—as well as a bottle of Jack Daniel's. "Dan showed up at the beginning of the party, left to do something, and came back at the very, very end of the party," she recounted. "He was so drunk, I wouldn't let him drive home."

But Wesley looked at his older friend and saw no wrong.

On Thanksgiving, 2007, Allyson and Wesley were both invited to the home of Dan's cousins, the Browns. In one photo, the collection of thespians are seen doing a synchronized Macarena. In another, Wesley poses, bending over the turkey and sweet potatoes, as the food comes out of the oven. In a third, Dan sits with an arm draped over the knee of the theater's musical director, grinning as if modeling for a billboard.

Onstage, Dan's continued acquiring accolades, especially for his portrayal of Mortimer Brewster, the male lead in *Arsenic and Old Lace,* a black comedy about a homicidal family. Mortimer, a drama critic, appears to be greatly alarmed by his two spinster aunts—and their fondness for poisoning lonely old men.

"Insanity runs in my family," Mortimer observes. "It practically gallops."

But the eeriest section—taken in the context of later events—occurs when Mortimer reminisces about a show he'd seen the previous week. "Yeah, what a play," he says. "When the curtain goes up the first thing you see is a dead body. The next thing . . ." He opens a window seat and finds not one but two cadavers. "Ye gads, there's another one."

After watching Dan onstage so often—and socializing with him at gatherings where the alcohol was abundant—Allyson accepted his invitation to go out on a date. "I thought he was cute, so we went out a few times," she said. "We went out on three actual dates. It seemed like every time we went out, we ended up doing karaoke with his cousins. And on the third date, we finally attempted to kiss, and it was nothing. Totally unromantic. He sweated like a damp mop. There was nothing sexy there at all, no sex appeal on his end. It was like kissing Mickey Mouse. That's the only thing I can equate it to.

"He dated a few of the girls at the theater, and it would always end up with them saying, 'Oh, he's just a big teddy bear of a friend.'

"It made me think about some of his performances. When he played Harold Hill in *The Music Man* and you tried to convince him that Harold was supposed to be seducing Marian the librarian, he had a hard time. You had to really say, 'Dan, turn here. Look this way. Show a little *oomph*.' He couldn't seduce a fly. He just didn't have that.

"He did *Seven Brides for Seven Brothers,* and there's a scene in there where Adam is on his wedding night and his wife kicks him out of the bedroom. And he's trying to get back in the bedroom to be with his wife. And when I saw that play at Golden West College, and the wife was finally inviting him to come into the bed, he looked back at her with a look of horror. That was Dan—neutered."

On MySpace, Dan described his ideal woman: "adventurous, bold, caring, different, energetic . . . goal-oriented, helping, interesting, jovial, kind, lively . . . personable, quick, radical, sweet, tender . . . yearning and zany."

By the time the body was found in his building, he'd informed his social media associates: "I'm really glad that I found her."

CHAPTER NINE

Later, much would be made of the fact that, among her other jobs, Rachel Mae Buffett—the pretty blonde Daniel Wozniak intended to marry—had played Princess Ariel, the title character from *The Little Mermaid,* at Disneyland.

Rachel grew up in Seal Beach—on the border of Long Beach and Los Angeles County—the starting point, city boosters liked pointing out, to Orange County's forty-two miles of coastline. In 2011, a year after Juri's death, Seal Beach would be the site of the deadliest mass killing in Orange County history, an incident whose ramifications would impact the Daniel Wozniak case as it ground its way through the preliminary hearing process.

When Dan was being investigated, Rachel would tell police that she and her three siblings grew up in a "sheltered" Christian household. Her favorite Bible passage, she said, was Psalms 23: "The Lord is my shepherd; I shall not want. He maketh me to lie down in green pastures; he leadeth me beside the still waters. He restoreth my soul; he leadeth me in the paths of righteousness for his name's sake" (King James Version).

Apparently, Dan was trodding the same path. After all, he'd listed "God" as one of his heroes on MySpace. And, like Rachel, his need to appear onstage was a compulsion as well as a calling.

Rachel's role at Disneyland—as well as another job, playing a princess at Medieval Times, a family dinner theater featuring jousting, sword fighting, and other games from the Middle Ages—reflected Rachel's theatrical zeal. After Dan's arrest, rumors would circulate about Rachel inciting unnecessary friction at the theater companies where she performed, while others described her as sweet natured and oblivious to her boyfriend's social manipulations.

"I first met Dan while doing a play," she'd tell the *Dr. Phil* show. "My first impression of Dan was he was a nice person. . . . He was eager to please and he always seemed like the guy who was going to give you the shirt off his back. Several years later, he started hanging out with me on pretty much a daily basis, and I quickly fell for him."

Rachel and Dan wanted to live together but feared the way her conservative parents would react. Instead, they came up with a scheme to delude her parents. Rachel told them that she was residing with her older brother, Noah. In fact, Noah and Rachel *did* live together—along with Dan. If the parents decided to stop by during the day, Dan was never there. He'd only come at night when he knew that he could be alone with Rachel in the room that they shared.

In 2008, Dan and Rachel became engaged. "He gave me this gorgeous, vintage ring that he said had come from his grandmother and was intended for him to give to whoever he was going to marry," Rachel said. "I looked at it as though we were going to have an awesome future."

Their fellow actors viewed the pair as a storefront theater version of Brad Pitt and Angelina Jolie and playfully dubbed them "The Royals." The same year, the two appeared together in the farcical play *Every Christmas Story Ever Told* at the All American Melodrama Theatre in Long Beach. In the plot, the couple, along with fellow performer Paul Villano, portrayed actors attempting to stage Charles Dickens' *A Christmas Carol*. "This is definitely not a lavish production," the blog *What the Butler Saw* reported. "The most extraordinary thing you can say about it is that it's non-stop funny. Divert your eyes from the stage to the audience and you'll see faces that beam like kids ripping open presents."

The actors, the review continued, "don't take themselves seriously . . . they have so much fun that the maintenance of character is next to impossible. . . . Take a gander. You'll be glad you did."

On New Year's Day, 2009, the couple was invited to a party at Dan's cousins' apartment. In photos from that day, he and Rachel bake cookies together, cuddle, and mug for the camera.

The two appeared just as close when they made a promotional video for their play, *The Green Room,* at the Orange County Theatre Company. Looking flawlessly coiffed, Dan grinned brightly into the camera and introduced himself: "Hi, my name is Dan Wozniak. I'll be playing the role of John Davidson—" Suddenly Dan became tongue-tied, laughed, and looked off-camera.

"Okay, take it again," said a disembodied voice.

"I'll be playing the role of John Davidson at the Orange County Theatre. . . ." He appeared to become confused another time and laughed again. "*God*damn." While others chuckled off-camera, Dan shook his head. "I'm just saying Orange County . . ." His eyes twinkled, and he laughed more.

The sequence then abruptly cut to Rachel standing with another actor in the play. Looking svelte and exuding a bubbly, youthful demeanor, she tried to pick up where Dan finished. "Hi, my name is Rachel Buffett. We're playing . . ." Now *she* started laughing and waved her hand. "Do it again please."

"Come see us!" shouted the other actor as Rachel giggled and raised two thumbs.

"Oh, this is sad," the actor joked while Rachel made the sign to cut.

Next, Dan, Rachel, and two other actors were seen on-screen as music played in the background. "Come see us!" one of the performers urged. While Rachel and the rest of the cast cheered the successful delivery of the line, an exuberant Dan thrust a fist into the air.

No group of people ever seemed more jovial and optimistic about life's prospects. But theater associates asserted that all was never as blissful as it appeared.

Although Dan and Rachel had visited his cousins on New Year's Day, Dan's old crowd apparently resented the woman Wozniak intended to marry. "I heard they wouldn't see him for months," Allyson Hathcock said. "They did not like Rachel. They thought she'd driven a wedge between them and Dan."

Six months before the murder, Daryl Wozniak claimed that his son stopped taking phone calls from his family. The elder Wozniak was bewildered. There'd been no argument or history of resentment directed at the parents who loyally attended every play.

"He just disappeared," Daryl told the *Daily Mail.*

According to Allyson, Daniel's family had grown suspicious of the influence that his fiancée was alleged to exert. "They'd only met her, I think, once or twice. They didn't know he was engaged. They'd been so close to Dan, and they found out he was getting married after everybody else did.

"Everything changed after he was with Rachel. He dropped out of Cal State Long Beach. He didn't see his cousins anymore. And he wouldn't even talk to his parents."

While being interviewed by detectives, Dan claimed that his parents disapproved of Rachel because "they wanted me to be with like a doctor or a lawyer." But when police probed further, they uncovered a different story. The separation in the Wozniak family occurred, they said, after Dan was caught stealing money from his parents.

Still, before the ties were severed Dan made a visit to his family's Long Beach home to procure an item that would change his future and obliterate the lives of so many others.

He took his father's .38 and moved it to Apartment D110 at the Camden Martinique apartments—less than fifty yards from Sam Herr's apartment.

CHAPTER TEN

Rachel and Dan moved into the Camden Martinique apartments in February 2010, some two years after they began dating and three months before Juri's body was found in Sam's apartment.

In March, they visited the Liberty Theater to see the show *King Arthur*. Some of Dan's former child students were performing, and he wanted to wish them luck. Immediately Jeff and Nancy Hathcock noticed that the perennially lively actor appeared strangely reserved, formally introducing Rachel to the cast.

"He had markedly changed from the last time I saw him," Jeff said. "He was hesitant. He was more reticent to be the jolly fellow. You could tell it was because of her. He used to be the one leading the group in. Now, she went ahead and he walked behind."

Nancy had the sense that Rachel was controlling Dan in some way. "He was like a puppy dog. I thought, 'Oh, this guy is really, really crazy about her.'"

The wedding was scheduled for Friday, May 28. The two planned to get married on the sand in Long Beach and have a reception overlooking the water. "He was bragging to everybody that they were going to have a big wedding, and then he was going to take Rachel on this special honeymoon," Allyson said. "But he wasn't working, so—like with everything else—I didn't know where he was getting the money. As far as I knew, he didn't invite any of his family to the wedding. His cousins weren't coming. The only guests I knew about were a couple he babysat for."

Although he didn't have a formal job, Dan and Rachel were in the midst of a three-month run of the musical *Nine* at the Hunger Artists Theatre Company.

"See me and Rachel in *Nine* at the Hunger Artists!" Dan wrote on Facebook. "Hope to see you all there. For those who have come . . . Thank You! It was amazing seeing you all! Have a good one everyone!"

The theater was named after the 1922 Franz Kafka short story "A Hunger Artist," about a performer who fasts for the public in a cage, observed by special minders who ensure that he isn't sneaking in food. "It's always been a very literate company," said *OC Weekly* drama critic Joel Beers. "A more sophisticated kind of literary fare was its trademark. Every storefront has its own niche. They've done Chekov. Obviously, they've done Kafka's productions. Over the years, they've had a lot of turnover, but they've always stood out."

The production of *Nine*—based on the Federico Fellini film *8 ½*—contained the kind of psychologically complex plot that appealed to the Hunger Artists crowd. The winner of the 1982 Tony Award for Best Musical, *Nine* is the story of Guido Contini, a self-possessed film director attempting to conceive the plot of his next work as he's pursued by various captivating women. As he flashes back on his life, he decides to recreate the Casanova story as a musical, an endeavor that forces Guido to experience a number of emotional upheavals.

It was one of the most exciting shows that the venue had staged. Originally, the theater was located in Santa Ana. But when Dan and Rachel appeared in *Nine,* it had moved into an industrial park setting, off South State College Boulevard in Fullerton, past a small shopping center that included businesses such as Burger Records, Future Tattoo & Body Piercing, and the Kayla Spa massage parlor. Unless you were truly a fan, the Hunger Artists Theatre would have been easy to miss, tucked into a corner of the complex alongside such businesses as Joe's Cabinets and Cortez Coral Saltwater Aquarium Suppliers.

"Every one of the storefront theaters has kind of a base of actors that they use quite a bit," Beers explained. "But because people have jobs or families or whatever, those people can't be in every play, but they'll all reconvene every so often. This wasn't one of those plays where a lot of the Hunger Artists stable was involved. There were a lot of people I didn't recognize."

That included Dan. "I wasn't aware of him until I saw *Nine* because he did a lot of musicals and dinner theater type of stuff, and that's not something we review," Beers said. "We're an alternative weekly. The light operas and stuff like that we don't really touch. It did turn out that he added me as a friend on Facebook maybe a few weeks before, but that's just random."

There was much that Beers didn't like about the production. "It was a small theater and the production standard wasn't great, and there was a very uneven field of actors. It happens a lot in storefronts. But I thought Dan Wozniak was very convincing in the role of Guido. It's not an easy performance to pull off. I mean, he's the lead. He's onstage ninety percent of the time. He was definitely the best thing in that play, and my review pointed it out."

The critique was effusive in its praise of Dan. "Dan Wozniak's Guido is superb," Beers wrote. "Though his character should be an unlikeable pig—he's self-obsessed, egotistical and a liar who uses women as checkers pieces— Wozniak somehow manages to make Guido eminently likeable and even sympathetic. This is a man absolutely into himself—both his virtues and his flaws. And Wozniak captures the angst of a man staring into the abyss of his own being and seeing his own frailty."

As with Harold Hill in *The Music Man* and Mortimer Brewster in *Arsenic and Old Lace*, Dan was able to deliver lines in *Nine* that seemed to come from his soul. "I would like the universe to get down," he sang. "on its knees / And say, 'Guido, whatever you please, it's okay / Even if it's impossible, we'll arrange it / That's all that I want."

Because of his habit of losing himself in roles—and the fact that he was the only man in the cast—Dan would have been an object of fascination for the actresses in the ensemble. But, backstage, Rachel managed to stay close to him. Some interpreted their constant proximity as possessiveness on Rachel's part. Others believed that they were simply in love.

Still, there were rumors that all was not well between them. When Dan and Rachel were out with friends, he'd reportedly flare over her spending habits, prompting companions to take him aside and calm him down. At the time, both were unemployed. After Dan wrote several checks for funds that he couldn't cover, he had a negative balance in his bank account. Recently, the couple had borrowed money to pay the rent. But they were on the verge of being evicted.

One night Ruben Menacho was visiting Sam at the Camden Martinique apartments and was introduced to several of his friends in the building. "Let's hit the Jacuzzi," someone suggested. When the group arrived, Dan and Rachel were in the hot tub with some other acquaintances.

Ruben had never met Dan before. After they shook hands, Dan mentioned his sales background. "But I'm really an actor," he stressed.

The way Ruben interpreted the comment, Dan was acting boastful, not a way to endear himself to someone who'd fought for his country.

"Well, I'm in the military," Ruben shot back.

He'd later remember, "I didn't like Wozniak from the second I saw him. He was pretty fake, the way he smiled. He seemed like a liar to me."

But Sam was acting friendly to Dan and Rachel, so Ruben looked away and tried to chat with the other people lounging around. Yet every time Ruben's eyes turned back toward Dan, there he was with that annoying grin. After a while, Ruben nudged Sam.

"Hey, let's go, bro."

Sam shrugged. He could see Ruben wasn't having a great time. "Yeah, let's go."

As they walked back to Sam's apartment, Ruben shook his head and motioned back at the Jacuzzi area. "I don't like that bastard."

Sam laughed out loud. "Ruben," he said, "you don't like anybody."

From that point forward Ruben, on the one hand, made an effort to avoid Dan during visits to the apartment complex. Sam, on the other hand, had the attitude that, unless someone did something egregious to him, that person was his friend.

"That was the problem with Sam," Ruben recalled. "He just trusted everybody. He was very open. And he made friends so fast. I mean, he just walked up to *me* in a classroom and decided he was my friend. That's the way he was. It was hard to keep up with Sam because people always wanted to be around him."

On May 15, Dan was arrested for DUI in Costa Mesa.

The police brought him to the Orange County Jail, where he began calling friends, looking for help. At some point, a mutual acquaintance contacted Sam, asking for his assistance. That's when Dan apparently learned about the significant amount of combat pay that Sam had acquired from the U.S. government. In the end, though, Dan managed to raise enough from other sources to post bond.

When he next saw Sam, they were both at the Jacuzzi again. Allegedly, Dan began complaining about his brief incarceration.

"I know all about being in jail," Sam replied, recounting his brush with the criminal justice system as a teenager.

Dan looked at Sam and listened. The actor's knowledge of the two hidden aspects of his neighbor's life—the past that Sam wanted to forget and the money he'd earned in the military—are said to have sparked a series of malevolent thoughts.

It was at this point, police would later hypothesize, that Daniel Wozniak formulated the scheme that ended Sammy's life.

CHAPTER ELEVEN

Sam never could have fathomed how soon it was all going to be over.

One night, Raquel drove Sam and his cousin Joey to a TGI Friday's chain restaurant. Joey was ten years older than Sam. They had spent time together when Sam was a child. But now they wanted to enjoy each other's company as adults. Both intended to drink, and neither wanted a DUI. When they were ready to end the night, they'd either phone a relative or call a taxi.

At closing time, after Sam had consumed a number of Jim Beam shots, the pair stumbled out of the eatery. For some reason, Joey had it in his mind that he wanted to walk to his in-laws' home.

"Where do they live?" Sam asked.

"About three miles from here."

The two began their journey, but Sam noticed that Joey was weaving. "Hey, I have a good idea," Sam suggested as they cut through a parking lot. "Why don't I *carry* you there?"

Joey tried climbing onto his cousin's back but slipped

off. The two were laughing, and Sam threw a playful slap at his relative. Joey crouched down and tried to snatch Sam around the waist.

"The police stopped them," Steve said. "They thought they were fighting. Then, they realized they were cousins who were just wrestling and having fun, cousins who were getting to know each other as men, cousins who loved each other."

Steve received a call at 3:00 A.M. It was up to him to retrieve the duo and find the house where Joey's in-laws lived.

Later, Joey would tell Steve, "I'm so glad we had that night."

It would be the last memory he'd ever have of his younger cousin.

On Thursday, May 20—two days before Steve came upon Juri's body in Sam's apartment—Sam's other cousin, Leah Sussman, was talking to her two-and-a-half-year-old daughter, Sonia, about safety. "You can't let just anyone take you when you want to go across the street," Leah emphasized.

Sonia seemed to understand.

"So who would it be safe to cross the street with?" Leah asked her daughter.

"Uncle Sammy. Because he's nice to me. And he's big and strong." Sonia paused. "Can we call him now?"

Leah dialed Sam's number, and he and Sonia had a brief conversation. Then, Leah got on the phone and she and Sam exchanged small talk.

As with Joey, it would be the final time that Leah would speak to her beloved relative. "I'm so happy that happened."

That night, Sam and Juri were going out to dinner with

Ruben Menacho and another friend named Lester Mc-Kinney. As they stepped off the elevator, they ran into Dan Wozniak and a friend named John Randolph. Because of Ruben's aversion to Dan, he immediately zoned in on John's dog, petting the animal while the others chatted.

"I wasn't really paying attention to what they were talking about," Ruben said. "I think they were talking about Dan's wedding or something."

Ruben and Juri were hungry, so everyone said their good-byes and Sam and his group continued to a nearby IHOP. It was a pleasant, jokey meal. As Juri went through her handbag, Ruben playfully grabbed it from her.

"What do you have in there?" he said as Juri laughed. "Makeup? Hair products? It must be really hard to be a woman." He pulled out a small jar of cream. "Man, how can you put this crap on your face?"

When the waitress came, Sam insisted that he wasn't hungry. However, after the food was delivered he began eating the fries off Ruben's plate.

"Sam, you always do that," Ruben complained. "Bro, if you're hungry, I'll buy you fries. You want me to get you fries?"

Sam chuckled. "No, Ruben, I like taking them from you."

For Ruben, it was a typical night with Sam and his friends—a night he likely wouldn't have remembered if two of the four people at the table didn't lose their lives within the next forty-eight hours. "Everybody was laughing," Ruben said. "We always had a good time. There was not one time when we hung out that we had a bad day."

The next morning—Friday, May 21, 2010—Juri sent a Facebook message to another person she knew from Sam's building, Dan's girlfriend, Rachel Buffett: "Hello, darling. I miss hanging out with you and I saw your fiancée last night when I was hanging out with Sam, Ruben and Lester. I hear you are getting married next week. Congrats. How are you?"

Rachel wrote back quickly: "Ha ha. So busy you can't imagine. We'll hang out when everything settles in the summer sun." She then alluded to meeting up at the complex's pool.

Dan appeared distressed that morning, according to Rachel, so upset that he was hyperventilating. "She told us that Dan woke up that Friday and that he was acting very, very weird," Det. Jose Morales would testify at a preliminary hearing. "He was stressed out. He seemed distant. And it seemed to her that he was acting as if he was going to have a heart attack.

"She had asked him what was wrong. He wouldn't come out and tell her. He eventually told her that he had to go see Sam upstairs and . . . he left shortly after that."

Rachel claimed that Dan was only gone a short time. He then returned with Sam. With an outsider as an audience, Dan appeared calmer as the two relaxed in the patio area outside Wozniak's apartment. However, Dan did admit to feeling stressed about money, and Sam suggested the military as a possible solution. "They take care of everything," Sam said. "Your housing is taken care of. There's no landlord threatening to kick you out. They expect a lot from you, but it's a way out of the financial situation you're in right now."

Sam had offered to help Dan move some items that day. As they prepared to leave, another friend of Dan's stopped by. Chris Williams told police that he had met Dan and Rachel a few weeks earlier. Dan was so strapped for funds that, almost instantly, he asked Chris for a loan.

"How much are you thinking about?" Chris asked.

"Three thousand dollars."

"That's a lot of money."

Dan explained how he was getting married and needed

the cash right away. He also pledged to pay everything back—to the penny. Chris didn't feel that Dan was being particularly pushy, just honest. And Dan and Rachel were so nice and fun to be around. Eventually, Chris lent them two thousand dollars. Dan was supposed to pay back the money that day.

Because Chris was new to the social network, he didn't know all of Dan and Rachel's associates. He'd later tell police that he thought the other man in the apartment was Sam based on the description of the veteran's tattoos. Ten minutes after Chris arrived, Dan and Sam abruptly left. Chris assumed that they'd return relatively fast. After all, Dan knew that Chris was waiting for the cash. In the meantime, Chris talked with Rachel while she sat at her computer and searched for items on Craigslist.

"For the next three hours, he remained in the apartment with Rachel," Morales said. "It seemed to him that he stayed there for a very long time, and was wondering what was taking so long because he initially thought that he was there to pick up the money that . . . Dan was supposed to pay him back."

Chris knew that Dan's family lived in Long Beach and thought that maybe the two were going there to retrieve the two thousand dollars. But Long Beach was just thirty minutes away—maybe forty-five with traffic. Why weren't Dan and his friend back by now?

Nonetheless, Rachel was an agreeable conversationalist, and she and Chris didn't run out of topics to discuss. She was deeply passionate about acting but nervous about whether she could ever support herself that way and mentioned a couple of other moneymaking possibilities that could sustain her. Eventually, Dan returned alone.

He didn't have the full two thousand dollars but handed Chris a wad of money as a gesture of good faith. Chris believed Dan when he said that the roll contained four hundred dollars; there was no need to count the money out. "While he was there, he noticed that there was some tension between Dan and Rachel that [Chris] . . . didn't want to be a part of," Morales said.

From a phone conversation they'd had earlier that day, Chris knew that Dan was beleaguered by debt and fretted about starting married life with so many creditors. When Chris slipped the wad of cash into his pocket without complaint, the burden appeared to be lifted, at least temporarily. "It looked like . . . he was relieved somewhat," Morales testified. "He wasn't as stressed out as he had been over the phone and when [Chris] . . . initially showed up."

Yet the friction between Dan and Rachel hadn't abated. Chris said that Rachel was staring angrily at her fiancé, as if she wanted to have a word with him in private. Satisfied that part of his loan had been returned—and not wishing to linger in the apartment any longer—Chris left.

A short time later, he looked at his cell phone and realized that he'd missed a call from Dan. When Chris called back, Rachel picked up.

"You left twenty dollars on the floor. You must have dropped it when Dan handed you the money."

"Don't worry," Chris said. "I'll pick it up later."

Generally, Rachel had an upbeat manner. But she seemed troubled during the brief conversation. Chris asked if everything was all right.

"She said she wasn't worried about his thing . . . referring to the money," Morales said. "And she said she was worried about something new. He didn't go into detail about what the something new was, and hung up the phone."

After Sam vanished and police began looking for him as a suspect, Jake Swett—the neighbor Steve had encountered in Sam's apartment—tried creating a timeline of his own. Jake discussed the worrisome circumstances with his roommate, Dave Barnhart, and suggested that they call Dan to gain perspective on what occurred that day.

Jake told police that Dan agreed to meet and arrived at the apartment with Rachel. "When's the last time you saw Sam?" Jake asked.

According to Jake, Dan maintained that Sam had helped him with some chores. Then, when they returned to the building, Dan said that Sam went off with a man wearing a black baseball cap. "At first, he said that it was a short Mexican guy," Morales testified. "And Mr. Swett said that he later changed that story to a short white guy. . . . And so Mr. Swett began inquiring even more, asking him what that person's name was. And Mr. Wozniak was unable to provide any further information."

The explanation didn't make sense. How did this mystery man suddenly appear at the building—and why did Sam go away with him? Did Sam introduce his associate to Dan? Could he have been a friend, or was there something more nefarious about the relationship? As Jake continued his questioning, he told police, Rachel looked over at her fiancé.

"Let's go," she apparently said.

Over the next several days, police continued operating on the assumption that Sam was still alive—and somebody in the building knew where to find him. "I didn't know if, at that point, [Rachel] . . . was harboring Mr. Herr or not," Det. Sgt. Ed Everett would testify, "or Mr. Wozniak was harboring Mr. Herr."

But Steve's personal investigation was painting a different kind of picture. On the morning that he called Dan to ask what he knew about Sam's disappearance, Steve was in Long Beach, still staking out locations where either money had been withdrawn from Sam's account or his credit card was used. Out of all of Sam's friends, Dan was the only one with a Long Beach number. It was too much of a coincidence. Although Steve was still uncertain about where his son might be, he was convinced that Dan knew the answers.

When Raquel called, Steve held on to the faint hope that she'd tell him that Sammy had been in touch. Instead, she said that Detectives Mike Delgadillo and Mike Cohen were at their house. Both were professional and as respectful as they could be under the circumstances. But Sam was their suspect, and they wanted Raquel to know that they were planning to hold a news conference, asking the public to help track down her son. Was there anything that the Herrs needed to tell them?

Steve rushed back to the house. Yes, he responded, there was a lot that he had to say. Dan had admitted to being with Sam on the day he disappeared—and offered the ridiculous story about Sam complaining about his issues with women, as well as "family problems."

"And look at this," Steve added, displaying a printout of Sam's bank transactions. "Somebody's pulling out money every day. And it's all coming from Long Beach. I don't care what you think—this guy Wozniak is dirty."

If the police persisted in their belief that Sam killed Juri, Steve intended to continue his probe—and pass on the findings to authorities. "I'll meet with Wozniak, and tell you what else I can find out."

"Please—don't meet him," Delgadillo urged. He wasn't sure what Steve was liable to do around Wozniak. Plus, the detectives wanted the chance to pursue this new information themselves.

The investigators promised the Herrs that they'd remain in contact and moved toward the door. But just before they left, Delgadillo turned to Cohen. In a voice loud enough for Steve and Raquel to hear, Delgadillo told his partner, "We might be looking for the wrong guy."

CHAPTER TWELVE

Up until this point, the police had treated the Herrs with a level of detachment. "They were not hard—that's not really the right term—but dry," Steve said. "Now, their attitude changed."

The next morning—Wednesday, May 26—Steve returned to Long Beach. He still had his list of locations where money had been withdrawn and was anxious to catch the perpetrator. But he didn't want to do it alone. He phoned detectives to tell them about his plans.

"I called and said, 'Are you guys staking these places out?'" he said. "And they told, 'Steve, we see you in your car right now.'"

At the same time, Det. Sgt. Ed Everett and his partner, Keith Davis, had been dispatched to speak to Dan. They located him with Rachel at the home of her brother Noah. Dan seemed surprised to see the police standing in his doorway.

"How'd you find me?" he asked.

Everett responded with another query: "Do you know why we're here?"

"Yes. It's about the murder."

There was nothing incriminating about this statement. By this stage, everyone in Costa Mesa was talking about the well-liked college coed found killed four days earlier in her friend's apartment.

Dan requested to speak to Everett privately, and the two went outside. "When is the last time you saw Sam?" the sergeant asked.

It was a question that Dan had already answered when Jake pressed him about his final encounter with his neighbor. Since then, he'd probably thought about his alibi dozens of times. "He had indicated that he had seen [Sam] . . . previously . . . Friday morning to Friday afternoon," Everett testified at a pretrial hearing. Dan was preoccupied with his financial challenges, and Sam handed him one hundred dollars.

"Just consider it an early wedding gift," Sam assured his neighbor, "and don't worry about repaying it."

They parted ways for the final time, Dan said, in the middle of the day. "He imagined that he had last seen him between two and three," Everett said. "And after having helped him run some errands for his wedding, Mr. Herr was with another unknown subject, and he left after dropping him off with this unknown subject in a Mazda."

As the conversation continued, Rachel came outside. "Is everything okay?"

Everett looked down at Dan's hands. They were shaking.

Shifting his attention back to Rachel, the sergeant said that he intended to speak with her in a few minutes. For the time being, though, he asked that she return indoors.

Rachel went back into the apartment and waited. When she finally spoke with detectives, her story was almost identical to that of her fiancé. "She indicated that they were having financial issues due to the wedding," Everett said, repeating the account of Sam giving them one hundred dollars as an early wedding present. "She told me she thanked him and then she had said she would save a dance for him at the wedding."

Like Dan, she claimed that Sam had been with a man she didn't recognize. "She said she didn't know who the subject was and didn't believe that he lived in the apartment complex." Everett said that Rachel told him that she'd seen the stranger herself. "She indicated he was in the apartment" with Sam and Dan.

By this point, detectives had a fairly vivid picture of what had occurred in the building that day. For example, they knew that Dan and Rachel had been visited by their friend Chris Williams. But, thus far, the only two people who said that they'd seen the man in the baseball cap were Dan and his fiancée.

It seemed like Dan and Rachel were covering something up. Maybe Dan was the one funneling the money to Sam, police thought. But why? Some detectives wondered if Dan and Sam were lovers. When Sam also became involved with Juri, the theory continued, the lovers' triangle turned violent. Maybe Sam killed Juri in some twisted sign of loyalty to Dan. For all detectives knew, Dan might have killed the pretty Japanese student himself.

Once they were done talking to Rachel, Everett and Davis returned to their car. "Let's follow him," Everett said, referring to Wozniak. "I think he'll lead us to Sam."

A team was assigned to surveille Dan from a distance, tracking him to Long Beach—the same general area that Steve had been watching. They spotted Dan exiting his car and meeting with a teenager, who handed the actor an envelope. After Dan left, the officers continued monitoring the teen. About twenty minutes later, a pizza deliveryman arrived on the block. The boy went outside to pay for a pie, then brought it across the street from his home—into a house where a party appeared to be going on.

Police followed the deliveryman several blocks and pulled him over. They learned that the pizza had been ordered from Ecco's—one of the spots where money had been withdrawn from Sam's account—and paid for with the veteran's ATM card. Detectives were alerted about the development and decided to crash the party.

"We thought that Sam might be hiding in the house," Everett said.

The teenager answered the door. When he looked up, he saw a helicopter banking over the building, and the officer inside literally pointing at him. As investigators searched the house for the missing veteran, the boy identified himself as sixteen-year-old Wesley Freilich—the same Wesley Freilich who'd played Winthrop in *The Music Man* and considered Daniel Wozniak his mentor. He tried to stonewall the police at first, denying any connection to the ATM card.

"Are you sure about that?" he was challenged. "This card's tied to a homicide."

Wesley was a kid who aspired to be an actor, not a criminal. Tears instantly ran down his face. "A homicide?" he repeated, terrified.

He immediately disclosed that the ATM card had been given to him by Dan Wozniak. Dan said that it wasn't a big deal. He was working for a bail bonds agent, and the card belonged to a client who'd posted bail, then disappeared.

For the past several days, Wesley said, Dan had had him withdrawing money from the account. When Wesley did this, Dan made it clear that it was important to wear a hat and sunglasses; you didn't want a security camera catching your image. He wasn't really supposed to be ordering pizza, Wesley admitted. But it's not like he wasn't doing his job. In fact, earlier in the day he'd handed Dan an envelope with his latest withdrawal—four hundred dollars.

Police still didn't know what had happened to Sam or what role he might have had in Juri's death. But they were beginning to view him as less of a perpetrator and more of a victim. After all, Wesley was delivering Sam's money back to Dan, not some enigmatic figure whom no one could name. At the very least, Dan—who'd continually suggested that he was desperate for money—was guilty of obtaining those funds through fraudulent means.

That night, Dan put on his effervescent grin when he met up with a group of friends at Tsunami, a Japanese restaurant in Huntington Beach, for his bachelor party. His wedding was just two days away, and if he was still panicking over money no one appeared to notice. Before the celebration ended, though, authorities entered the establishment and arrested the groom for financial improprieties.

Dan would later complain that the lawmen waited until he'd finished paying the check.

Sam's Army friend Miles Foltz learned about the arrest from Rachel. Miles had come to the building to discuss the case with Sam's neighbors Dave Barnhart and Jake Swett, hoping to make sense of the disappearance. Although both men had been friendly with Sam, they seemed exceptionally close to Rachel, and she was in the apartment as well. It was the first time that she and Miles had ever met. As they spoke, Rachel received a text and looked over at Miles.

"Dan got arrested," she told him.

Because no one reacted with dismay, Miles assumed that he was the only one hearing the news for the first time. Certainly, Rachel seemed perplexed by the circumstances. Yet Miles had the sense that all three had expected the arrest to occur.

"She wasn't really freaking out," Miles said. With the wedding date so close, he expected a stronger reaction. Maybe that was just the way Rachel processed information, Miles thought. Still, something wasn't right. Miles wondered what Rachel and her friends weren't telling him.

"It was really weird," he said, "just a really weird atmosphere around her."

But Rachel said she didn't grasp the extent of Dan's problems. "I didn't know what to think," she'd tell the *Dr. Phil* show. "And my first response was"—she smiled—" 'Oh my gosh. What trouble could this idiot have gotten himself into now? And is he going to be out for the dress rehearsal tomorrow?' "

At the time, Dan was simply charged with bank fraud. No one said anything about Sam's ATM card being used, but Miles instinctively knew that the crime was tied to his friend's disappearance.

"Rachel said something about Dan owing money to a loan shark," Miles said. "The others seemed to know about it, and were saying things like, 'You know Dan; he can't keep his fuckin' mouth shut' and 'he's not going to be able to keep his story straight.' And so I was like, 'Is everyone in on this?' "

Not wanting to reveal his suspicions, Miles looked down at his phone and quietly sent a text to Steve. Rachel needed to be investigated, Miles suggested. She might know what had happened to Sam. In fact, Miles thought that maybe the whole building was part of the conspiracy.

To add to the confusion, police noticed that somebody had logged on to Sam's Facebook account. It seemed like Sam was still alive and posting messages from Northern California.

Costa Mesa detectives contacted authorities there. They

quickly discovered that the poster was a buddy of Sam's who knew nothing about the disappearance. He just knew Sam's password and was putting up some nonsensical post as a gag.

It was just around midnight when Dan arrived at the Costa Mesa Police Department and was taken to an interview room. From two monitoring rooms on the same floor, detectives gathered to watch a telecast of the conversation.

Det. Mike Delgadillo—the investigator to whom Steve had initially handed the list of banking transactions—sat across from Dan. Delgadillo had been a member of the Costa Mesa Police for thirty-one years. At his side was bald, bull-necked Det. Mike Cohen.

Reaching for a lanyard he kept around his neck, Cohen read Dan his Miranda rights from a laminated card.

Police had quickly determined that the crime was not drug related. Although Dan drank and dabbled in Ecstasy, he wasn't a daily drug user, nor had he attempted to alleviate his financial stresses by dealing cocaine, methamphetamine, or OxyContin. Likewise—despite his fondness for consuming alcohol with friends—Sam wasn't even a recreational drug user.

Nevertheless, Dan told detectives that it was Sam who conceived the plot to defraud the bank. "He told us that he had been approached by . . . Sam Herr to get involved in a fraudulent credit card scam," Delgadillo said, "where he was orchestrating use of Sam's ATM card.

"He explained to him that he could make money by using Sam's ATM card, and requesting the assistance of a third party to use Sam's card and go to the ATM, withdraw money from Sam's account, and Sam could make the claim later that his card was being used fraudulently, and the money would be refunded to him."

Dan claimed that Sam agreed to stay far away from the bank or ATM when the money was being withdrawn. This way, if there was a sighting of Sam at that time he'd be able to maintain his argument that he had no connection to the plot. In addition, Sam intended to use his cell phone, Dan said, in case authorities attempted to determine his location with telephone company records.

Wesley was chosen to participate because he was underage, Dan said. "He got ahold of Wesley and asked him if he would engage in using the card at the ATM," Delgadillo said. Dan's rationale: "Because he was a juvenile . . . more than likely, if he was ever caught, they would do nothing, as far as prosecution."

But what about Juri? It was one thing to steal a few hundred dollars from a bank and quite another to kill a young woman. Dan anticipated that detectives were going to ask about the murder and was eager to provide an answer.

He blamed Juri's death on Sam.

"He did it," Dan said. "I'm not going to protect him anymore. I'll tell you everything."

According to Dan, he'd met Sam downstairs on Saturday, May 22—hours before Steve discovered the corpse in his son's apartment. Sam appeared nervous, Dan claimed. "He said that Sam . . . asked for some help to get out of the area," Det. Jose Morales would testify, "that he had done something. He wouldn't go into detail."

What Sam did reveal, Dan said, was that something bad had happened in his apartment.

"Dan got dressed and left with Sam in Sam's vehicle, as they drove just to drive," Morales said. "They weren't really going anywhere. He said that Sam . . . admitted that he had killed somebody, and that he needed to get away. Eventually, Sam admitted that he killed Julie."

The reason Dan hadn't disclosed this information previously, he said, was that he was scared. After all, he'd claimed to have seen Juri's body with his own eyes. "At one point, he finally confessed to going up to the apartment and seeing what was there," Delgadillo said. "Apparently, Julie was deceased. And he agreed to take Sam, drive him into Long Beach, and, over the course of time, take money out of his account and funnel it back to him so that he could flee the area.

". . . He said he did it because Sam had threatened that if he didn't help him, he would come back and get him, as well as . . . Rachel."

Delgadillo and Cohen let Dan talk. But neither of the seasoned detectives believed much of what he heard. "There were a lot of [inconsistencies] . . . ," Delgadillo said. "I mean, we asked him about where he dropped [Sam] . . . off, where he was staying. He was very evasive as to a lot of this, the way he had driven up there. I mean, we asked him a lot of questions about the area that he dropped him off at, as far as how we can contact him. It just didn't seem right."

While Dan was busy with the two investigators, Det. Jose Morales drove to the Camden Martinique apartments and looked for Rachel.

He wasn't sure how Dan's fiancée would act when he found her. But, at this stage of his career, Jose believed that he was prepared for just about anything. The detective had grown up in the neighboring city of Santa Ana after emigrating with his parents from Mexico's Guerrero State at age four. He remembered his parents each working two—and sometimes three—jobs while the family attempted to gain a foothold in the United States. Both labored in factories. Jose's father also picked oranges for Valencia Growers in Irvine, while his mother worked in a series of bakeries.

The one thing the two generations shared was an appreciation of Los Tigres del Norte, a San Jose, California–based band with its roots in drug-ravaged Sinaloa, Mexico. Jose was aware of the fact that traffickers from both sides of the border enjoyed the group's songs about gangsterism, but that wasn't the part of the music that appealed to him. "They talk about the Mexican government not fulfilling people's dreams," he said, "and the way people suffer after they come to the United States for a better life."

He saw signs of that struggle all over Santa Ana, as well as a hesitance to cooperate with the authorities. "People respected law enforcement," he said. "But they weren't going to be forthcoming with information. We used to live across the street from a rock house"—a place where addicts purchased crack-cocaine—"and people would knock on *our* door, thinking that was the place. You wouldn't call the police. People used to break into our house all the time. You wouldn't call the police. We'd buy bikes every other month because people would steal our bikes. They'd jump over our fence and steal them. But you wouldn't call the police for that.

"You didn't want to get involved with the police coming over to your house."

Among the city's immigrant population, the Santa Ana police had a reputation for manhandling thieves and other miscreants. "They were very tough," Jose said. "You didn't mess with the Santa Ana Police Department."

His family largely approved of their tactics. "My mom was the law enforcer in our house," he said, "and she told me, 'If the police ever catch you doing something bad, they're not bringing you home. You can stay in jail and forget about getting bailed out.' "

Nevertheless, Jose had little fear of law enforcement. They'd never do anything to him, he reasoned, as long as he followed his mother's edicts about staying out of trouble. "I was attracted to the uniform," he says. "My uncle was a first sergeant in the Mexican military, stationed out of Mexicali. We'd go out and visit him once in a while, and he'd tell me about confiscating drugs and burning them in the mountains, and all the duties he had. He'd show me his shooting trophies, and I was attracted to that."

Whenever the police passed Jose on the street, he made it a point to acknowledge the men in blue. "My friends would say, 'Why are you waving to *them*?' But those were my guys. They were it."

Because his parents couldn't afford college, Morales decided to join the U.S. Marines Reserve after high school and have the government pay for his education. He attended Golden West College in Huntington Beach while working the graveyard shift as a security guard. And since he'd been in the Santa Ana Police Department's Explorer group in high school—a type of scouting program in which young people learn about law enforcement policies and training—he was offered a second, paid position as a part-time cadet. At age twenty-two, he was given a full-time job.

Dealing with drunks and bar brawls was relatively easy. Jose was confident in his physicality and could easily break up fights. And if the situation became heated, he had both the weapons and the training to wrest the confrontation in the direction that it needed to go. Interactions with the mentally ill were more confusing. "It's hard when you're trying to help somebody who doesn't want to be helped," he said. "You say one wrong thing, and you're going to get the kind of reaction that can trigger something very negative. So you have to think quick.

"I remember being called to one lady's home who tried to cut her wrists. She was upstairs. We were downstairs. What I tried to do was connect with her not like a police officer who wanted to lock her up, but another human who cared about her personally. We talked about the people who needed her, like her kids, the things that were important to her. And, eventually, she dropped the glass, and we were able to take her into custody to get her some help."

After six years on patrol, Morales began working undercover as a narcotics officer. In one operation, he'd arranged to buy a collection of guns, along with cocaine, methamphetamine, marijuana, and pseudoephedrine. But when the conspirators' affiliates were busted in Northern California, the suspects became paranoid and demanded a meeting.

"It wasn't, 'Let's go meet for some beers,'" he said. "It was, 'We want to talk to you *now*. We need to get to the bottom of who the snitch is.'"

After conferring with his superiors, Jose found an excuse not to attend, then continuously delayed the meeting for several more weeks until tensions eased. Although the dealers suspected Morales, they were anxious to make the sale—and the police department was able to make the bust. "It's always the greed," Jose observed. "It's always about the money to them. They'll forgive and forget as long as the money's coming in."

With each passing year, Jose acquired more knowledge about the criminal psyche. A year before Dan's arrest, Jose was promoted to detective, specializing in Crimes Against Persons.

At the Camden Martinique apartments, Morales found Rachel with Jake Swett and Dave Barnhart in the apartment that they shared, and asked to speak with her outside.

After briefly discussing Dan's arrest, Morales asked Rachel if she'd be willing to accompany him to the police department. "You're not under arrest, and you can end our interview at any time," he said.

"Okay."

When she arrived at the building, Dan was interrupted in the interview room and told that his fiancée was outside. He asked if he could talk to her.

"The police said . . . , 'Okay, we're going to have him talk to you 'cause what he has to say, you're not going to believe it, coming from us,'" Rachel recalled. "At that point, I realized that he was seriously in trouble."

Rachel was brought into the interview room. With the detectives listening, Dan "told her that he had been involved in a fraud scheme with Sam," Morales said, "and that Sam had killed Julie, and that he had helped him clean up the crime scene."

Morales watched Rachel closely to gauge how she was absorbing the news. "There was no reaction," the detective said. "That's what kind of caught us off guard is that he's telling her what's going on, and she has no reaction. . . . There's nothing."

After the exchange, Rachel left the interview room and met privately with detectives, telling them about Dan's behavior the previous Friday, when he'd been hyperventilating and acting as if he were going to have a heart attack. She maintained that she asked what was wrong and he explained that he'd borrowed money from "bad people" and had to repay the funds that day.

She insisted that she was ignorant about whatever occurred later on. "After hearing out of Dan's mouth that he had any involvement in a murder, I went into shock," she said on *Dr. Phil*. "The wedding's the next day. We were supposed to have our dress rehearsal that evening, and I'm finding out he's not the person I thought he was."

* * *

After Rachel went home, Dan was led out of the interview room to a jail cell down the hallway. After his DUI arrest, it was his second night in police custody in less than a month. But in this case, it seemed like he'd remain behind bars far longer.

At noon, Det. Sgt. Everett received a message from the jailer. Daniel Wozniak had more that he wanted to say.

Delgadillo rushed back to the jail. Dan was in a holding cell, waiting. The detective would describe him as "extremely agitated, anxious. He seemed kind of upset."

According to Delgadillo, Dan said, "I need to talk to you."

"Okay. You'll be able to talk to me, but we have to go back into the interview room."

Dan nodded and Delgadillo led the suspect down the hallway—into the room where Det. Mike Cohen was already waiting. Once again, Delgadillo repeated the Miranda warning, and Dan waived his rights.

"After I advised him of his rights, I asked him if he wanted to talk to me," Delgadillo said. "And he asked me where his attorney was. And I told him, 'I just got done advising you of your rights. . . . Do you understand that?' And he says, 'Yes.' I asked him, 'Do you want to speak with me?' 'Yes.' 'You said you had something to say. Go ahead and tell us.' And he goes, 'Okay.'"

It was the third time in less than twenty-four hours that the detective had gone over Dan's rights with him. In the detective's mind, Dan understood that he could ask for an attorney at any time and the interview would abruptly end. But Delgadillo believed that Dan didn't want an attorney. Dan wanted to talk.

The Daniel Wozniak who looked at Delgadillo was not the same man who entered a room grinning, telling boisterous jokes, and backslapping both friends and strangers.

Now Dan's face was serious. His eyes were wide, and there was clearly something that he needed his questioners to know.

Delgadillo returned Dan's stare, and Dan started to talk.

"The first words out of his mouth," the detective said, "were, quote, 'I'm crazy and I did it.' "

CHAPTER THIRTEEN

Within the space of a few short days, investigators had gone from viewing Steve and Raquel Herr as the parents of a killer on the run to victims themselves. When the investigators finally informed the couple that they had Daniel Wozniak in custody for Sam's death, the news was delivered with sensitivity, as well as a resolve to bring the family justice.

"Underneath, I felt he was already dead," Steve told the *Orange County Register* when asked about that painful moment when he learned that his son had been killed, "but when they confirmed it, it was a tough go. Your lives are crushed when you get news like this."

As Steve and Raquel mourned with their extended family, details about the arrest and double homicide trickled out in small dosages.

It was chilly when Jeff Hathcock drove onto the Joint Forces Training Base at Los Alamitos in the hours after

Dan's confession. He was planning on a typical day, calling actors and making improvements at the theater. He found a parking spot close to the performing center and exited his car. When he did, he was met by a number of official-looking men in military uniforms.

"We're going to have to close the theater down."

Jeff was bewildered. "What, for repairs?"

"No, no, something else."

"What? What else?"

"I can't tell you."

Flustered by the stupefying information, Jeff drove to the security office and asked about what was occurring. This time, the answer was slightly less vague.

"I can't really tell you, but the police are at your theater. There's been a murder there."

It was the last scenario that Jeff expected. "Holy shit," he blurted.

"My theater!" he later recalled. "I'm praying it's no one I know. So I got into my car again, and drove to the back of the theater. The Costa Mesa police, the FBI, military security, and other police officers were all there. I told them who I was and asked them what happened."

Once again, Jeff was informed, "Somebody was murdered in your theater."

"Oh, my God. I can't believe this."

An investigator from the Costa Mesa police introduced himself and asked Jeff for identification. The detective studied Jeff's driver's license and nodded.

"Let's go around to the front of the theater so we can talk."

The inside of the building was now cordoned off. The two sat down on the steps, and the detective began asking questions.

"Do you know anyone named Dan or Sam?"

"I don't know anybody named Sam. But I do know a Dan. Dan Wozniak."

"What do you know about him?"

"He's a hell of a nice guy. I think he's a great guy."

Perhaps pondering the state of Juri's body at the time she was located, the detective switched topics. "Do you know if the adult males in your cast get along with their wives?"

"As far as I know, they do."

"What about guns? Do any of them own guns?"

"Well, some of them do." He explained how actors had occasionally dressed up in Western clothes, complete with rifles, and posed for photos in frontier settings.

The temperature seemed to be dropping, and Jeff was only wearing a T-shirt, so he asked for permission to sit in his car when the interview was completed. The detective agreed. As Jeff studied the activity from the driver's seat, he saw a gurney being wheeled into the theater. Once again, he told himself that he hoped that he didn't know the victim.

Who could possibly have died in the Liberty Theater? Jeff tried to visualize what had occurred. He imagined a confrontation in either the theater seats or the aisle and someone producing a gun. After all, the detective had mentioned a firearm.

Exiting the vehicle, Jeff found a member of the base's security team.

"Where'd the murder take place?" Jeff asked. "Was it in the seats?"

"No, it was upstairs."

Suddenly the security guard started to cry.

"What's wrong?" Jeff asked.

"They're all up there, looking at the body."

"Did you see it yourself?"

The security guard nodded.

"Well, what did it look like?"

"I don't know." The sobs grew louder. "It didn't have a head."

Now Jeff started shaking. He needed to talk to his wife. Tracking down the Costa Mesa detective, Jeff asked if he was needed any longer.

"No. Go home. We'll call you if we have any more questions."

It wasn't always easy to receive news from the States in Afghanistan. But since Sam vanished, Theresa Glowicki felt as if she was in constant contact with people who'd heard rumors or theories. When she finally learned that her friend had been killed, though, she was as puzzled as when she heard that he'd gone missing.

"I knew the kind of person Sam was," she said, "and I knew that if were in any kind of danger, he'd fight for his life. I could easily see Sam fighting a seven-foot man and coming out the winner."

Theresa had never met Dan Wozniak and knew little about him. But she felt as if she understood exactly how the murder transpired. "I figured that whoever had done this to him was a coward, and had to have done it fast—and without Sam's knowledge at all. Because if Sam saw it coming, there was no way that anyone could take him down."

For Ruben Menacho, the situation was even more confusing. Although he didn't like Dan, the actor never had appeared menacing or violent. Plus, Dan and Sam seemed to be friends.

"When I found out it was Wozniak, I wanted to know why," Ruben said. "I didn't think he had anything against Sam. Sam had helped him out a bunch of times. And the way Julie was killed, it was horrible. I found it hard to believe that Dan Wozniak would do something like that to her. I'm not saying I thought he was innocent. It was just hard to believe. It didn't make any sense.

"I was thinking, 'There has to be more to this story.'"

Over and over again, Jessica Wolf Googled Dan Wozniak's name, hoping to find a new clue that would explain why her friend Juri Kibuishi was taken so suddenly.

"I was looking up his name, and then I found his fiancée's name and started Googling her," Jessica said. "I looked on Facebook because I wanted to see what their deal was, just trying to put all the pieces together myself.

"Already, there were people on the fiancée's Facebook page, bashing her. And her brother was on there, arguing with people, saying; 'She had nothing to do with this.' I felt so stupid, creeping on these people. But I wanted to know who they were, and what happened. Because it was just so baffling to me.

"It still is."

At a press conference, Juri's mother, Junko—or June, as her American friends called her—recalled how her daughter always communicated with the family. On the night she died, Junko's concern had been nothing more serious than Juri's commute to her brother Taka's home. "I told her she better leave early because traffic is hard in Long Beach," Junko said before dissolving into tears.

Juri's father, Masa, could barely muster the energy to tell the assembled reporters, "I don't want to say too much. Still, I don't believe this has happened."

Each member of the family continued rerunning the events of May 21, wishing they'd done something to prevent Juri rushing to the Camden Martinique apartments. Taka said that, if he could do the night over, he would have ensured that Juri was too drunk to drive and forced her to stay at his home.

"It is horrible to think that anyone in the world can derive this kind of plan," he said, "and take innocent victims."

In her mind, Junko continued to replay the moment when police informed her that her daughter was found murdered in the apartment of the man she'd described as a friendly, helpful "teddy bear." Junko had shaken her head from side to side, telling herself, "No. No. That's not my daughter."

On both the storefront theater and the karaoke networks in Orange County, people who'd considered Dan a friend were reevaluating their assessments of him.

"I found him charming," actor and costume designer Molly Dewane told the *Orange County Register.* "He was really good with little kids. He was always on time. He had a great sense of humor. I went to a karaoke bar with him and had a wonderful time. I never saw a temper."

A blogger who called herself "A Mad Mom" wrote about her two daughters meeting Dan while auditioning for *The Music Man.* Like so many others, they were instantly enchanted.

"The lead role, the Music Man himself, was played by Dan Wozniak," the writer said. "The now-infamous Dan Wozniak. You know, the freak from Costa Mesa who just murdered two people . . . perpetually happy guy with the aw-shucks personality and gentle disposition, the guy who everyone loved and admired, including both my daughters, was not the gentle soul he pretended to be. . . . Who would have known?"

She described Dan as a person who always smiled and joked, elevating the moods of the people around her. Children, as well as parents, admired Dan, the blogger said. Once, she recalled, she approached him in the green room, praising him for both his dramatic skills and the positive energy that he seemed to spread everywhere.

"It makes me wonder," she continued. "Was Dan harboring those psychopathic thoughts when he was sharing the stage with all those kids? . . . What was he thinking when he put his arms around my two daughters and posed for one picture after the next."

Her final encounter with Dan occurred when he was directing her children in the musical comedy *Once Upon a Mattress*. She wrote, "I had this feeling we'd be hearing a lot more from Dan in the future. I was right. I just didn't expect the news to be so grisly—and so disappointing."

Readers of the blog were equally as stunned. "The story is still so heavy on my mind," wrote one anonymous respondent. "Dan was a fellow karaoke singer. . . . You couldn't help but smile or laugh when Dan was around."

Two days before the murder, the writer said that she texted Dan to invite him to her birthday party. He sent back a characteristically amiable message. "I still cannot believe what he did and am soooo saddened to think that a person I admired could be capable of such a heinous crime."

Most of the replies to the blog were composed in the same spirit. Although no one defended Dan, everybody seemed to wish that the perpetrator had been another person. "My mind keeps coming back to Dan, too," another reader wrote. "Total disbelief. Do you think he was psychopathic all the time?"

Dewane told the *Register* that she was disappointed over not being able to detect the dangerous side of Dan. But she knew that she was far from alone: "I suspect he was one of those people who was really good at holding things in. Still, it's very difficult to reconcile what I know about Dan with this awful . . . crime."

Forensic psychologist Michael Perrotti, Ph.D., speculated that Dan's actor friends might have disregarded some of his curious behavior as simple nonconformity.

"I think because of the nature of their work, actors can be more sensitive to human emotion. They are probably more accepting and less critical . . . because of the process they go through when working on roles. He may have been showing signs of trouble and people saw it, but dismissed it or minimized it."

Perrotti estimated that those who'd shared dressing rooms with Dan—and relied on him while performing— might not come to terms with his role in the crimes for months or even years.

Dewane said that she intended to cope by thinking of Dan in the past tense. "It's like he died. You want to remember the person that was. How could I have possibly worked with someone who could do something like that? I just can't wrap my mind around this. It's impossible to."

As *OC Weekly* drama critic Joel Beers probed the sentiment in the local theater community, he heard a number of statements that he considered justifications for the extreme brutality that claimed the lives of Sam and Juri. "Some people said things to the effect of, 'Well, we all possess this inside us. There's nothing surprising. Theater people are screwed up,'" Beers recalled. "And that's bullshit. We don't all possess the ability to kill two people. This was unbelievably gruesome. And two people who are your friends? What the fuck?"

As he attempted to comprehend Dan's mentality, Beers combed the actor's social media pages. For Dan's last birthday, in March, there had been dozens of Facebook greetings. That alone was fairly routine. What Beers found interesting was the tone of the messages. "They weren't just, 'Happy birthday, blah, blah, blah,'" he said. "I mean, it was like, 'You're one of my best friends.' 'You've done nothing but support me and help me.' 'You're the greatest guy.' There seemed to be a lot of genuine affection and love for the guy. And after the murders, people started posting more critical things, and one that really stood out to me was somebody saying that Dan always had a smile on his face, and it bugged the person. And he always offered everyone beer at parties, and this guy said he was trying too hard. You know, it was one of those twenty-twenty hindsight things. Like, 'No one can be in that kind of a mood all the time.'"

Unlike Dan's acquaintances, who knew him in social settings, the one time that Beers had observed the suspect was when the actor was starring in *Nine*. Now the similarities between Daniel Wozniak and Guido Contini were unmistakable. "Here's the megalomaniac in the play who basically gets away not with murder, but he cheats and he lies," Beers said, "and everybody loves him because he's so talented and brilliant and all of that. And by the end of the play, he looks at all the things that make him unhappy and he has this redemptive moment. And I wrote about just how weird it was that here's the actor who played Guido Contini also dealing with issues of his own doing."

When the media visited the Starting Gate, part of the circuit of bars where Dan and his friends sang karaoke, one of the customers drew a parallel between the suspect and Anthony John, the central character of the 1947 film *A Double Life*. Like Dan, Anthony is an actor who appears to lack the barometer to measure the difference between fictional and actual violence. While playing Othello on Broadway, Anthony fatally strangles his mistress and later attacks his press agent.

Ronald Colman received an Academy Award for his portrayal of Anthony. But there'd be no such prize in Daniel Wozniak's future. As he sat in a jail cell and police continued investigating the double homicide, the pinnacle of his theatrical success was behind him.

The only distinctions that he'd garner would come from his newfound infamy.

Jeffrey Kociencki knew Dan from high school and college and feared that he was destined for some kind of clash with the law. Around Halloween, Dan had texted his old friend about a possible insurance scam. Kociencki unambiguously turned Dan down. Then, a week or so before the double homicide, Dan called Kociencki and mentioned that there'd been a murder at the Camden Martinique apartments. At the time, Dan insisted, he was taking a serene walk by a duck pond. But because no one had seen him there, he wondered if Kociencki was the type of guy who'd be interested in providing an alibi.

"I couldn't help him out with that," Kociencki later testified. Believing the tale about the murder at the complex, he told Dan to talk to the police and be honest with them. If he was telling the truth, Kociencki assured Dan, it would all turn out fine.

Still, there was something about the conversation that just didn't feel right.

At the Liberty Theater, the members of the Hathcock family finally understood why Dan had played such a convincing Harold Hill in *The Music Man.* All the hints about the peculiarities in his personality were forming a larger picture.

When she wasn't busy at the theater, Nancy Hathcock earned money by managing a real estate office. After hearing about the commissions that some of the brokers were earning, Dan made an appointment to see her. "I was telling him that he had to get licensed," Nancy said, "and he let me know that he was already doing real estate with another broker, and he was doing it without a license. He'd make the deal, and the broker would pay him under the table and call it a referral fee.

"Well, if somebody goes out and actually shows you a home, even if they don't sign the contact—they'll fill the contract out, and the broker or agent signs it—that is so illegal. The broker can go to prison for allowing that. If Dan was involved in that kind of activity, he'd never get a license in the state of California.

"The way he was talking to me, I realized that this was one guy I wasn't going to recruit into my office. I didn't even tell him, 'Go and get your license, then talk to me.' We don't need that type in the real estate business."

Dan never noticed the disapproval. When the Liberty Theater tried to expand its base, Allyson remembered Dan being eager to assist. One day, he walked into the building with a disc containing the mailing list for the Orange County Children's Theatre. "He'd done some work for them," she said, "and I guess he just took it."

After the arrest, Jeff recollected his interactions with Dan in and out of the theater. "We talked about how jolly he was, and his charisma," Jeff said. "But now, when I think about it, there was always an underlying tension." At times, Dan's inner turmoil worked for him, Jeff said, particularly when the actor was able to channel it into a character onstage. "I've directed almost five thousand actors in over one hundred and seventy-five plays. And in Dan's case, that tension was always there. You could feel it. It was a very palpable thing."

In December 2009, six months before the murders, the Liberty Theater was presenting *Babes in Toyland*. Each night after the performances, the family would lock the doors to the lower level of the theater. But if someone was really determined to access the stage, he or she could enter the balcony, where there was a ladder leading to an unlatched trapdoor. This led to a loft, from which one could enter the backstage area.

One day, when the family arrived to prepare for rehearsals, they discovered that someone had come into the theater after it had closed, removing set pieces and costumes. An extension ladder was spread over the seats. "We had two wooden nutcrackers in the show, beautifully painted," Jeff said. "And those nutcrackers were missing. There was a hole in the ceiling where someone had started to fall through, probably drunk, and plaster on the seats. Someone had tried to pull the Plexiglas off of our control room up there."

At the time, the family concluded that some of the Marines from the base had invaded the space. Then, in March, while the cast was rehearsing for *King Arthur,* the Hatchcocks heard footsteps on the catwalk—about thirty-five feet up. Jeff contacted security at the base. "They went up there and found some cigarette butts, Coca-Cola, and a half-consumed bottle of Jack Daniel's," Jeff said.

"Jack and Coke. That was Dan's drink. That's when I remembered that Dan knew how to get into the theater through the balcony, and began to think that he was the one who went up there."

Both invasions occurred within days of Dan's visits. "The two times when he came to the theater, he was on edge, like he was thinking about something," Jeff said. "And the costumes that were stolen, those were male costumes. Also, why would someone just take set pieces? So I began to think, no, it wasn't a soldier who broke in. It was an actor. It had to be somebody in theater." Remembered Allyson, "Dan kept coming in, and then things would disappear."

When Allyson saw Dan again, she'd mentioned the thefts. "By the way," she told him, "there was some stuff missing after you were here that last time."

Dan replied by flashing her a sly smile. "*Ya, ha, ha,*" he said dramatically. "You caught me."

Allyson smiled, as well. But she felt that Dan was hiding the truth. "The attitude I got was, 'Let's see you try to prove it.'"

CHAPTER FOURTEEN

One day after the confession, a reporter contacted Dan's father, Daryl. Stunned by the recent chain of events, Daryl Wozniak said that his son was in a coma.

A Costa Mesa police spokesperson told the press that Dan had been taken to Western Medical Center on Thursday, May 27, with self-inflicted head injuries. Authorities believed that, when Dan was alone in his cell, he'd attempted to commit suicide.

Whatever rage Dan had been hiding had now been unleashed on himself. To those who'd seen him onstage, it was easy to imagine him uttering a line by Guido Contini in *Nine:* "Nothing in my life makes sense."

It was a statement that not only applied to Daniel Wozniak. Friends and family of both Sam Herr and Juri Kibuishi were experiencing the same feelings.

Sam Herr's friend Ruben Menacho wondered if Dan had been trying to kill himself—or take himself out of commission before his words got other people in trouble. Like Miles Foltz, Ruben suspected that those close to Dan might be part of the plot. "I was thinking, 'There has to be a reason why Dan Wozniak tried to commit suicide,' " Ruben said. " 'Maybe the cops aren't doing the right investigation.' "

In the *OC Weekly,* Joel Beers wrote that he'd wished the public was more interested in the loss of Sam and Juri than the killer himself. Yet Beers—like almost everyone else following the case—could not contain himself from analyzing the alleged perpetrator. That the accused was also an actor—an actor many in the community knew and considered a friend—made the crime even more mystifying and, Beers admitted, more tantalizing.

"Making the accused murderer rather than his victims the focus of any conversation about a crime is an unfortunate reality," Beers wrote. "Victims of violent crime can be anyone; perpetrators are the agents who break our collective social covenant, exposing the rank currents that lurk beneath the apparent placid surface of daily reality. As such, they are fascinating, if wholly unsavory, train wrecks.

". . . It's tempting for creative-minded people to look at this story as a case study of a highly talented actor obviously wrestling with deeply disturbed and submerged issues finally snapping during a well-received run in a challenging play and on the verge of marriage. A case of self sabotage to an unimaginably horrible degree."

Beers speculated over a legal strategy that might depict Dan as

> a young man with serious psychological issues and under economic and emotional strain . . . led to the breaking point through the process of laying his emotions bare by crawling into the skin of a greatly tortured egomaniac (on stage).
>
> Not inconceivable perhaps, but it would be really shitty. Because the simple truth is if Wozniak indeed

did commit the murders, he deserves no empathy, analysis or explanation. . . . Those who choose to take the stuff of dramatic fiction out of the theaters and into the sunlight are not tragically flawed heroes. They're just evil fucks.

Head scars and bruises notwithstanding, Dan rallied in the hospital and his health quickly returned. After two days, he was sent back to the Orange County Jail while investigators continued to use the suspect's words to piece together the circumstances surrounding the double homicide.

On Friday, May 21—the day after Dan ran into Sam and Juri by the elevator—he told detectives that he lured Sam to the Liberty Theater on the Los Alamitos Joint Forces Training Base. The theater was empty that day, and Sam thought that he was going to help Dan move a few items. But when they were alone, Dan said, he shot Sam in the head, stole his ATM card, wallet, and cell phone, and left him in the building.

On the same day that Dan was smashing his head against the hard surfaces of his cell, police found Sam— naked and headless—upstairs in the theater's loft area, near the lighting booth. His hands had been chopped off, as well as the upper portion of his left arm, in a bizarre effort to camouflage the victim's identity.

"It's a very cold, calculating and heinous crime," Det. Sgt. Ed Everett told the *Los Angeles Times*. "He probably took some time to plan it."

Later, the sergeant would remember the conversation: "I told the reporter that it was very heinous because it appears to have stemmed from a financial gain kind of thing. The fact that we have our first victim and then the second victim is lured to the location . . . I just can't fathom that."

But what he did sense was that there was more to the

story. Police were continuing to question Dan's associates to determine who "may potentially have assisted in it or may have helped him after the fact," Everett said. "My guess is that there'll probably be some future arrests."

When Ruben learned the details, he reexamined everything he had done that Friday. Early in the afternoon, he'd been invited to Huntington Beach with Sam's neighbors Jake Swett and Dave Barnhart. "I asked if they were with Sam," Ruben said. "And they told me, 'No, just come over.'"

Ruben thought that the group was going to meet Sam at some point. "We started driving to the beach," he said, "and I get a text message from Sam's phone, saying, 'Some issues with my family.' Issues with his family? That was kind of weird. And something else—Sam always called me 'Rube,' but in the text message he was calling me 'bro.'"

Confused by the digital exchange, Ruben attempted to call his friend. "The first time, no one answered. I called back and someone picked up. You could hear a lot of wind over the phone. And it's like, 'I'm dealing with some stuff with my family. I'll call you right back.' And I'm thinking, 'What? What are you talking about?' And he hangs up.

"I knew it wasn't Sam."

At the beach, Ruben again inquired about Sam. "Dave tells me, 'Oh, Sammy's helping Dan set up some tents.' For the wedding. So we had a regular beach day—hot dogs, beer."

As the afternoon was winding down, the group struck up a conversation with a beachgoer who'd come on his bicycle and gave him a ride home. Eventually, the trio ended up drinking at the Goat Hill Tavern in Costa Mesa. "We're talking in the bar," Ruben said. "Everything was normal. But it just didn't seem right that Sam wasn't answering and he didn't call me back all day."

But maybe the process of putting up tents took longer than Sam realized, and then he'd rushed over to his parents' house to work out whatever family difficulties they were having. Only later did Ruben dissect the terminology of the text message and the fleeting phone call—but that was after he knew that, while he was drinking beers and walking along the surf, Sam was being murdered at the Liberty Theater.

Ruben would also ponder Dave and Jake's motives that day. Were they simply being friendly by inviting an acquaintance to the beach, or did they purposely want to isolate Sam from a friend who would have intervened before Wozniak's plan could be carried out?

"I mean, everything is questionable," Ruben said. "Out of anger, I wanted to blame everybody."

Before detectives ruled out accomplices, though, they had to question not only the members of Dan's social circle but everyone associated with the theater—in order to ascertain that nobody assisted Dan with the murder.

They discovered that no one was more shocked by the details of the macabre scene than the Hathcock family.

They remembered walking across the base one night while the investigation was under way and running into Wesley Freilich—the teen accused of siphoning Sam's funds back to Dan—and his mother.

"What are you doing here?" Allyson asked.

"Well," the mother answered. "Wesley's going to join Sunburst."

The Sunburst Youth Academy was a military-style program run by the National Guard and the Orange County Department of Education. Over a period of five and a half months, students lived on the base in a disciplined structured environment while developing academic and leadership skills, as well as badly needed self-esteem.

The program's motto: "Change your life and be proud of yourself."

Most of the attendees were falling behind in school and struggling socially. Wesley hadn't visited the theater in a while. As he aged, he'd developed something of an attitude. But since he'd been such a prodigious young actor, Allyson was surprised that he required this type of regimentation. She lowered her voice.

"I wouldn't expect Wesley to be involved in something like Sunburst," she told the mother. "What happened?"

"Oh, don't worry," the mother answered. "You'll hear all about it on the news."

At the time, because of his age, Wesley's name was not being released to the public. Det. Sgt. Ed Everett had told the press that the teen was not considered an accessory to murder. Nevertheless, it was possible, the sergeant said, that Wesley might be charged with other crimes.

The Hathcock family's befuddlement over Dan's involvement in a double murder eventually gave way to anger. Not only had he snuffed out the lives of two people, but he also had greatly complicated the life of the teenager who idolized him.

"I don't think Wesley knew that Dan had killed anybody," Nancy said. "But here he was, just a kid, and now he's mixed up in a murder case. Maybe Dan said, 'I have a source of money here. Don't worry. It's nothing at all.' He was a habitual liar, and the Pied Piper leading Wesley."

As the particulars of the crime were being slowly filtered to the public, Nancy became convinced that Dan never thought about the impact that Wesley's participation would have on the boy—the same way that the suspect hadn't bothered to consider the way that the arrest would hurt the doting parents who'd turned up at his every performance. "Dan was the golden child. The sun rose and set on him. He didn't talk to his parents for months, and then this. They weren't in the best of health, and something like this could have killed them. But I don't think he cared."

Contemplating the events that had occurred at the Liberty, Allyson noted that Dan never realized how close he'd come to leaving an extra body behind: "When Dan chopped Sam up, he missed the live wires by centimeters. There were live electric wires back up there. So Dan could have electrocuted himself."

From what the family understood, after Dan shot Sam he left the body in the theater but returned a day later to begin dismembering it. At one point, Allyson said, Dan entered a barbershop located near the theater space and borrowed a pair of scissors. "He came back a few minutes later and said, 'I need a bigger pair.'"

After authorities removed Sam's body from the building, the Hathcocks walked along the crime scene in an effort to retrace the chronology of the incomprehensible crime. In the ceiling above the lighting booth, they noticed a series of round, recessed lights. "When we looked up," Allyson said, "one of the lights was covered with blood. So that was off-putting. It was eerie when we realized that."

Just across the border from Los Alamitos in Los Angeles County sits El Dorado Park. Bordered on the east by the San Diego Freeway and on the north by the Long Beach Towne Center mall, the park appears to be self-contained. Molded largely from soil used to create the San Gabriel Freeway, the 450-acre oasis includes a campground, soccer and baseball fields, basketball, volleyball, roller hockey and tennis courts, a skate park, rock walls, a one-hundred-acre nature center and three lakes where visitors can ride pedal boats, race remote-control sailboats, and fish for trout, catfish, carp, largemouth bass, bluegill, and redear sunfish, among other species.

On the northern end of the park, the Long Beach Police Academy trains its new recruits. After Dan's arrest, a contingent from the Long Beach Police Department—as well as agencies from Costa Mesa, Orange, Los Angeles, and Ventura Counties, the FBI, and the Los Angeles Coroner's Office—converged on El Dorado to find the body parts that Dan claimed to have discarded there. For two days, they searched the grass with cadaver dogs, finding an arm and a hand in a shallow hole covered by leaves on Friday, May 28.

It was the day Dan and Rachel were supposed to get married.

It wasn't until June 5 that authorities discovered the final missing body part: Sam's severed head. Like the arm and hand, it was partially decomposed and had been scavenged by animals.

"Our son was cut into pieces," Steve told the Web site Patch. "He was just a guy, a regular guy. He was a guy going to college and a decorated combat veteran. He died just before his twenty-seventh birthday."

Despite the gruesome findings, Raquel was relieved that Sam's body had been located. Finally, indisputably, the authorities knew that her son was a true victim, not a suspect who had chosen to go on the run.

CHAPTER FIFTEEN

There was so much investigators still didn't understand. "I think when people look at Dan," Costa Mesa detective Carlos Diaz said, "they just can't believe that he actually did what he did."

Diaz noted that if he were to run into Dan at a restaurant or party, his instincts would probably not alert him to the possibility that the smiling actor was dangerous. And Diaz—who'd been hanging around police stations since his teens—believed that he had pretty good intuition about that type of thing.

Growing up in a strict Central American household, Diaz was repeatedly warned to stay away from the Hispanic gangs he saw in Santa Ana. Like fellow detective Jose Morales, Diaz became involved with the Explorer Scouts in high school, training with the Costa Mesa Police Department and assisting with chores such as traffic control and manning parade routes. As he observed the veteran police officers, he was enticed by their sense of mission.

"Nothing was routine," he said, "and it looked like exciting work."

After graduating from high school at seventeen, Diaz was hired as a cadet by the Costa Mesa police. Meanwhile, he took classes at Orange Coast College and then Stanford University. By the time he graduated, he was already a full-time police officer.

Very quickly he learned that there was a price to pay for wearing the uniform: "There are people out there who really want to hurt you. But there's also good people you meet as a police officer, good people dealing with bad situations. You see the whole spectrum of life.

"It's weird to be twenty-two years old and you're expected to tell someone forty or fifty years old what to do. You get a domestic call, and you have to make these bold decisions, and you're a single guy who's never been in that kind of relationship. It's just a very eye-opening experience. You really have to earn your keep. It's a sink-or-swim world."

Early on, he was privy to homicide investigations because he was one of the few officers at the time who spoke fluent Spanish. It was heart pounding as he looked at a blood-covered corpse and observed the emotionality of the witnesses. But he had to keep himself calm and translate every word properly.

One misinterpreted phrase, he understood, could mean a mistrial or an acquittal.

Because of his awareness of the nuances of the criminal justice system, he was chosen as an investigator in the Crimes Against Persons division without ever working in Crimes Against Property. "I leapfrogged in a way," he said. "But I felt prepared for this job. It's not the kind of unit where someone's going to hold your hand and walk you through things. You're a homicide detective. You're in this unit because, obviously, you know what you're doing. Start doing it.

"I had great partners who helped me the first couple of

months get into it and really get on the ground and start running. There's a lot of unwritten rules. You have to be a hard worker. You have to be a person who's willing to put in the time. You have to earn your keep on some things—taking cases other people don't want. And then, you have to sink into it, dive into cases that are hard and complex. You need to get that experience so that when the big one comes you have the ability to solve that case."

Even when interviewing hardened criminals, Diaz strived to be honest and relatable. "I like to be straightforward," he said. "People don't look at me as an abrasive person. I always try to be a good listener. My style is to let people just talk and tell me their story, and then we go back and start going over the facts. I tell everybody from the start, 'Hey, I expect you to tell me the truth. If you don't, I'm going to catch you in the lie. I always do. And then, I'm going to really come after you, plain and simple.' But I do it in a friendly manner."

In the early days of the Wozniak case, Diaz was guarded about what he could disclose. But it was clear that the investigation was going to be a long, difficult process. "This was pretty strange," he said. Detectives were particularly bewildered by the logic Wozniak applied to justify killing two people whom he appeared to like. "It's almost like you can't write a story like this."

At first, authorities were hesitant to tell the public why Dan and Sam were together on the day of the murder, how they ended up in a theater on a military base, and why the thespian was driven to homicide. Even the victims' families were uncertain. Through Miles, Steve had heard the theory that Dan owed money to a loan shark and needed a fast windfall of cash. But Steve wasn't sure if the story was true or Dan's associates had planted it with Miles in order to cover up either their involvement or the collaboration of others close to them.

As much as possible, Steve tried to convey his misgivings to law enforcement. In the days after Sam's body was located, he accompanied Det. Sgt. Ed Everett to the Liberty Theater and ascended to the spot where the murder took place.

"This is where we found Sam," Everett told the grieving father.

Steve stood back and studied his surroundings. "It was up in the rafters, a very small area," he recalled. Looking around, he tried to imagine the last few moments of his son's life. "I began to think that maybe somebody was up there with Sam, somebody who got Sammy's attention away, and Dan went behind him and blew his brains out. I truly began to believe that.

"Everybody told me they didn't think Dan had the brains to do this alone—so somebody had to be in it with him."

Steve told Everett his theory. After the investigators had mistakenly thought that Sam Herr was the number one suspect, there was nothing that they were going to discount now. Steve wasn't the only person who'd expressed cynicism about Dan being the lone architect of the crime. Detectives weren't taking any possibility lightly.

In his mind, Steve wished that he had been lurking somewhere in the theater to help Sam. It was impossible, of course, but the thought was comforting. Any scenario that had Sammy alive and well soothed the agony that tormented the Herrs while they were awake and haunted their dreams when they went to sleep.

"Sam was my child, my strongest link and my weakest link," Steve said. "When I say 'weakest link,' I mean it's the fear of something happening to our children that's our weakest link. I'm still thankful I had Sam for twenty-seven years. But I envision how that bastard put two bullets in his head and dismembered him every single day. But you know what hurts me more? As a father, I wasn't there for him. Logic says I couldn't have been. I get that. But it still hurts that I couldn't be there for my son. I just wish I could have protected him, thrown myself in front of the bullets. I think about it all the time."

Long after the case was adjudicated and the detectives had moved on to other tragedies, Steve would be alone with those pictures playing in his head. He understood why the detectives were hesitant to apprise him of every finding, particularly when there was so much that they were still learning about the events of May 21. But Steve felt like he couldn't wait for the case to play itself out. He needed to understand every detail right now.

"I want to know the whole story of the murder," he said. "Why did Dan Wozniak choose Sam? Why did he choose Julie?"

Everyone who'd been following the case had a theory. Online, people who'd never met any of the actual players began to weave their own plotlines. In one, Dan was so desperate for cash that—after killing Sam—he began calling the slain veteran's friends to shake them down. When Juri refused to provide more money or Sam's PIN, the premise went, Dan killed her, too.

But it was a flimsy supposition. As a college student, Juri did not have the kind of funds Dan needed. And as much as Sam liked her as a friend, the only person with whom he'd share his PIN was his father.

Plus, if Dan was only interested in money, why did he stage what appeared to be a sexual assault?

In the Internet age, Steve and Raquel were able to read every hypothesis. Indeed, some were provided by readers of the *Los Angeles Times, Orange County Register,* and *OC Weekly* directly following the legitimate online stories about the case. At times, Steve stopped and considered the suggestions. More often than not, the dearth of knowledge intensified his frustration.

While friends and relatives were able to offer comfort, Steve realized that the only people who truly related to his feelings were the members of the Kibuishi family. A few weeks after the double homicide, he and Juri's brother Taka met to compare notes.

Later, when authorities found out, the pair were told not to meet again. Steve was not persuaded by the directive: "Don't tell me about any rules. There are no rules. My son and Taka's sister were killed. We want to find out how it happened—and exactly who is responsible."

Once Dan was in custody, neighbors said, they'd regularly see his fiancée, Rachel Buffett, and her older brother, Noah, in Dave Barnhart's apartment. Depending on their opinion of Rachel, observers believed that she was either coming to terms with the crime or strategizing about how to protect herself from law enforcement.

Rachel claimed that she was thunderstruck by the revelation that the man she intended to marry was capable of such cruelty. "After we found out that Dan had actually committed both of these murders, I'm finding out random, different lives," Rachel told the *Dr. Phil* show. "Jobs that he never had. People that he talked to on the telephone that never existed. A condo he never owned. Overdrawn bank accounts. On top of everything, I found out that the ring that he had given me was not his grandmother's. His parents had never seen it before.

"After I'm finding all of this out, I'm starting to question if I've ever known him. I absolutely feel like I was duped by Dan."

Noah had been at his sister's side almost from the moment that Dan was handcuffed. After her first interview with police, Rachel had a friend drive her to Noah's home. "She wanted to let everybody know that the wedding was off," Detective Jose Morales would testify at a pretrial hearing. "She notified her parents of what happened with Dan and the arrest. And they were trying to make plans to cancel their wedding."

With her friend, Rachel said that she then drove to the Wozniak family home in Long Beach to inform his parents of their son's legal predicament.

"They were there for about an hour or two, I believe," Morales said. "And on the way out, they came across Tim Wozniak, Dan's brother. It appeared that he was driving to the parents' house. [Rachel] . . . had a brief conversation with him where she notified Tim that Dan had been arrested.

"She said that Tim had gotten very nervous and was fumbling with his phone . . . and said that, he, Tim, had some kind of weapon. She told me that she didn't want to stick around any further for any other information and left."

Perhaps Rachel was worried because she knew that Tim Wozniak might soon be arrested, as well. The weapon he'd mentioned turned out to be the gun used in the murders. Some members of law enforcement believed that Tim might not have initially been aware of the precise way that the pistol had been utilized. But he knew that Dan hadn't taken the gun from the family home to shoot sparrows.

Just putting his hands on the gun tied Tim to a very serious crime.

After the murders, Dan had apparently given his brother a box—along with explicit instructions not to open it. But the next morning, Dan purportedly became upset when his brother called to ask about the contents in the box.

From Sam's extensive travels, he'd accumulated quite a

bit of foreign currency. Dan had stashed a backpack in the box that included the wallet containing the foreign money—along with the killer's bloody clothes, the murder weapon, and the tools used to dismember Sam.

Once Dan was in custody, detectives discovered that Tim had possession of the incriminating items. As a result, police charged Tim and his girlfriend, Lisa Golledge, with being accessories to a murder after the fact—or helping Dan hide or dispose of evidence. Both would plead not guilty.

Tim was released on twenty thousand dollars bail. Lisa's bail was higher, since there were unrelated charges pending against her, but she was soon home, as well.

When the story of Tim's arrest appeared in the local media, Steve's brother-in-law brought over a newspaper and pointed to a photo of the captive. Steve studied the picture and immediately recognized the face.

On the night that he'd been staking out Ecco's Pizza in Long Beach, hoping to catch the person who'd been withdrawing Sam's money, Steve had seen Tim Wozniak in the restaurant. He was the guy who'd been highly agitated, speaking into a cell phone and pacing in the aisle by the bar.

The pizzeria was close to the Wozniak family home, and Steve surmised that Tim had been on the phone with his brother. Whatever Tim was hearing on the other end wasn't making him happy.

It was one of the few pieces of the story that Steve believed actually made sense.

Noah Buffett would draw the attention of law enforcement, as well.

The day after Sam's murder, police said that Dan visited Noah's home and left with a saw, an axe, and a number of garden tools. Dan then "drove to the Los Alamitos base, where Sam's body was," Morales testified, "and he proceeded to cut his head off, cut off the hands and the forearm, the left forearm of the body," in an attempt to make the cadaver less recognizable.

Not only had Dan used Noah's tools to dismember the body; the killer was also seen driving his future brother-in-law's pickup truck.

In fact, during the weekend of the murders Noah had complained on social media about Dan keeping the truck too long—so long that Noah joked about possibly de-Friending his sister's fiancé on Facebook.

When Noah realized what Dan had done with the vehicle, he allegedly deleted the post. Nevertheless, police were able to tie him to the crime. Like Tim Wozniak, Noah was arrested on suspicion of accessory after the fact, or assisting in the disposal of evidence.

Noah pleaded not guilty, and the charges were eventually dropped. He'd later contend that both he and his sister had been misled by Dan. As with Wesley Freilich, Tim Wozniak, and his girlfriend, Noah had gotten too close to the actor, he'd argue, becoming just another character in the tragedy Dan scripted.

"It's bewildering to find out that you don't really know somebody," Noah told Dr. Phil. "He duped all of us."

CHAPTER SIXTEEN

Police estimated that it could be two or three years before Dan went to trial. The suspect's father had had a good career in the aerospace industry, and detectives imagined that he'd hire one of the region's better attorneys. However, investigators heard that while Daryl Wozniak initially took this proposition seriously, he eventually determined that the weight of the evidence was so strong against his estranged son that Dan's guilt was a foregone conclusion.

Dan's parents had assisted him his entire life. But this time, they were not going to jeopardize their savings to protect a murderer. There had also been a rumor that Steve Wozniak might contribute to the legal fund. Although Dan had told Jeff Hathcock that he wasn't related to the Apple co-founder, he'd apparently boasted to others about a family tie. But this, like so much else about Dan Wozniak, turned out to be fiction.

Before Juri's body was cremated, her family asked that she wear the tiara that her brother gave her on the night that she died. In August 2010, the Kibuishis traveled to Japan with Juri's ashes. A fund drive, sponsored by the *Orange County Register,* had raised approximately four thousand dollars for the family, who subscribed to the Japanese belief that the remains of unmarried children should be reunited with those of their ancestors.

"This was definitely an emotionally challenging, but needed, trip for the family to take," Juri's brother Taka told the newspaper. "Our pain and our sorrow will never go away, but this trip will be the closing of the first chapter of our lives after Julie was taken away from us."

Juri's mother, Junko, also placed some of her daughter's ashes in an urn and surrounded it with flowers, photos, and another tiara to remind her of Juri's spirit. Junko said that she planned to keep the item in her bedroom for the rest of her life. After her death, she specified, she wanted the ashes of mother and daughter to be mixed together.

Because of the way that Juri's body was found, investigators naturally assumed that the killer had some kind of an emotional—or, at the very least, sexual—connection to the victim. Very quickly this notion was obliterated.

"At first thought, it was, 'Okay, we have a homicide,'" Det. Jose Morales recounted. "'Must be some kind of boyfriend involved.' Then, the case started taking so many other turns. I think we were all kind of surprised, just scratching our heads. Bizarre? Yeah, very bizarre."

In June, a special circumstances committee had gathered at the Orange County District Attorney's office to consider the details of the case. Under California law, the death penalty could be considered if aggravating factors outweighed mitigating factors. Mitigating factors were conditions that diminished the defendant's guilt and supported a more lenient punishment. Aggravating factors were defined as "any facts above and beyond the circumstances of crime that increases the wrongfulness of the defendant's conduct, the enormity of the offense, or the harmful impact of the crime."

Based on the nature of the double homicide and the vulnerability of the victims, among other factors, the committee instantly and unanimously decided to pursue the death penalty.

"Some murders are committed with such a depraved heart and in such a callous manner that the only punishment that fits the crime is the death penalty," District Attorney Tony Rackauckas said in a statement.

The Wozniak investigation was now designated a Special Prosecutions Case, supervised by Rackauckas and a team he'd selected. Among other trials handled by the same unit was the largest medical fraud prosecution in the United States, the Unity Surgical Outpatient Center case. According to prosecutors, healthy people were enlisted from all over the country for unnecessary surgeries, including tummy tucks and hysterectomies, enabling the medical center to bill insurance companies approximately $154 million.

The Special Prosecutions team also targeted Alejandro Avila, who, in 2005, was sentenced to death for killing five-year-old Samantha Runnion in the city of Stanton in western Orange County. She'd been playing a board game in her yard with a friend on July 15, 2002, when Avila approached the girls and asked for help finding his Chihuahua. Samantha's interest was piqued. "How big is it?" she asked.

Avila quickly grabbed her and threw her into his green Honda. The girl tried to hit and kick her abductor but couldn't escape. As Avila drove away, the child screamed out to her friend, "Tell my grandma! Tell my grandma!"

The next day, Samantha's nude body was found in an isolated area near Lake Elsinore, sixty miles away. It had been posed conspicuously to display the killer's handiwork. An autopsy would reveal that Samantha had been sexually assaulted, as well as strangled.

The death inspired California to implement a statewide Amber Alert program.

Avila had been on police radar after being accused of molesting an ex-girlfriend's nine-year-old daughter and her cousin. Although he'd been acquitted in the case, investigators continued to view him as a sex offender and found his DNA on Samantha's body and Samantha's DNA in his vehicle.

Detectives believed that the genetic material might have come from the little girl's tears.

"For the heinous crime he committed against Samantha Runnion, the only appropriate punishment is death," Rackauckas said when the penalty was imposed, "although it still falls short of justice."

For the Herrs and Kibuishis, though, the thought of hearing a judge pass sentence on Daniel Wozniak both motivated and comforted them. Yet almost from the beginning, they realized that that day would be a long way off.

CHAPTER SEVENTEEN

At the time of Dan's arrest, the Orange County Sheriff's Department was eager for positive publicity.

In 2009, Sheriff Mike Carona—dubbed "America's sheriff" by national talk show host Larry King—was convicted of trying to convince an aide to lie to federal investigators probing department corruption. Carona, a thirty-two-year veteran, had been one of the most popular public figures in the region, greeting constituents with hugs rather than handshakes and telling a compelling story about growing up in an alcoholic household and finding purpose in law enforcement. When a child killer from Orange County went on the run, Carona looked into the camera and pronounced, "Don't eat. Don't sleep. Because we're coming after you."

After Carona was elected three times, his name was touted as a possible candidate for lieutenant governor when Arnold Schwarzenegger ran for the state's highest office.

But, behind the scenes, Carona was exchanging favors with political donors, including one who recorded him for investigators. In 2007, he was indicted on six felony corruption counts. While the sheriff's wife sat supportively in the courtroom, his mistress stood trial, as well.

Although he was only convicted of one charge of witness tampering, he was sentenced to sixty-six months in a federal prison.

It was one of a series of embarrassments for the department. In 2006, John Derek Chamberlain, an inmate booked at the jail for alleged child pornography possession, was fatally beaten by a group of fellow prisoners who believed that he was a child molester.

One inmate would later claim that sheriff's deputies ordered him to deliver a "touch up"—or beating—to Chamberlain.

Three deputies resigned after an Orange County District Attorney's report claimed that guards at the jail were napping, texting, and watching television instead of monitoring—and stopping—the violence.

In the wake of these and other scandals, the department decided to allow a TV crew into the five facilities comprising the Orange County Jail system to interview inmates for the MSNBC TV show *Lockup*. "In six episodes, the show achieved its mission to air nothing but positive, rehabilitating OCSD imagery," R. Scott Moxley opined in an *OC Weekly* blog.

If that was the intention, the effort would later be complicated by the inclusion of Daniel Wozniak in the program.

The producer remembered scouring the jail, marveling at the variety of inmates. "There's everybody from someone who looks like your neighbor—who's been arrested for a DUI—to a gangbanger who's tattooed from head to toe. I didn't expect that. But when you consider that Orange County is right next to Los Angeles, it does make sense."

Most of the seventy-thousand inmates in the county's

jail system were awaiting trial for crimes ranging from petty theft to homicide. Some would be released or bailed out within hours of their arrests. Others, like Dan, could sit in jail for years before their cases were adjudicated.

With deputies standing nearby, the producer and associate producer walked from cell to cell, introducing themselves and asking inmates to tell their stories. At one point, the producer said that she briefly met Dan. But her attention had been on other details, and she hadn't had a chance to speak with him and find out how he ended up behind bars.

Still, she couldn't forget his face.

Several weeks later, while the show was already in production, the two crossed paths again in the jail. "There was a guy walking past me in a line of inmates," the producer said. "He was quite tall and really stood out. His jail-issue uniform was way too small for him. He was wearing these pants that were up to his shins. It was completely bizarre. Usually, the jail-issue uniforms are too big. And this guy just looked like a giant in there.

"He smiled and called me by my name. I knew I'd met him before, but we meet literally hundreds and hundreds of people when we're doing these shows. But he had one of those faces.

"Besides being really good-looking, that smile was unique. He didn't *look* like a criminal. Usually, if you meet people who look like him when you're doing this job, they're just seeing the inside of a jail for the first time. It's a pretty heavy experience. They're depressed, struggling. And he wasn't like that at all."

The producer turned to the deputy accompanying her. "What's that inmate's name?" she asked.

"Wozniak. Daniel Wozniak."

With the associate producer trailing behind her, the producer introduced herself. Dan was pleasant, chatting as if they were meeting inside a restaurant or outside a theater. "Would you be interested in being interviewed?" she asked.

"Sure."

"Okay. Let me set that up."

There was another room where the camera crew had arranged their lights and audio equipment. It was a quiet space, where the subject wouldn't be distracted by the stares and comments of other inmates. While Dan returned to his cell to shave, the producer told the cameraman and audio engineer to get ready. She'd found someone who looked like he'd make an interesting interview.

Soon Dan came by with a paper bag lunch, provided by the jail. "I usually ask the guys to give me a cell tour," the producer said. "He was in a, I don't know, maybe an eight-by-ten room. Just a box in an older part of the jail where there's metal bars on these long tiers. It's very depressing. And here he was, acting like he was entertaining guests."

When he knew that the camera was on, Daniel began his monologue: "Yeah, you just have little things around here. Got the sink, toilet. It's small, but, you know, it is what it is."

Although he was living in cramped surroundings, Dan claimed that his spirituality was sustaining him. "It's small." He chuckled. "But, yeah, you got the bed. You got the Bible. Coffee, milk. Jesus is with me."

He also described the jailhouse cuisine. "Bag lunches every day." He flashed his smile. "Sandwiches, hard-boiled eggs. Most of the time, it's either bologna or ham." He looked through the contents of his bag. "Uh-oh. Extra bread today. Look at that." He chuckled and started performing in earnest. "You get your little carrots like this. And, of course, plenty of mayo. So then, what you do is pretty much eat the carrots and then"—he squirted his mayonnaise packet into a bowl—"you have this . . . little bowl. You can mix everything up, like egg salad sandwich, stuff like that. You know, on some days, it gets really good. You can put vanilla pudding or chocolate pudding, mix it with your milk, stir it up, you got a milk shake." He assembled a sandwich together on bread. "So you learn little secrets like that. Bon appétit." He took a bite.

While this was transpiring, an associate producer had done a Google search on Dan and forwarded a number of articles to the producer. She scrolled through them, astonished that the jokey character in front of her was accused of beheading a friend and scrawling obscenities on the body of a woman he'd shot. "I couldn't believe it. We sat down for the interview, and just started talking, and it went from there. I think the strangest part for me was trying to connect the charming, affable man with the crimes that he was being charged with."

Like the investigators and the families and friends of the victims, the producer wanted to know more about what occurred on the weekend of May 21, 2010. But Dan was cautious about what he was willing to divulge.

"He would get uncomfortable when I would question him about certain aspects of the charges," the producer said. "He didn't want to incriminate himself, understandably so. He hadn't gone to trial yet. It's always tricky doing interviews with people who are in the middle of that phase."

"I want people to know that I'm a good guy," Dan stated, then tried to make light of his circumstances with humor. "I'm easygoing. I enjoy long walks on the beach. I'm an Aries." He laughed.

His manner became slightly more serious. "I just want people to know that, no matter what, throughout all this, I'm a really good guy. Almost everyone in my life will say so."

At times, the producer wondered if Dan was really as

nice as he appeared. "He would kind of slide back and
forth, getting agitated and then slipping straight back into
actor mode—charming, smiling, maybe feeling a little
remorseful. You know, I live in Los Angeles and have
grown up around aspiring actors, and there are certain personality traits that seem kind of across the board that you
need to succeed as an actor. And one of them is to be able
to turn it on. He knew how to turn it on. He knew how to
connect with people."

Not surprisingly, Dan questioned the veracity of news
coverage about the case. "The honest truth of what they're
saying I'm not really sure," he said. "Since I've been here,
I haven't been able to read the paper. I don't know what
they're saying. One time, I turned on the TV in the pod or
whatever, and then, I just saw my picture on television. It
was a mug shot that they got from the police department.
They put together some old YouTube videos of me. I was
in theater, so they were just flashing that all over the news."

When the producer went online to show Dan other news
reports, he became tense. Looking at his photo on-screen,
he muttered, "Oh, great, that mug. Oh my God." He shook
his head and appeared to tear up. "It makes me look like
Satan himself, that I orchestrated and planned all this. This
is, that's, I'm sorry. I can't."

The producer showed him an image of Sam. "This is
your friend," she said.

"Yeah,"

"Why did this happen to your friend?"

Dan stammered. "I, I can't get into that. I can't get into
that. I can't. I'm, I'm sorry. I can't. I really can't. I cannot."

What he would offer was, "I know his body parts, they
say, were found in a park."

And Dan acknowledged being connected to the theater
where Sam was killed and dismembered, but only as an
actor. "There were two shows that I did there," Dan said.

"One was *Charley's Aunt,* and the other one was *Arsenic and Old Lace.*" He laughed, at either the memory of being onstage or the irony of appearing in a play about homicide. "Yeah, I played Cary Grant's character. So a lot of fun."

Dan emphasized his great affection for Sam and Juri. "The two victims were two of my close friends," he claimed. "Sam lived in the same complex that me and my fiancée lived at. He had helped me out on several occasions. Just, he was there for me, you know? I needed him, and Julie was just a friend in the group. Just very, two of the nicest people. Two of the nicest people that I've ever known."

While avoiding the fine points of the case, he asserted his innocence. "They were saying that I shot both of them and decapitated one of them." He shook his head. "That's not true."

In describing the arrest at his bachelor party, Dan tried to affect a comedic air, as if he were telling a story about receiving a parking summons. "You know, our meal was over. We paid the bill. And all of a sudden, this. It was a swarm. It was a swarm of police. Came in, grabbed me, pulled me up, put me in handcuffs, and dragged me out of the back of the restaurant. And I said, '*Uh, ok-aay?* Hello? How are you? My name is Dan. What can I . . .'" He chuckled. "You know?"

Once he got to jail, though, he said he realized the gravity of situation and felt the compulsion to end it all. "I was alone in a room and there was, there was a wall. And I, they're all stone, so I saw the corner and I said, 'If I jump and hit my head, maybe all this will go away.' And, um, it's still here."

Among the most difficult aspects of his incarceration, he maintained, was the separation from Rachel. "If I was given the opportunity to talk to my fiancée right now, I'd either say, 'Can I be with you out there?' 'Can you be with me in here?' Just, I mean, the bond, I just love her. Like, that's, that's the hardest part about getting through my day is just knowing that I can't be with her, period. It's, you know, it's, it's, it says: 'Absence makes the heart grow fonder.' It does. It really does."

But, according to Dan, God would help him weather this challenge. Opening his New American Bible, he read from Psalm 39: " 'Lord, let me know my end, the number of my days, that I may learn how frail I am.

" 'You have given my days a very short span; my life is as nothing before you. . . .

" 'Turn your gaze from me, that I may find peace before I depart to be no more.' "

He looked at the producer. "It's one of my favorite ones," he said of the verse.

"Why?"

"It just touches home. It, to me, it's just exactly just how short life really is, you know. It makes it a lot easier in here, knowing, you know, our time here is just so short, you know. Life is just a short time, but eternity's forever."

Nevertheless, he told her, he intended to fight the government's effort to convict and sentence him to death. "The death penalty is something that they are seeking," he said. "Whether it happens or not . . . I have full faith in the truth, and the truth will set me free. And everything will come to be. I just pray daily. That's it. And not so much for myself, but for all the lives that have been shattered through this event."

After the interview ended, the producer was uncertain about how to interpret Dan Wozniak's words or behavior. "Another bizarre interview with another bizarre inmate," she said. "We try not to judge. It's really hard to know."

But, because she'd conducted so many jailhouse

interviews before, she realized that she couldn't part company with Dan without having him sign a release, allowing the production company to use his words and image on television. When the task was complete, the producer took a photo to match his face with his name. "It was as though he was posing for headshots," she said. "I noticed it. The whole crew noticed it.

"Most people will go through phases in a situation like this. They're trying to escape from the horror of being arrested. Somebody who's an actor has found a way to be somebody else who can take him away. I don't know if reality had landed for him yet."

Dan's story was broadcast on MSNBC on March 26, 2011. At the time, there was much that the public didn't understand about the details of the crime. After the episode ended, the uncertainty persisted.

But those who'd known the suspect were largely certain of one thing: in customary fashion, Dan Wozniak was lying.

The Hathcocks were particularly surprised by the sight of the actor reading the Bible out loud. "He used to make fun of his parents' Catholic faith," Allyson claimed. "It was kind of like, 'Oh, aren't they quaint in their beliefs?' "

To Jeff, Dan's talk about Jesus being in his cell was almost laughable. "He was not sincere about it at all. I guess they all get religion in jail, when the chips are down, don't they?"

Orange County District Attorney Tony Rackauckas had seen that type of behavior before. "He's an actor who considers himself to be a star, and all other people to be living props in his play," the prosecutor told *OC Weekly*.

Sheriff's department spokesperson John McDonald

had a similar reaction. "I thought it showed Wozniak is a bad actor," he said, noting that his sympathies were not with the inmate's struggles behind bars but the victims' families.

In Anaheim Hills, Steve and Raquel Herr studied every gesture as they watched Dan on the screen, attempting to elicit compassion. "It made great television," Steve told the newspaper. "But it's not fair and balanced to let Wozniak say anything he wants before the trial, and not have the Costa Mesa police, a prosecutor, or me on the show even for a minute to tell the public the truth. This monster killed my son and Julie. That's the truth."

As Steve sighed heavily, tears formed in his eyes as he looked at reporter R. Scott Moxley. "Do you know how hard it is to watch him smiling and laughing on that show after what he's done? He decapitated my son. Let him say he's innocent. He's an actor. He knows how to fake emotions.

". . . My whole life is now dedicated to winning justice for my son. That show wasn't about justice. It was about letting Wozniak perform. Everyone who saw it thought it was very sympathetic to him."

In reality, though, many viewers shared Steve's cynicism, as well as his conviction about the fate that Dan deserved.

"I don't want him to escape with life in prison," Steve said. "I want revenge. I want Wozniak dead."

CHAPTER EIGHTEEN

One of the few consolations for the Herrs was the concern that Sam's friends expressed for their well-being. Even as they struggled with trying to pry information from investigators and prosecutors, their son's Army companions regularly called and visited.

"As a matter of fact," Steve said in an interview one Friday afternoon, his features relaxing into a smile, "two more are coming on Sunday. And another one just flew in. He was with Sam his last few months in the Army. He's on leave from Hawaii, and he wants to come down. They come all the time. They'll call up and say, 'Look, I'll be in town soon, so could I come and spend a few days?'"

In particular, the couple had grown close to Miles Foltz and Ruben Menacho. "Miles is just the opposite of Sam," Steve said. "Miles is very quiet and laid-back. Very introverted, but he's the sweetest guy. We love him. He's like our adopted son. Just like Ruben. But Ruben's a very different type. He's a big tough Marine who's just a knucklehead like Sam."

Every day, it seemed, another soldier was Friending

Steve Herr on Facebook. When the number exceeded twenty, the group decided to form a page called Sam's Buddies, featuring photos of Sam in Afghanistan and Germany, updates about the murder probe, military humor, and holiday greetings. "You look at the camaraderie," Steve said, "and you realize that these guys are going to carry Sam's memory the rest of their lives. People can say whatever they want about the case, but when you go through Sam's friends, you'll get the true story."

Despite the passage of time, Sam's friends remained loyal. On Valentine's Day, Raquel received flowers. When a veteran graduated from college, the Herrs were invited. Another former soldier invited Steve to be the best man at his wedding "to fill in for the *real* best man, Sam."

The murders not only impacted the lives of the people close to the accused and the victims. In Los Alamitos, the Liberty Theater received more attention for the murder and decapitation than it ever had for its plays.

The building had been the realization of a dream that Jeff and Nancy Hathcock had harbored since they'd met as idealistic drama students at Cal State Long Beach. With their daughter, Allyson, assisting, the two enjoyed a status about which many in their position fantasized: parents and an adult child laboring at a mutual love together and succeeding.

Now they had to fight to stay in business.

"We had pictures in the lobby of all our shows," Nancy said. "All the ones that had Dan in them, we took them down."

As she did, her anger rose at the actor who'd once mockingly called her facility the "Mayberry of theaters." "We'd been so nice to Dan over the years," she said. "And he had to choose *our* theater to do something so terrible. The gall, the nerve. He killed two innocent people, destroyed their parents' lives, broke his own parents' hearts, and then did this to us with no regard for the work we put into the theater. It just added insult to injury."

After the police investigation began, the family painted over the white plywood where Sam's blood had splattered. But they could never erase the horror of what had transpired in a space that had been designed to teach children the art of theater and bring joy to the families in the audience.

Nancy claimed that visitors to the Liberty heard noises that completely unnerved them. The family already believed that the place was haunted by ghosts. But those had largely been benevolent spirits, they said. The new creatures, according to the Hathcocks, were more menacing and represented the gruesomeness that had occurred on the grounds.

"One lady told us she saw them and they were about nine feet tall and dark," Allyson said. "They just kept popping up, making growls and screams."

The Hathcocks consulted a psychic and met with a priest from St. Hedwig, the Roman Catholic church on Los Alamitos Boulevard, near the base. He asked Allyson to gather a group of friends who shared her Catholic beliefs, then led them to the scene of the murder to pray.

The ritual seemed to calm the family's nerves about dark forces lurking in the theater. But in the secular world, reports of the murder continued to distress actors and patrons.

"One thing we were grateful about was that, when there were news reports about Dan, they never showed a sign for the theater on TV," Nancy said. "But everyone knew what happened, and it greatly disturbed our child actors and kids who came to our shows. The old ghost stories about the theater never bothered them. Those were old ghosts, not fresh, harmful ghosts. It was like Casper for them. But this was so different. Some parents told us their kids didn't want to come back after the murder. And it made it worse that Dan—Mr. Personality—was the one being accused of killing these people."

Like Wesley Freilich, another teen actor had viewed Dan as a mentor. When others began referring to Dan as a murderer, the boy would react with rage.

"He refused to believe that Dan would have anything to do with that," Jeff recalled. "He was very adamant about it. Several of the other kids sided with him."

As the troupe attempted to perform their next play, the young man was "very surly, very rude," Allyson said. "He had a personality change, and caused a lot of trouble. All he wanted to do was get back at anybody who talked badly about Dan."

Every two years, the commander of the Joint Forces Training Base changed, leaving the Hathcocks nervous about the new regime's receptiveness to their endeavor. After the murders, though, the family was burdened with an even greater cause for concern. Although they'd done nothing to cause the crime, the Hathcocks were treated differently than they'd been before.

"The military was angry about the media attention," Jeff explained. "The murders were giving negative publicity to the base. Every story mentioned that Dan was an actor. They were trying to build up that angle. He was an actor, and he committed a murder in the theater. But the base was mentioned over and over again because that's where the theater was."

From that point forward, the once-hopeful aura of the theater changed. Even when people came to the shows, they couldn't resist looking up and pointing, trying to discern where Sam Herr had been killed and decapitated.

"It wasn't fun anymore," Allyson said.

To Jeff, "it was like a pall was over the theater. It had lost its innocence."

As it was, the aging building needed retrofitting. The roof leaked. The Hathcocks wanted a new stage floor. The military began to consider other uses for the venue once used to host USO dances.

In 2012, the Liberty Theater closed—one more victim, the Hathcocks insisted, of Dan Wozniak's self-centered explosion of violence.

CHAPTER NINETEEN

In May 2012, a Grand Jury finally convened to consider the evidence that police had spent two years compiling against Daniel Wozniak.

"It's been long overdue," Steve told the Patch Web site after learning about the proceedings. "I wanted this to be done a year ago. I just want to find out the whole story. We still don't know everything that happened."

In senior deputy district attorney Matt Murphy, Dan was facing an adversary who'd never lost a murder trial. Murphy had started out as a junior clerk in the Orange County District Attorney's office during the summer after his first year of law school, working on small misdemeanor cases. He never left.

In 2008, he prosecuted a pair of white supremacists accused of fatally bludgeoning and stabbing a clerk during a 7-Eleven robbery. Suresh Dass, fifty-five, was looking forward to visiting his oldest son in India as he worked an overnight shift at the Irvine store on March 2, 2004. "His wife wanted him to stay home with the family, since he

was going to be gone in a few days," his brother, Rejen-
bra, told the *Los Angeles Times*. But Shuresh needed the
money and decided to go to work anyway.

At 2:30 a.m., Travis Justin Frazier, twenty-five, and
Spencer William Fox, twenty-four—both heavily tattooed
with racist insignia—entered the convenience store, masked
and clad in black. Wielding a heavy metal flashlight, Frazier battered Shuresh seven times over the head, fractur-
ing his skull. As the clerk lay bleeding on the ground, Fox
climbed over the counter and stabbed him with a large
hunting knife, piercing his heart.

Yet the robbers didn't know how to open the cash register. While Shuresh lay dying, Fox ordered him to explain
how they could gain access to the money. He either refused
or was incapable of telling them. Using his knife, Fox attempted to pry the device open but was unsuccessful.

The intruders would leave empty-handed that night, yet
they seemed to derive pleasure from stealing the life of a
hardworking immigrant. Glancing at the victim on the
floor, the two peeled off their layers of clothes and fled,
running through the parking lot in hysterics, either too ar-
rogant or obtuse to comprehend that the entire incident
had been captured on video.

Several yards away, two security guards in a parked car
saw the men running from the crime scene and instantly
became suspicious. One raced into the store to attempt to
help the clerk. The other drove behind the suspects, pur-
suing them to an Anaheim apartment complex. Police were
immediately alerted and set up a perimeter. A police
canine named Rambo followed the discarded clothes to
Frazier, while Fox was taken into custody a day later.

As murder cases went, this was far easier for law enforcement than the killings of Sam and Juri. Murphy used
the video surveillance to demonstrate the viciousness of

the crime to the jury. By June, both Frazier and Fox were convicted and sentenced to life without the possibility of parole.

In 1999, Vincent Choy Cheung—who, like Daniel Wozniak, occasionally worked as an actor—became irate that his onetime boyfriend, Guy Thomas Whitney, a voice and music teacher at an Irvine conservatory, was now dating Lawrence Wong, an internationally known pianist. On July 27—after failing to ingratiate himself to Whitney with gifts that included one hundred videotapes of Academy Award–winning films—Cheung snuck into his former lover's home, where Wong was now living. Police would find Whitney at the bottom of his stairs with thirty-six stab wounds, including seven to his face. Upstairs in the master bedroom, Wong had been stabbed twenty-five times.

After learning that Cheung had been stalking the new couple, detectives began investigating him, discovering a diluted water droplet in his car. When forensic experts tested the material, it fluoresced positive for a mixture of blood that could be traced to all three men.

During a five-week trial in 2003, Murphy told jurors how Cheung had "stepped in blood at the crime scene, so there's bloody footprints all over the house. That's probably the most compelling evidence we had."

The jury was convinced.

Murphy would settle for nothing less in the Daniel Wozniak case. The first major hurdle would be persuading a Grand Jury that Dan's crimes were worthy of prosecution. Although it seemed like a foregone conclusion, prosecutors were unwilling to leave anything to chance.

Grand Juries differ from criminal trials in that the purpose is not determining guilt or innocence but rather if there is probable cause to believe that the defendant may have committed the crime. This is not a miniature trial with the defense calling rebuttal witnesses. In fact, suspects are often unaware that the Grand Jury is taking place. Nineteen Grand Jurors are selected to consider the evidence. If the prosecution is persuasive, twelve of the nineteen will submit a report with the presiding judge calling for an indictment.

On May 3, 2012, Matt Murphy faced the Grand Jurors in the California Superior Court building in Santa Ana—an institutional structure of concrete and glass—and inquired if any had a conflict of interest. "Do any of you know socially or have any of you heard anything about the case or any of the persons named which would cause you to not render an unbiased decision?" he asked.

He looked from person to person. No one appeared to know either Dan or the victims.

"Let the record show," the jury foreperson announced, "that no member of the jury has retired" from the proceedings.

Det. Mike Delgadillo was then asked to recollect his exchanges with the defendant. Delgadillo assured the panel that Dan had not been coerced into making his confession.

"Was he threatened in any way?" Murphy asked.

"No."

"Did anybody point a gun at him or hit him or anything like that?"

"No."

"Okay. So after waiving his Miranda rights, there were no threats or promises made to him to secure any of these statements? Is that right?"

"Correct."

The detective described how the initial interview with Dan focused on the suspected bank fraud rather than murder. "When we found out through Wesley," Delgadillo

Juri "Julie" Kibuishi in high school with friend and fellow dancer Natalie Jameson. Natalie admired Julie for her artistic talent, sense of humor and positive worldview. They'd take dance classes together until Julie was killed. (*Natalie Jameson Sommer*)

Before a high school recital, Juri Kibuishi and friends attempt to take a group photo outside, in front of a backdrop. Juri playfully throws back her arm in a type of pinup pose. (*Courtesy of Jessica Wolf*)

Steve Herr was raised in New Jersey, and his wife, Raquel, in Argentina. Both became teachers in southern California. As their only child, Sam, grew into adulthood, he remained close with both his parents and extended family. (*Costa Mesa Police Department*)

After struggling as a teen, Sam Herr found focus while serving with the US Army in Afghanistan. Afghan soldiers viewed him as a mentor, while the other Americans viewed him as a friend and leader. He was considering reenlisting as an officer when he was murdered.
(Courtesy of Steve Herr)

Police identified this .38-caliber, semi-automatic pistol as the murder weapon. It had previously been taken from Dan Wozniak's parents' home. (*Costa Mesa Police Department*)

According to Dan Wozniak, he drove Sam's car after the veteran confessed to murdering Juri Kibuishi, then left it near a Long Beach mall. "This is the honest, true story," Dan said. (*Costa Mesa Police Department*)

The Liberty Theater, located on the Los Alamitos Joint Forces Training Base, was a wholesome, family-run enterprise until the double-murder case scared off both patrons and children in the drama program. (*Costa Mesa Police Department*)

Even in his mugshot, Daniel Wozniak looked like he was posing for a head shot. On the storefront theater circuit of Orange County, CA, he was one of the most popular actors. (*Costa Mesa Police Department*)

Daniel's fiancée, Rachel Buffett, was charged as an accessory to his crimes. The news stunned family members, who insisted that she was as good-natured as the princesses she played at Disneyland and Medieval Times. (*Costa Mesa Police Department*)

After the deaths of Sam Herr and Juri Kibuishi, Tim Wozniak was handed a crate of evidence by his brother, Dan. Tim would be charged as an accessory, and testify against Dan at his trial. (*Costa Mesa Police Department*)

Daniel Wozniak is questioned by Costa Mesa detectives. At first, he appears
confident and eager to assist, but his mood changes when he learns that he
won't be released in time for his wedding. At one point, investigators bring
his fiancée, Rachel Buffett, into the interview room to question him.
Ultimately, he realizes that police are never going to believe his story
about Sam Herr being the actual perpetrator.
(Costa Mesa Police Department)

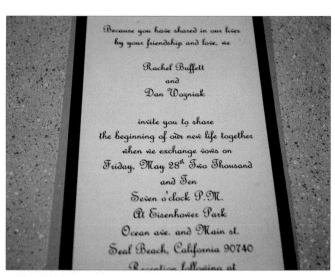

Because you have shared in our lives
by your friendship and love, we

Rachel Buffett
and
Dan Wozniak

invite you to share
the beginning of our new life together
when we exchange vows on
Friday, May 28th Two Thousand
and Ten
Seven o'clock P.M.
At Eisenhower Park
Ocean ave. and Main st.
Seal Beach, California 90740
Reception following at

As police searched through Sam Herr's apartment,
they found an invitation to the upcoming wedding of
his neighbors, Dan Wozniak and Rachel Buffett.
(Costa Mesa Police Department)

said, referring to the actor's sixteen-year-old accomplice, "that he was implicated as the orchestrator of this credit card–ATM scam, we felt that there was enough to arrest him on that. When we brought him in, during the interview, this thing basically exploded on us."

During the first interview, Murphy told the Grand Jurors, Dan "kind of said, 'Yeah, I know, Sam is on the run, and he is taking money out, and I am sick of covering for him,' and things like that. And then, the interview ended. He went down to his jail cell and said, 'I want to talk to you guys again.' He informed the jailer, and the jailer brought detectives back in.

". . . At which point, Mr. Wozniak told [Delgadillo] . . . , 'Okay, here is the deal. I murdered Sam. I took him to this theater and I shot him in the head.'"

The deputy district attorney asked Delgadillo how Dan had described the murders.

The suspect initially "indicated to me that he lured Sam," Delgadillo said. "They both drove together to the military reserve base at Los Alamitos. The location on the base was the theater. . . . [Wozniak] had done rehearsals there at the theater on the base.

"They both arrived at the theater. There is an attic, with a ladder leading up to the attic. And he told Sam, 'I need you to help me move some stuff up in the attic.'

"They both walked up to the attic together. Sam walked up to a piece of furniture in the attic, and Wozniak indicated to him, 'I need you to help me move this.'

"Sam went down and started moving this article. Wozniak had a .38-caliber, semiautomatic pistol with him, pointed it at the back of Sam's head, and shot him once in the back of the head. At that point, Sam fell to his knees, looked up at Mr. Wozniak, and said . . . , 'Something happened. I just got electrocuted.'"

Realizing that Sam was still alive, Dan attempted to fire

a second time, Delgadillo testified. But when Dan pulled the trigger, the weapon apparently jammed.

"He reached for the slide," the detective said, "pulled the slide back, ejected the jammed round out of the gun, and shot Sam one more time, as he looked up at him, in the temple. At that point, Sam fell to the ground."

Although Dan appeared to have accomplished his goal, police said that he now shifted tactics from committing murder to purging the crime scene of evidence. With blood pooling around Sam's body, "Mr. Wozniak said he attempted to find the discarded shell casing, but he couldn't find it," Delgadillo told the Grand Jurors.

Thinking about the next series of crimes that he hoped to commit, Delgadillo said, Dan rifled through Sam's pockets for his ATM card, keys, and cell phone, utilizing the device to convince Juri to make a late-night stop at the victim's apartment.

Playing off of Juri's consideration for others, Delgadillo said, Dan had little trouble setting a trap for the talented fashion student. "He had taken Sam's telephone, and had made contact with Julie Kibuishi," the detective said. "He was texting her, leading her to believe that Sam was texting her."

Investigators said that the texting had begun while Dan was backstage at the theater where he was performing hours after he left the scene of Sam's death. In essence, he was singing and dancing while orchestrating a second murder.

"Okay," Murphy replied. "And what did he tell you about those texts? What did he say the purpose was? Take us through that."

"The following night, he had texted Julie, who was at her brother's house in Long Beach. Julie believed that the texts she was receiving were coming from Sam. . . . 'I need you to come to my apartment. Stuff going on. I am having family problems.' "

Dan told detectives that he'd been downstairs in his own apartment, trying to get Rachel Buffett to go to sleep. When Juri arrived, Dan claimed that he came upstairs and met her at Sam's front door, using the veteran's key to enter the residence. In the living room, Dan apparently said that Sam was anxious to talk to her about some problems. While Juri waited for Sam, Dan went into another area of the apartment and loaded his gun. He then supposedly summoned Juri into the bedroom to look at something. When she did, she was shot twice in the head with a .38 that Dan said he'd stolen from his parents' closet approximately two years earlier.

According to authorities, Dan explained that his motive had been "to basically make it look like Sam had been involved in a love triangle situation," Murphy said, "that he murdered Julie as a result of this love triangle, and that that would explain why nobody could find him, and why money was being taken from his account."

Dan told his interviewers, "I killed Sam first, and then, I killed Julie," Delgadillo testified to the Grand Jurors. "He said it was all about the money. It was one hundred percent about the money."

Delgadillo elaborated about Dan's monetary issues. "He was a financial mess," the detective testified. "He had a pending marriage coming up. He had bills to pay. He was in arrears on his rent for two months. He had no way of paying for the wedding or the reception. He wanted to go on a honeymoon or a cruise, and he had no way of paying for it. He basically had no money to his name at all."

Hoping to underscore Dan's intentions for the Grand Jurors, Murphy queried, "Okay. And did he say that in the context of his motivation for the murder?"

"Yes."

Even before Juri was killed, Delgadillo said, Dan was trying to procure Sam's funds. After the murder of Sam, the detective claimed, Dan "left the base. He ended up going and picking up Wesley . . . and they went and withdrew money from Sam's account."

The plan was to siphon off the cash in small increments, according to police—from the sixty-two thousand dollars Sam had received from the Army. "Mr. Wozniak was aware of that, and he planned on eventually draining that account and making withdrawals every other day for four hundred dollars," Delgadillo said.

Before he was captured, Dan had acquired approximately two thousand dollars, the district attorney's office reported.

It was a number that would plague Steve Herr's thoughts. "I cannot believe that somebody would do something like this to a young man and a young woman just for a few thousand dollars," he'd say. "My boy is gone, and I'm thinking, 'What a waste. What a waste.' He saved all his money so he could buy a house, go to college, and get married, and this guy takes it all away."

CHAPTER TWENTY

At the California Superior Court building, Det. Mike Delgadillo was telling the Grand Jury about what Dan Wozniak did after he shot Sam twice in the attic of the Liberty Theatre at the Joint Forces Training Base at Los Alamitos.

"I believe at that point, he went home," Delgadillo testified, "went on with his business . . . However, the following day, he came back to the . . . base."

"What did he do there?" the senior deputy district attorney, Matt Murphy, asked.

"Well, the first thing he did is he said he went to the [base] barbershop, and asked the barber . . . to borrow a pair of scissors. The scissors that he was borrowing from the barbershop, he took them up to the attic, where Sam was at. I should say prior to doing that . . . he went to his future in-laws' house."

"And what did he say he did there?"

"He went into the backyard and got an axe and a saw, which he brought back to the . . . base with him."

Fully prepared for the next phase of the crime, Delgadillo maintained, Dan used the scissors to cut off Sam's clothes. "Then, he proceeded to sever the head with the axe. He sawed Sam's head off. He sawed one of his arms . . . and he sawed the hand off the other arm. I asked him why he sawed the arm off. He said it had an identifying tattoo."

In fact, Sam had a number of recognizable tattoos: a skull, a lone wolf, and a parachute with the 173rd Airborne emblem. But Dan missed the heart and rose—and the words "Mom" and "Dad"—etched on Sam's chest. Although the head and portions of both arms had been cut, police would immediately spot that tattoo when they discovered Sam's torso and legs at the theater, identifying him before a scientific match could be made through forensic testing.

"At that point, he wrapped all the body parts that he had severed from Sam's body into . . . plastic bags," Delgadillo said. "He used Sam's backpack, and put all the body parts inside the backpack, wrapped."

From there, the detective said that Dan admitted to transporting the body parts to El Dorado Park. "He discarded Mr. Herr's head and hands," Murphy told the Grand Jurors, "for the purposes of trying to conceal his identity. Which is kind of silly in a lot of ways because he had distinct tattoos and, of course, was a member of the U.S. military and would have had DNA anyway."

At the time, though, Dan apparently fancied himself as an astute criminal, who was about to cast suspicion on Sam by murdering his good friend. "He didn't intend on us ever locating Sam," Delgadillo testified. "He intended to get rid of the rest of the body, and he wanted us to believe that Sam was the killer. And the only way he could do that was by killing Julie."

What the investigator didn't mention to the Grand Jury was that the search for Sam's body parts occurred on the day that the victim would have turned twenty-seven. "Saturday, May 29, was Sam's birthday," Steve Herr told the

Orange County Register. "And I'll never forget that on my son's birthday, I was praying that they would find his head."

After Delgadillo described his interrogation of the suspect, lead detective Jose Morales testified about what he witnessed at Juri Kibuishi's autopsy. "The pathologist, after the body was prepared, was washed down for the examination of the skull," he said. "We could see that there were two bullet holes to the head."

"All right," Murphy responded. "And did you actually see bullet fragments being removed from her skull?"

"Yes, I did."

The image, when compared to the photos of Juri's kind face and mischievous smile, was a difficult one for Grand Jurors to disregard. But Murphy wanted to further accentuate how the congenial, trusting student had been robbed of her life and asked that Juri's death certificate be entered into the record. "The official cause of death," he emphasized, glancing at the document, "was contusion, laceration of brain with skull fracture and gunshot wounds to the head. And she was twenty-three years old."

Without Dan in the room—perhaps looking concerned for the victim he claimed to have never harmed or dramatically dabbing his eyes—it was easy to arouse the wrath of the Grand Jurors. The fact that Juri had allegedly been sacrificed just to form an alibi for the actor's warped story line was equally infuriating.

While questioning Delgadillo, Murphy asked about the way that Juri had been stripped and defiled with profane slogans—all because, authorities claimed, Dan hoped to divert police into believing that she'd been sexually assaulted. "He said he tried to orchestrate it to make it look like it was Sam who had done it out of a rage of jealousy," Delgadillo said. "He got some scissors and cut open the back of her . . . [clothes]. She was still wearing a tiara that her brother had given her before she left Long Beach earlier that night. He had also written on her back with . . . a Magic Marker, a black writing instrument. I believe it said something like, 'Fuck you. You can have her.'"

According to authorities, Dan was hoping to convince police that Juri was the focal point of a bitter love triangle—involving Sam and Juri's online boyfriend, Corp. Mark Johnson. "Over the course of your investigation," Murphy asked, "you determined that it was not, in fact, a love triangle? Is that right?"

"That is correct."

"And specifically, during your interview with Mr. Wozniak, what did he tell you about this love triangle? Did he say that was real or fake?"

". . . I asked him if he had anything, any type of relationship, going with Julie, or there was any jealousy motive here. And his words to me were, 'I'm not into yellow fever,' meaning that he didn't have a preference for Asian women."

Murphy still wanted to spell out Dan's purported strategy for the Grand Jurors. "Okay. So based on your involvement in the investigation, as well as your interview with him, the love triangle was something he faked to make it look like Mr. Herr was involved in the murder?"

"Yes."

It was a testament to Dan's cunning that, for several days, police and the public suspected that Sam was guilty of murdering his friend. However, detectives believed that Dan's decision to conscript a teenager who immediately led them to the perpetrator was a statement about his ineptitude—as both a criminal and a member of society.

The process of determining whether a suspect deserved to be indicted was something that the authorities took seriously. In order to allow the Grand Jurors to consider their decision in isolation, witnesses were cautioned not to "discuss or repeat at any time outside of this jury room the questions that have been asked you, or your answers in respect to this matter." Failing to adhere to this rule could result in contempt of court charges.

But the detectives who'd come to bolster the district attorney's position had heard this admonishment before. Like the prosecutors and the families of the victims, their goal was to see Dan tried for the double homicide in the very near future. There'd already been so many obstacles in simply determining the facts, as law enforcement saw them. No one intended to do anything else to weaken the case.

As the proceeding neared its conclusion, Murphy thanked the Grand Jurors for their patience and elaborated on the nature of the charges. "We have two counts of murder," he said. "Murder for financial gain, which was established during the interview with Mr. Wozniak. And based on the autopsy information as well as the confession, and seeing some of the [crime scene] photographs, the use of a firearm. So I would ask that the Grand Jury indict on those two counts of murder."

He asked the foreperson of the Grand Jury if anyone had any questions about the evidence. No one did, and the panel gathered to consider the charges.

When the group filed back into the jury room, the foreperson formally announced the result that the detectives and members of the district attorney's office expected: "May it please the court, the Grand Jury of Orange County in its deliberation has returned an indictment in the *People of the State of California v. Daniel Patrick Wozniak.*"

Officially, Dan was facing two counts of murder, as well as the "special circumstances" charges of committing multiple murders and killing for financial gain.

CHAPTER TWENTY-ONE

Daniel Wozniak was arraigned the next morning at 8:30. Unlike the Grand Jury, this hearing was a public event, drawing the victims' relatives, as well as the media.

During the two years he'd been incarcerated, Dan appeared to have gained some weight, lengthened his sideburns, and grown a goatee. Hints of gray could be seen in the twenty-eight-year-old's beard, as he chatted with his lawyers, Tracy LeSage and Scott Sanders, in a mustard-colored jumpsuit, limbs shackled.

Despite what appeared to be a powerful prosecution position, Dan continued to insist that he had nothing to do with the crime. When the judge asked how he intended to plead, spectators strained to hear the defendant pronounce, "Not guilty."

It was the first time that Sam's cousin Leah Sussman had ever seen Dan in person. "Just being in the courtroom, in his presence, I shook the whole time," she said. "It literally made me sick. I felt nauseous."

To those who knew Dan from theater, it did not seem

implausible to imagine him addressing the court as the main character from *Arsenic and Old Lace*:

"*Well, usually, I'm Mortimer Brewster, but I'm not quite myself today.*"

"*I'm sorry, Judge. But a thing happened.*"

"*Even the cat's in on it!*"

But there were no theatrics in the courtroom that day. The entire proceeding took less than five minutes. Then, Dan returned to his cell while the reporters, detectives, and attorneys spilled out into the hallway with curious onlookers and the victims' loved ones.

The indictment was "long overdue," Steve Herr told the *Orange County Register*. "If it can expedite the trial, all the better."

In Steve's mind, Dan's guilt was already determined, and a jury reaching the same conclusion would not be enough for him. Alluding to an upcoming referendum to reconsider capital punishment in California, he said, "If there's a case for keeping the death penalty in the state, this is it."

Once the press published the details of the Grand Jury hearing, Juri's friends finally understood how easy it had been to set the bait for the considerate girl they knew from dance class. Jessica Wolf could visualize Juri relaxing at her brother's home with a tiara on her head and receiving an urgent text from a friend. "It was so in her character to run out to help somebody," Jessica said. "I thought, 'God, she would totally do that. She would come in the drop of a hat.'"

Recalled Natalie Jameson Sommer, "She always put other people before herself."

It was the same reaction that Juri's family had had. "She

did what she always did," her mother, Junko, said, "for friends." In fact, Junko would later wonder if she'd made a mistake by raising her child to always show kindness.

As they gathered at the dance competition at the Disneyland Hotel to reminisce about Juri, both Jessica and Natalie felt her absence. "You meet a friend who's never danced and they ask how it's going, and, you know, it's awkward," Natalie said. "It's so easy with a dancer. Even if you haven't seen each other in a while, you start talking and it's like all that time never passed."

Now they'd never have the opportunity to bump into Juri again, muse over their childhood memories, and laugh about their fellow dancer's new stories.

But Natalie would never forget the day, five years earlier, when she realized this sad truth. She'd been in her car, going to modern dance class at Orange Coast College, when she was struck with an unsettling feeling. Usually every day she received a text from Juri—nothing specific or detailed, just a friendly reminder that Juri was looking forward to seeing her at school. When there was no message, Natalie's intuition told her that there was reason for concern.

Then, her friend Faye Creedon texted three cryptic words: "Have you heard?"

A few minutes later, another friend from New York texted: "Have you heard about Julie?"

Now Natalie was truly scared. She'd already parked her car when her phone rang, and she felt a chill run through her body. It was her mother on the other end of the line.

"Natalie, I need you to sit down. I need you to stay calm. And I need you to listen to me." There were already tears in Natalie's eyes when her mother continued, "There's an article in the newspaper about Julie."

Natalie listened, but the words didn't fully register. Julie murdered? Who would want to murder Julie? "There was head trauma; that's all I knew," Natalie recalled. "I mean, 'head trauma.' What does that even mean? Nothing like this had ever happened to someone I knew, and somebody so nice, who everybody loved. I still cry, just talking about it.

"I had a friend die in a motorcycle accident. One of my grandparents died of cancer. Another one of my grandparents died of a heart attack. But how could someone have killed Julie in cold blood? It blows my mind to this day."

That morning, Natalie was supposed to have a modern dance final. She entered the classroom but quickly realized that she was incapable of functioning. "I'm really sorry," she told her teacher. "I just found out that Julie Kibuishi was murdered."

"Julie Kibuishi?" The teacher appeared to be shaken by the news. "Just leave, Natalie. You can't dance right now."

After she drove home, Natalie attempted to distract herself by turning on the television. But a fictional crime show was on. The topic: detectives investigating a murder. Now Julie was like one of those characters on television. *Julie. Why Julie?* Natalie began bawling all over again.

Without any additional information, Natalie began weaving scenarios in her mind. Maybe Julie met a psychopathic guy who took advantage of her trusting nature. Or maybe she wasn't really killed at all. "The article said 'head trauma," Natalie said. "Maybe she fell."

Natalie was still obligated to teach her dance classes. "I was driving to the studio in San Clemente, with a heavy heart, just thinking about everything," she said. "I didn't know Sam Herr. But the police seemed to think Sam had done it. And now Sam was missing. Where was he hiding? I was so angry at him."

Prior to leaving her home, she'd copied a link to the article about Juri's murder and sent it to all the parents of her students, as well as friends and relatives. She wanted everyone in Southern California to be vigilant and help the police find Sam Herr. When she arrived at the studio, her face was streaked with tears. "A couple of my students came up to me, and they just hugged me," she said. "And I remember just crying. Because when children hug you, they really understand what's going on. That was a big moment, being comforted by my students. They knew I was hurting inside.

"I was in a funk for weeks. My husband—who was my boyfriend at the time—didn't know how to make me feel better. Because how do you feel better when something like that happens? You can't."

Jessica Wolf was also trying to come to terms with the crime. "The dance world is so small. So I remember my phone just blowing up. Everybody was trying to put the pieces together. And now, with social media, it's like, 'boom, boom, boom.' My sister dances, too. She's three years older than I am, and teaches at the studio where we trained. So she was hearing her own rumors and theories. And then, we'd get on the phone, and try to figure things out. It was just a roller coaster of emotions.

"I don't think I've ever really talked about it until now. I tend not to vocalize things. I remember keeping things inside, but doing things like choreographing a number, and saying, 'Do this for my friend, Julie.' Little things to make me feel better therapeutically. But I could never really think about the details of *how* she was killed. I didn't want to think about what actually happened to her. I couldn't wrap my head around it."

Whenever Jessica logged on to Facebook, she immediately went to Juri's cousin Cathy Katagiri's page to see if the family was providing updates. But Cathy appeared as baffled as everyone else. Jessica also had vivid memories of seeing Juri's parents at performances and tried to imagine what they were experiencing. "I can't even fathom going through that as a parent. As a parent myself, it kills me."

Two years after the double homicide, it still seemed incomprehensible. Yes, the Grand Jury testimony had reinforced the concept that both Sam and Juri were guiltless players in the scheme of a madman. But, to Juri's friends, Sam was chosen because he had money. Juri provided nothing to Dan Wozniak, they believed, other than a dead body that could help cast suspicion on someone else.

"It was like, 'I need this other person to cover my tracks,'" Jessica said. "And that just made the whole thing more senseless."

She had no idea how random Juri's death had been.

What detectives couldn't tell the public was that Dan had initially targeted another young woman to divert suspicion to Sam. A few months earlier, Sam and a group of friends had been out together and the veteran ended up going home with a girl named Petra. Dan knew the story and, after the shooting in the attic of the Liberty Theater, he used Sam's phone to text Petra in an effort to entice her into coming to the victim's apartment.

Thankfully, Petra never responded. Unfortunately, at that very moment, Juri happened to text, asking: "What's up, buddy?"

The poor timing turned the kindhearted dancer into the most ill-fated person in Orange County.

"I am convinced that if Dan Wozniak hadn't been caught, he would have killed again," Det. Sgt. Ed Everett said. "He couldn't reach Petra, so he killed Julie. Who thinks like that? Serial killers do."

As she pored over the detectives' statements about what they claimed Dan told them in the interview room, Natalie felt like she was reading the synopsis of a movie. Then, she was struck by the fact that Juri was part of a horrible true-crime story. "That's when the anger would come back," Natalie said. "Juri was beautiful in every way. She was so sweet and didn't deserve that. I've heard people say that life isn't fair. But when someone you know becomes the example of that, you just feel helpless."

Remembering how she was incapable of teaching her dance class after learning about Juri's murder, Natalie was puzzled by the allegation that Dan stepped out onstage and performed after slaying two people. "How could you have the capacity?" she asked. "I'm getting the chills just talking about it."

At times, Jessica wished that Juri had lived away from the familiar cocoon of Orange County, where the glow of Disneyland's lights often lulled residents into believing that danger was elsewhere. "When I'm in LA, I always feel like I need to protect myself," she said. "When I came to New York to audition, I zipped up my belongings and made sure I was paying attention to where I was going. But maybe this would have happened anyway. You're never guarded when you're around the people you're close to. She thought she was going to help Sam. No one would have imagined that there's someone on the other side of the door, waiting to kill you."

If there was any common ground that Jessica could find with Dan, it was experiencing the pressure of planning a wedding. Jessica and her husband, Mark, had married six months after the dual murder and were living some of the same anxieties as Dan and Rachel. "Weddings are hard and expensive," Jessica said. "We wouldn't have had a honeymoon if my husband's parents hadn't gifted us one. But is it worth killing someone to have the money for a *honeymoon*? I mean, we live in Southern California, five minutes from the beach! Was it really *that* important? It's crazy to think that that would be a motive to kill people."

* * *

Like Juri's friends, Steve was also digesting the Grand Jury testimony, hoping to find some hidden truth in the statements uttered by the detectives and the senior deputy district attorney. Along with Jessica and Natalie, Steve wished Juri had been more cynical and realized that the texts that she was receiving from Sam's phone were being sent by someone else. "When she got the message 'Please, no sex. I need to talk to someone,' she had to know that wasn't Sam," Steve said. "She did kind of laugh it off, and say, 'What are you talking about? You're like my brother.' But Sam would never talk to her like that. That all came out of Wozniak's mind. I wish she'd stayed away. Then, at least *she'd* be alive today."

Just as Steve felt survivor's guilt for outliving his son, he was burdened with a sense of responsibility for Juri's death. If she hadn't befriended Sam when she started tutoring him, nothing bad ever would have happened to her. At Orange County College, she would have continued with her classes, then graduated and ended up in the fashion industry while teaching dance to children. Maybe she would have married her boyfriend in the Marines and started a family, giving her parents joy instead of sorrow. As Steve attempted to decipher the details of the case, he was determined to see justice served—for his own family, as well as the Kibuishis.

The problem was that, even after the indictment, Steve continued to feel closed out of the investigation. "The cops don't tell me much, and neither does the DA," he complained in 2012. "I want to know more, but they won't let me. I just wish I could look at the evidence, but I know that's not going to happen."

What Steve did have was the phone records from the day his son died. In Steve's living room, he'd pull them out of a file and read them over, desperately trying to re-create the final hours of Sam's life.

At 10:32 a.m., the documents indicated that Dan called Sam and asked him to assist with moving some objects at the Liberty Theater. At 11:28, Sam phoned Dan, possibly to confirm the appointment. At 12:12 p.m., Dan called Sam, probably to tell him where specifically to meet.

Steve pictured the two of them leaving together a few minutes later, with the rugged Army vet naïve to the fact that the actor was about to end his life in the playhouse.

At 12:25, Raquel, who'd been assisting Steve at his school, phoned her son. Sam sounded happy but kept the conversation short. "I'm helping somebody," he said. "I'll call you back."

The casual exchange marked the final time that Sam—with his murderer positioned beside him—would talk to his mother.

Spreading out the phone records in front of a writer, Steve wanted to continue dissecting the case. But he couldn't. Authorities had told him that he was going to be a witness at the trial and needed to choose his words carefully. Nonetheless, he continued talking to reporters. Maybe a member of the media could pass on a piece of intelligence that he hadn't heard. At the very least, he hoped that the press would continue to advocate for the family.

"I feel I need friends in the media," he said. "I'm being left out of the investigation of my son's murder, and I'm being treated unfairly. If they take Dan's word as gospel, and don't investigate other possibilities, they're making a mistake. A lot of times, I feel that the people involved in the investigation aren't competent. I might be absolutely wrong. I hope I am. I've given them a lot of information, and they don't tell me what they've followed up on. So I vent to these newspeople."

Detectives regularly assured Steve that they were dedicated to ensuring that anyone involved in the crime was punished. But in an area as populated as Orange County—

there were more than three million residents in 2012—other cases constantly arose, and resources were spread thin.

In the meantime, Steve continued talking to Sam's friends and neighbors, hoping to discover something that hadn't been uncovered. "I knew Sam and I knew his friends," Steve said. "Friends tell the father more than they're going to tell the police."

Sam's acquaintances were not always as forthcoming. "When you speak to certain people, you can feel their discomfort," Steve said. "If someone tells me, 'Well, I don't feel comfortable talking about this,' I have to ask if he's hiding something. Then, I go back to Sam's true friends, and see if they've felt the same bad vibe from this person. If they do, then something's amiss."

Although authorities suspected that Dan had learned about the money in Sam's account directly from the victim, Steve wasn't so sure. Perhaps Sam had mentioned his savings to another associate who then conveyed the information to Dan. Whether the person had simply made an innocent remark or been in on the plot Steve wasn't sure.

Steve knew that he sounded paranoid. But when he considered the way that his son had died and the manner in which Juri was lured to her death, Steve believed that the mistrust was justified. "I know that there are more people involved," he said. "I don't know the reason they got involved. All I can do is speculate, and hope that the police and the DA are doing the same thing.

"I want answers, and I've been promised that they'll go over every question I have. But when? I want them to do it now. And I want arrests. I want more arrests."

CHAPTER TWENTY-TWO

If the authorities were going to parcel out information in cautious doses and some of Dan's associates continued to show trepidation when certain topics were broached, Steve had his own plan about gleaning details about the case.

He intended to go directly to the source.

"I decided to just go to the jail and request to see him," Steve said, "The old adage is 'Get it from the horse's mouth.' The worst he could say was no. I had nothing to lose. But at least, I gave it a shot."

Arriving at the Orange County Jail, Steve filled out the necessary applications, then waited about thirty minutes until he was ushered to a room in which Dan was seated behind Plexiglas. The two were making eye contact as they each lifted a telephone receiver to communicate. According to Steve, Dan immediately said, "I'm sorry."

"I saw you on MSNBC," Steve said. "And you said that you were reading the Bible and were into Jesus. So you know what? I'm never going to forgive you, but I might hate you less if you tell the truth."

Dan stared back. "I respect you," he said with apparent sincerity.

Steve remembered being at the jail for forty-five minutes. Since the arrests, he'd been pondering how Dan secured access to Sam's PIN. Now Dan promised to provide the answer.

"He said that a few days before, he went to the bank with Sam. He said he watched Sam put in his PIN number and saw how much money was in the account." That's when Steve claimed that Dan told him about coming up with the concept of robbing Sam of his savings.

While Dan explained his motive, Steve contained himself, knowing that if he revealed anger or even disbelief the suspect might stand and ask a deputy to take him back to his cell.

"I don't know what made me do it," Dan allegedly said.

Steve tried not to shake his head. But he didn't accept Dan's version of events. "Two things don't jibe," Steve said later. "Number one—Sam wouldn't let anyone get that close to him when he was putting in the PIN number. Number two is your balance comes out on a small sheet. It doesn't come out on the screen where everyone can see it. Sam would look at the sheet, rip it into little threads, and throw it away. He wouldn't let Dan look at that."

In an effort to rationalize his actions, Steve said that Dan then outlined his financial issues. He was insolvent, he said, repeating what had become something of a mantra, to the point that when Sam gave him hundred dollars as a wedding gift Dan converted it to a cashier's check to use for the rent.

"He told me, 'I owed a lot of money. I did it for the money,'" Steve said.

Despite his not guilty plea in court, Dan apparently was willing to confess to his victim's father about behavior that could lead to the death chamber. But Steve had become convinced that others were involved in the conspiracy. "My guess was that somebody else—maybe someone who'd been tight with Sam—might have known the PIN number. Maybe Sam was drunk one night and said the number out loud while he was withdrawing money. I don't know this. It's just a theory. But I wanted to know who else was involved."

On three separate occasions, he maintained that he asked Dan about cohorts in the plot. "He said, 'I can't tell you,' " Steve said. "He didn't say, 'Nobody helped me.' He didn't say, 'I did it myself.' It was, 'I can't tell you.' So that, to me, is covering something."

Straining to identify the co-conspirator, Steve mentioned the arrest of Dan's brother Tim for being an accessory to murder after the fact—hoping the discussion would stir something in the suspect. In a tone that sounded frank, Dan, looking over at the victim's father, purportedly declared, "Tim had absolutely *nothing* to do with this."

Looking back on the conversation, Steve would conclude that Dan was either attempting to protect his brother or actually revealing a snippet of truth. "Maybe he was telling me, 'Other people had something to do with this, but not Tim.' "

Dan also wouldn't provide particulars of the murder, Steve said. Indeed, at one point Steve alleged that the actor asserted that he'd forgotten certain aspects of the crime. "Why did you kill Julie?" Steve claimed to have asked.

"Sometimes, you just black out. I don't remember certain things."

Steve struggled not to raise his voice. Nonetheless, he felt compelled to let Dan know that his story was less than convincing.

"I looked at him and I said, 'Dan, I'm a Marine from New Jersey. I was in the service during Vietnam. There are certain things in my life I've done. I remember everything. Don't bullshit me.' "

In reality, it was Steve who was toying with the truth. "I never went to Vietnam, but Dan doesn't know that,' " Steve said. "So I was just telling him that he was full of crap."

One of the few things that Dan apparently did concede was his disappointment with Wesley. "He was pissed off because this kid was using Sam's ATM card to buy pizza, and he was even driving Sam's car around," Steve said. "The way I interpreted it was Wesley wouldn't listen to him. Dan wants to be the Alpha guy, the one making plans. 'Don't drive the car. Don't do this.' Obviously, Dan didn't want to get arrested. And the kid was doing things his way."

At times, Steve thought about crashing through the Plexiglas and pummeling Dan, meting out justice without the intervention of detectives and district attorneys. "I wanted to kill the fucker," Steve admitted. "But I'm not stupid. If I start ranting and raving, they're going to come and take me away. What's most important to me is finding out the whole story."

In fact, when Dan referred to his visitor as "Mr. Herr" he was told, "Just call me 'Steve.' "

"I fear you the most," Dan apparently said, without elaborating.

Steve wanted Dan to keep talking. "You have nothing to fear from me," Steve responded, "as long as you tell me the truth."

Indeed, the actor's reverential tenor was disarming. It appeared that, in some way, Dan was attempting to atone for his crimes. But Steve did not believe that Dan was legitimately penitent. The suspect's main regret, Steve presumed, was getting caught.

* * *

How could someone sit calmly across from the father of the person he killed, respectfully calling the man "Mr. Herr" while claiming to have blacked out on details of the double homicide? If everything described in the indictment was true, he suffered from some type of anti-social personality disorder. According to the American Psychiatric Association, the world's largest psychiatric organization, both sociopaths and psychopaths fall into this category and share a number of traits, including a disregard for the rights of others, failure to feel remorse or guilt, and a tendency for violence.

Sociopaths—known for emotional outbursts and fits of rage—are able to form attachments to individuals or groups but have no consideration for society's rules. Their crimes are said to be disorganized and impulsive, rather than carefully planned out. But under certain, uncommon circumstances, the sociopath can feel compassion for other people.

By contrast, psychopaths are described as charming and manipulative and able to gain people's trust. Because of this, some can thrive at jobs, marry, and raise families. However, they are unable to form real emotional attachments or feel empathy. As a result, they observe how the rest of society behaves and imitate the emotions that others expect them to show, exhibiting signs of sadness when informed about a tragic situation or expressing sympathy over a death.

In the business world, psychopaths have been known to conceive elaborate swindles, using their personable qualities to convince their victims to make debilitating investments. When the psychopath commits a violent act, it's often meticulously planned, down to the alibi. Experts describe psychopaths as the more dangerous of the two groups. To the psychopathic serial killer, for instance, human beings are perceived as objects to be sacrificed for entertainment and pleasure.

Another difference between a sociopath and a psychopath involves the cause of the anomaly. Experts define psychopathy as a neurological disorder, involving a defect in the part of the brain responsible for emotions and impulse control. Psychologists have described sociopathy as a learned condition, sometimes brought on by abuse or other childhood trauma.

Was Dan Wozniak a sociopath or psychopath? In some ways, his alleged actions appeared to fit both classifications. In other ways, he seemed to be in a category all his own.

CHAPTER TWENTY-THREE

Rachel Buffett was in the California Superior Court building when the Grand Jury convened to indict Dan. Although she was prepared to testify, senior deputy district attorney Matt Murphy decided not to have her address the Grand Jurors. "Now, Rachel Buffett is on my witness list," he told them. "I don't think at this point, I am going to call her, after all. I think that she may . . ." He carefully adjusted his words. "Well, depending on how things go, she is here now, but we will see how that goes. She may need an attorney."

Like Steve Herr, Murphy, as well as the detectives who'd been covering the case, suspected that there was much that Rachel didn't want to reveal. And that meant that the former Disneyland princess was in a good deal of trouble herself.

On November 20, 2012, Rachel received a phone call from police, asking if she could meet with them to sign some papers. She arranged a rendezvous at a shopping center. But the moment that she arrived, she was placed under arrest.

Rachel had been "within the focus of this on-going investigation for the past two years, and has been previously . . . interviewed by detectives," Lt. Paul Dondero of the Costa Mesa police investigations bureau explained in a statement. "Detectives compared information obtained in those interviews with information gleaned from interviews of other witnesses, as well as additional aspects of the investigation, and determined there was probable cause to arrest Rachel Buffett."

Allegedly, she cried and asked about the statute of limitations. She was apparently told that there was no statute of limitations for murder.

Bail was set at one hundred thousand dollars.

"I sat in jail for six days, through Thanksgiving weekend, before anybody could get ahold of the district attorney's office and find out exactly what I was being charged with," she complained on the *Dr. Phil* show. "I ended up being in there three weeks. I was charged with three felony counts of accessory to murder."

For Steve Herr, the case finally appeared to be moving forward. Not only was Dan in custody, but now his fiancée was, as well. On December 13—seven months after Dan's indictment—some of the same players returned to the Superior Court building for a pretrial hearing to consider whether the pretty twenty-five-year-old actress manufactured a number of tales to help Dan—in the words of the district attorney's office—"avoid and escape from arrest, trial, conviction and punishment for the felony."

Once again, lead detective Jose Morales outlined the circumstances of the double homicide: the discovery of Juri's body in Sam's apartment, Steve's 911 call, and Dan's confession at the Costa Mesa Police Department.

But rather than simply rehashing what had been discussed at Dan's indictment, law enforcement hoped to convince Judge Kazuharu Makino that Rachel was entangled in the plot.

Morales explained that, on May 27, 2010, Dan told detectives that he'd murdered Sam the previous Friday: "He . . . had lured him over to the theater base so he could help him move some furniture, some, I believe it was theater props. He shot him twice in the head and took his belongings, his wallet, his identification, his bank card, and drove, took his car and drove out to the city of Long Beach, where he picked up Wesley.

"He instructed Wesley to remove money from the ATM using the bank card. . . . He returned to his apartment and later, sometime in the evening, he went to the show with Rachel."

The investigator was referring to Dan and Rachel performing in a production of *Nine* hours after Sam was killed. Following the show, Morales said, the couple went home. It was in the apartment they shared, detectives testifed, that Dan used Sam's cell phone to send the texts that led to Juri Kibuishi's death.

"He pretended to be Sam . . . texting Julie, asking her to come over," Morales said. "He didn't really go into big detail about, you know, each text message that was sent."

Satisfied that the detective had appropriately explained the system that Dan used to ambush Juri, Murphy asked Morales to set the scene inside the apartment. "[Dan] said . . . that he was using Sam's cellular phone to text Julie," the detective replied. "Rachel was on the couch with him, trying to fall asleep."

Did that mean that Rachel knew what Dan was trying to do?

She told detectives that she was oblivious to his lethal designs. After she and Dan returned from the play, Morales said, Rachel asserted that "they popped in a movie"—*Men in Black*—and an episode of *Family Guy*, to be precise, "and went to bed, and didn't give any details about what they did." Reportedly, Rachel also went on Facebook around this time, responding to a message Juri had sent earlier. Rachel also scanned ads for topless dancer jobs, hoping a stripping gig would bring in funds that the couple hadn't been able to earn through any other means.

But investigators claimed that, in one of their interviews, Rachel said she never realized that she and Dan were in financial trouble. The excuse seemed laughable when police learned that the couple had already been evicted from another apartment and were about to be ejected from the Camden Martinique complex.

According to detectives, on the night that Juri was killed Rachel "could not remember whether she used a computer or anything else," Morales stated.

"Did she ever say that after they got back, Mr. Wozniak left the apartment for a period of time?" Murphy asked.

"No. She didn't tell us that."

"Okay. And again, just so the court is clear—in Mr. Wozniak's confession, they got back from the show and he had been using this cell phone to lure Miss Kibi-ushi to the apartment, right?"

"Correct."

"And then, he left and went and committed the murder of her. Is that right?"

"Correct."

"And then, returned to the apartment?"

"Yes."

But, according to Rachel, she could not recall her fiancé departing or coming back to the bedroom after Juri had been killed, stripped, and sullied with an obscene message. Rachel would tell the *Daily Pilot,* an Orange County newspaper, that, by the time Dan committed the crime, she'd fallen asleep.

"I told . . . [detectives] I can't really remember" what

occurred that night, Rachel would say in a TV interview. "I usually go to bed pretty quickly after coming home, maybe pop in a movie. I was speaking [in general terms], trying to tell them what happened because I didn't remember at first."

Law enforcement was less than persuaded. "She told us a story we know not to be true," Det. Sgt. Ed Everett told the *Daily Pilot*. Orange County District Attorney Tony Rackauckas suspected that Rachel was trying not only to absolve herself from any wrongdoing but protect her fiancé as well. "In particular, that . . . statement is meant to give Dan an alibi," Rackauckas said. "They would be in bed at the time of the second murder."

Rachel would deny doing anything to excuse Dan's actions.

The first time that she heard anything about a murder, she maintained, was at the end of the cast party after the Saturday night performance of *Nine* at the Hunger Artists Theatre. That's when she said that both she and Dan were contacted by their neighbor Dave Barnhart, who'd run into Steve Herr in Sam's apartment and discovered that a homicide had occurred. According to Morales, Rachel claimed to have been told that "something was happening . . . [Dave] wouldn't relay what was happening, but . . . their presence was needed back at" the Camden Martinique Apartments.

Yet the couple's friend Chris Williams—who'd tell police that he saw a man he believed to be Sam leaving for the Liberty Theater with Dan—claimed that Rachel seemed unusually emotional twenty-four hours earlier, following the Friday night performance. After spending part of the afternoon with the couple, Chris decided to see their show that evening. "He thought that Dan had done a great job and texted him" about his exceptional acting, Morales testified. When Chris watched Rachel onstage, though, "he didn't think that she was going to get through the show," Morales said, "because she had been crying throughout the whole show or at least during her crying scenes. She had been crying after the show.

"They got together before Dan and Rachel left [the theater]. . . . Chris had talked to them about their performance, and Rachel had stated that the tears were real tears. And . . . it wasn't because of the show. It was because of everything that had gone on during the day."

While Rachel didn't elaborate, law enforcement believed that this statement suggested that she was already aware of Sam's murder. "It indicates she knows something," prosecutor Matt Murphy would later theorize before adding sardonically, "It could be because she's marrying [Dan]. Who knows?"

Another actress in *Nine*, Cynthia Lee, contributed to the suspicions about Rachel's behavior. "She said that on Friday . . . she saw Miss Buffett," Morales said, "that she appeared to be sad and distant, and that she was sitting on a trunk adjacent to the stage area. Mr. Wozniak approached her and he tried to kiss her, and she turned away from him. [Cynthia] . . . thought that it was odd because . . . they were always together and he would always kiss her before a play . . . to wish her well, but on that evening, she turned him away.

". . . During the play, there was a scene where Miss Buffett was supposed to be upset. But normally, throughout all the plays preceding this evening, she had never cried before. But on that particular night, Miss Buffett was crying during one of the scenes. And after . . . the scene was over, she continued to cry and was trying to compose herself."

Even for an actress who took her roles seriously, the behavior seemed intense. Cynthia told detectives that Rachel was "a wreck" the entire night.

The next evening—after Juri had also been lured to her death—Rachel arrived at the theater characteristically late, at 7:15 p.m. In the dressing room, Cynthia and Rachel sat across from each other, separated by a small partition. "Miss Lee said they were so close that she could reach over and touch her if she wanted to," Morales said. "And she could see Miss Buffett sitting down. . . . She was putting on makeup, and she continued to be kind of sad."

Because of her mood the night before, Cynthia was worried that something was truly wrong and asked how the pretty blond actress was feeling.

According to Morales' report, Rachel responded, "My friend is missing. I think she's missing. I think she's dead. I think my friend did it."

To stress that Rachel indeed understood exactly what Dan had perpetrated, Murphy asked the investigator when Juri's body was discovered.

"Miss Kibuishi was discovered on Saturday night around midnight," Morales replied.

"Okay. So midnight after seven fifteen? Is that right?"

"Yes."

"Okay. And was there some big search going on? Was there flyers being posted, anything like that, regarding missing persons, that you're aware of?"

"No."

In other words, if the recollections of Chris Williams and Cynthia Lee were accurate, Rachel knew about the crimes before she said that she did. This alleged elasticity with the truth led some of her detractors to believe that Rachel was not just an accessory to the crime but a co-conspirator. A few wondered if she'd been in the apartment when Juri was killed.

If anyone in the district attorney's office subscribed to this concept, it was not the version of events that the prosecution presented in the courtroom. Rather than depicting

Rachel as a direct participant in the bloodshed, they portrayed her as an accomplice who undercut the investigation by providing data that were deliberately untruthful.

In the eyes of investigators, that was damning enough.

Rachel, Morales said, maintained that between ninety minutes and two hours after Dan left the apartment with Sam he came home. "She said . . . he had money with him," Morales said, "that he was still acting very weird. It looked to her like he was going to have a heart attack. They . . . went to the pool, tried to relax, but then, he said he had to go to his parents' house.

"His explanation was he had to go talk to his parents, or try to reconnect with his family. . . . Then, he said something like, well, he needs to go to his parents' house to get some childhood memories. At which point, he took off."

More than a half hour passed, Rachel told Morales, before Dan called again and reported that his parents weren't home and he was unable to enter the house. "He had left the keys behind in the apartment. So he came back. When he came back, that's when he picked her up and went to the show."

This was a contradiction of Chris Williams' account of lounging in the apartment with Rachel until Dan returned from his journey with Sam and repaid a loan. In fact, the four hundred dollars that Dan paid Chris was likely the first withdrawal made from Sam's account after his murder.

"Does Miss Buffett mention anything to you about Chris Williams being in the apartment?" Murphy asked the detective.

"No, she does not."

". . . Does she say anything to detectives—you or anybody else—about him paying Chris Williams back at the apartment?"

"No, she didn't."

When Dan told detectives about his whereabouts that day, he initially described Sam stopping at the apartment before the two left to run some errands. Dan claimed that they'd been accompanied by one of Sam's friends—a person Dan characterized to his friend Jake Swett as a nameless male in a black baseball cap. After Dan's arrest, however, Morales said that Dan "told detectives that he wanted to be honest, and there wasn't a third person. . . . He wanted us to know that he had lied about this third person."

This reinforced Chris Williams' statement about Dan and Sam leaving the apartment complex alone. Why, then, did Rachel tell Det. Sgt. Ed Everett that *she'd* seen the stranger in the baseball cap?

She also informed investigators that she had another piece of information that might be helpful to the case. According to Morales, this occurred after her first interview, at approximately 3:00 or 4:00 a.m., on May 27.

"You finish your interview with her in the early-morning hours," Murphy asked the detective, "and you, did you drive her back to her apartment?"

"Yes, I did."

"Okay. And when you drove her back to the apartment, did she say anything to you at that time, as you were walking through the parking lot?"

"Yes, she did."

"What did she say?"

"We were just having a conversation about her going back to see her parents and whatnot, where she was going to go after the interview, and she said something. She [asked] . . . whether or not we had looked into Sam's background because he had been involved in something like this before."

She was talking about the fatal beating of Byron Benito

by a large mob—a crime for which Sam had been arrested and later acquitted.

"I asked her how she had come across the information," Morales said. "And she said that Sam had been talking about it in the Jacuzzi."

With Sam missing—after Juri was found dead in his apartment—it seemed that Rachel was implying that her neighbor might have a propensity for murder.

In a later interview, she'd also contend that Sam had an uneasy relationship with his family—a detail that both police and prosecutors noticed. On June 9, 2010, four days after searchers finally discovered Sam's head, Rachel told Morales about an exchange she'd had with Sam on the balcony just outside her apartment. "She told us that during that conversation that she was aware that Sam had lent Dan one hundred dollars and that if Dan couldn't pay it, [the] one hundred dollars would be considered a wedding gift," Morales said. According to Rachel, "during the time that they were on the patio, he continued and said that he was having family problems. He wouldn't go into what these problems were. She noticed that . . . he looked like he was down, and said that he was going to see his folks for the weekend."

Apparently, Rachel wasn't aware that Sam regularly met his father to work out, eat dinner, and socialize with friends. Nor could she have realized that the allegation about family problems would be broached during Dan's Grand Jury hearing.

"During the course of your investigation," Matt Murphy asked at the time, "did you learn any information that Mr. Herr was having any sort of family problems?"

"Yes, we did," Morales answered.

"Okay. What information did you receive?"

"That he was not having family problems."

Now, Murphy and Morales were together at another proceeding, arguing that Sam's supposed issues with his parents were invented, first, to guide Juri to her death and, then, to mislead investigators. And, the way law enforcement saw it, Rachel was just as guilty of deception as the man she'd intended to marry.

"When she tells police that she had a conversation with Sam Herr on the balcony, and he said that he was having problems with his family, that echoes the exact ruse that Wozniak was using to lure Kibuishi over there that night," Murphy insisted in front of Judge Makino. "There's no confusion about it. . . . The court has evidence, heard evidence, that's absolutely not true. That's part of the ruse."

Still, Rachel would continue to assert that her greatest transgression was picking the wrong guy.

CHAPTER TWENTY-FOUR

From the perspective of Rachel's lawyer, the former Disney princess' sole intention was aiding the detectives attempting to solve the murders of Sam Herr and Juri Kibuishi.

"Miss Buffett was put into a circumstance where her brother and her fiancé were arrested two days before her wedding," defense attorney Ajna Sharma-Wilson argued in front of Judge Makino. "Her life basically fell apart. And, in trying to figure out what happened, she did go to the police. She volunteered [giving] to the police any information that this young lady had."

The lawyer referred to Rachel telling the detectives about her encounter with a nervous Tim Wozniak after Dan's arrest: "She . . . let them know that Tim Wozniak may have been the one." The implication was that Tim's behavior led Rachel to suspect that Dan's brother could have committed the crimes. "I don't think that the police would have gotten as far in their investigation without the assistance of Miss Buffett."

Nonetheless, Sharma-Wilson conceded that Rachel

hadn't conveyed the absolute truth: "I understand some of her information were lies because Dan told her them. . . . And that has come out today with the testimony of the [prosecution] witnesses. Other than that, I do believe that my client did her best to tell the truth to the police officers, and did her best to try to put her life together over those past two years.

"And I will submit to that."

But Matt Murphy continued to insist that Rachel was part of the problem, not the solution.

"There's been a murder that's been committed," he maintained. "We know there's a plot. We know there's a plot based on Wozniak's confession that he planned this whole thing out."

"That he did it?" Judge Makino attempted to clarify.

"Right. That he did it."

"There's a plot involving him?"

"Right."

". . . But you're saying the plot involves her?"

"That's right, because it has to involve her because when Wozniak tells police, 'Yeah, there's this third guy,' that's obviously a part of the plot. I don't have to prove what little twisted thought [Rachel and Dan] . . . have together about how that's going to . . . protect them. But I can submit to the court that, based on this, when Sam Herr's body is eventually discovered, they want to blame it on this mystery guy.

". . . Wozniak is the very first one to make the statement, 'I lied about the third guy.' Okay? And so, that's part of the plot. Third guy—part of the plot . . . When she's first interviewed . . . [she] tells the exact same lie . . . about this third guy being at the apartment. That's a material falsehood."

In addition, the senior deputy district attorney claimed that Rachel deliberately omitted the fact that Chris Williams had been at her home on the day that Sam disappeared. "She doesn't mention Chris Williams at that point," Murphy said. "That's an affirmative falsehood because Chris Williams has been waiting" in the couple's apartment and saw Dan return alone. "The witness knows there's no third person."

And, according to the prosecutor, Rachel also knew that Juri had been murdered before Steve Herr found the body in Sam's apartment. On Saturday night, prior to Rachel's performance in *Nine*, "Miss Buffett announces to this other actress that her friend is missing, she thinks she's dead, and she thinks her other friend did it," Murphy stressed to the judge. "If Julie isn't found until later that evening, and we've got evidence that this woman, our defendant here, knows about her death before anyone has discovered her . . . the only place that she can get that information is from Wozniak."

Because of her intimacy with Dan, as well as the odd timing of Rachel's revelation to Cynthia Lee, Murphy contended, she knew about Juri's sad fate, as well as who committed the crime.

But Sharma-Wilson had issues with some of the sources used by law enforcement. As sincere as Cynthia may have been when she spoke to authorities, the lawyer pointed out that the actress was interviewed on October 26, 2010— about five months after the double murder. And detectives admitted that neighbor Jake Swett, who found Steve Herr in Sam's apartment, was intoxicated when he was first interviewed.

Even so, Murphy said, Rachel's actions during that weekend proved her culpability. Besides lying about the man in the baseball cap, Murphy claimed, Rachel's story about returning home from the play and going to sleep was "akin to an alibi."

"What was the false statement?" the judge challenged.

". . . They came home and they went to bed. Okay? As opposed to, 'We came home, my fiancé left and came back, and we went to bed.'"

"How about, 'We went to bed, he left while I was asleep, I didn't know it, and he came back'?" Judge Makino suggested.

"Which would be great. And that's a wonderful thing at trial. But she doesn't say that. She says, 'We came home and we went to sleep.'"

Speaking over Murphy, the judge continued to question the notion that Rachel was being economical with the truth: "Where's the evidence that that's false? I mean, how is it not possible that did, in fact, happen? And that he left and killed the other person and came back?"

"Well, for one thing . . . I believe we had testimony that they usually go to sleep about one. Julie Kibuishi is murdered right around midnight." The prosecutor noted that Juri's cell phone records indicated that that was when Juri's text communication with her brother stopped. "So according to the defendant's own statement, they usually go to sleep between one in the morning and three in the morning. So it's before her bedtime for one thing, and she says nothing about her fiancé leaving."

The adamant tone of Murphy's voice sounded convincing. Still, Judge Makino warned that he wasn't interested in having the case tried in front of him. "This is not a trial," he said. "This is a preliminary hearing." As with the Grand Jury, the purpose of the proceeding was determining whether there was enough evidence to try Rachel for being an accessory. "I would say you have enough for the preliminary hearing," the judge told Murphy. "But I would also say that I have my doubts whether that's going to get you a conviction at trial."

Either way, Makino expressed his opinion that the testimony had convinced him "that there's a reasonably strong suspicion that the crimes alleged [at the proceeding] were committed, and that this defendant was the person who committed those offenses."

Rachel was incredulous about being in any way associated with the crimes attributed to Dan. "It's such a preposterous notion," she'd later say on the *Dr. Phil* TV show. "I had nothing to do with the murders, and I had no knowledge of the murders until after the police did."

In the courtroom, Murphy appeared to be looking forward to proving her wrong: "I have no doubt it's going to be interesting."

CHAPTER TWENTY-FIVE

If Rachel was convicted on all three charges of accessory after the fact, she would have to defer her acting aspirations for as much as three years and eight months. That was the maximum sentence that she could receive in the event that she was found guilty on every count.

Shortly after her arrest, she'd vigorously pleaded not guilty. She told the *Daily Pilot* that she was perplexed about why she'd been charged with anything at all.

"You go over it in your mind. 'How could I possibly give someone wrong information?' " she said. "I was trying to be helpful and give them every conception in my mind."

Although they were trying to be circumspect in what they disclosed to the media about the case, members of law enforcement found it difficult to mask their contempt for Rachel's excuse. Like Steve Herr, a number of investigators suspected that she might have been guilty of more than what the charges indicated. Despite their efforts to prove this, though, they were unable to support the theory.

"By the time we finally got to the point where it seems

it's going to be pretty clear additional evidence isn't going to come out," Orange County District Attorney Tony Rackauckas said, "it was decided Rachel could only be charged with accessory after the fact."

Behind bars, Rachel struggled. "It's hard to eat when your stomach is in knots," she told ABC News.

Despite the accusations, she maintained that she blamed her circumstances completely on Dan Wozniak: "I'm innocent. It was like the person I loved never really existed."

Indeed, she was so appalled by the nature of the crimes that she appeared to share Steve's view of how Dan should be punished. "I think they are very justified in going for the death penalty," she said of prosecutors. "You can't believe anything a sociopath tells you. He did fully confess."

Yet some wondered if it was Rachel who was showing some form of anti-social personality disorder. When she mentioned her affection for Sam and Juri, Rachel sounded strangely like Dan on MSNBC's *Lockup*: "They were just amazing people, and I'm sorry such evil has occurred."

Nonetheless, Rachel's brother Noah—who'd also been arrested as an accessory—insisted that his sister was speaking from the heart and the hostility leveled at her was misdirected. Had she been involved in anything of this magnitude, he assured people, he would have known. "We tell each other everything," he said. "She wouldn't lie to me."

In an interview with LA TV station KTLA, Noah referred to Rachel's former job at Orange County's best-known landmark. "Rachel is a Disney princess," he declared, speaking for his family. "She's our little princess."

The notion that the police would handcuff the sweet-faced blonde and place her in a cell alongside methamphetamine dealers and gang members both stunned and disheartened the family. And, like the Herrs and the Kibuishis, Noah was frustrated that the case had the potential to linger in the courts for years "We're still kind of in shambles," he told the news platform Patch, "just waiting for a very slow system of law to get in gear."

Out of all of Rachel's siblings, her bond with Noah seemed to be the strongest. And he contended that this enabled him to provide insights about his sister that others couldn't. "I've known her since she was a baby," he argued. "She just wasn't part of anything like this."

From his perspective, Noah believed that law enforcement was targeting Rachel because of her relationship with Dan. "It's a little unnerving to see what they'll try to pull out of thin air," he said.

It was a position that Rachel's attorney, Ajna Sharma-Wilson, was also espousing to the press, describing Rachel as, "in essence, collateral damage of Dan Wozniak."

But Steve had no sympathy for the young woman he'd grown to perceive as a manipulative actress, who may have had more in common with Dan than she was willing to admit. "I would assume it's a strong case," he told Patch. "They wouldn't have charged her if it wasn't."

Immediately after her arrest, the family began lobbying for a deduction of Rachel's one-hundred-thousand-dollar bail. The Buffetts' finances were spent, Noah said, and they hoped to raise money online. "We all want to see our sister come home," he said. "She had no idea what was going on."

Two days before her pretrial hearing—after twenty days in the Orange County Jail system—Rachel was released on a reduced bond of fifty thousand dollars. It was near midnight when she passed through the door and was whisked to her family's house. "She's feeling okay," Sharma-Wilson told Patch. "She's happy to be back with her family again, and she's very thankful for her family and community for supporting her during this."

Exactly which members of the community were standing behind Rachel was uncertain. But she realized that she couldn't rely on Noah and other loved ones to evaporate the cloud of suspicion that hovered over the actress—particularly after Judge Kazuharu Makino's ruling at the pretrial hearing. There was going to be a long battle ahead, and Rachel needed to drive a greater wedge between herself and the man accused of slaying Sam Herr and Juri Kibuishi.

After participating in a number of small news stories, Rachel made a dramatic decision to appear on a national TV show and take her case to people who had never heard of Costa Mesa, the Liberty Theater, or Daniel Patrick Wozniak.

CHAPTER TWENTY-SIX

After his birth in Vinita, Oklahoma, Phil McGraw was raised among the oil fields of northern Texas, where his father was an equipment supplier who harbored dreams of becoming a psychologist. By the time Phil had graduated from college, he had the same goal and began conducting self-help seminars, alongside his father, who'd now established a practice in Wichita Falls, Texas. In 1998, Dr. Phil—as he branded himself—started appearing weekly, as a relationship counselor, on Oprah Winfrey's show. Four years later—after publishing four best-selling psychology books—he became the star of his own syndicated show, *Dr. Phil,* produced by Winfrey's Harpo Studios.

On February 5, 2013, he invited Rachel Buffett on to the program to address the question of whether she was yet another innocent victim of Dan Wozniak's treachery or a co-conspirator who had helped her fiancé cover up the murders.

The show began with McGraw confronting Rachel in a forthright manner. "If you were falsely accused here, and

[were] pulled into this cover-up, then, a lot of people are going to owe you an apology for accusing you of it, and trampling on your reputation," he said. "If you were, then that was a mistake and you need to own it and move on with your life. At this point, there's a lot of open wounds here." He motioned at Steve Herr, who was also in the studio. "And you need to understand why this man here is hurting."

Rachel's features dropped in an apparent show of sympathy. "I do," she said.

"He hasn't gotten justice for his son." Dr. Phil crossed his arms. "How do you feel about what happened to his son?"

It appeared that Rachel was ready to answer. But before she could, Dr. Phil cut her off to continue his monologue: "It breaks my heart and I didn't know him, and wasn't even close to him." McGraw raised his hand to gesture. When he did, his sleeve slipped down, revealing a large, gold watch. "And I watch you . . . and you seem to have no reaction at all."

The actress was quick to defend herself: "It's absolutely horrific. But I think, I know I'm not the main victim. Sam and Julie were the main victims. And then, I think even secondary would be their families. I'm after all of that. I realize that. And that's why I didn't come out in the limelight. . . . I tried to keep it to myself and work through it, and tried to do my little healing process or whatever. But because of how much these people are hurting, and they think I had anything to do with that, it's bringing up a lot of pain for me, and I guess that's why I don't want to wait for it to go through court. I'm so happy that it will, so they can see that I had nothing to do with it. But I want"—she moved her head slightly from side to side—"some sort of healing." She looked down and blinked quickly. "Or at least for them to know that I didn't have anything to do with their pain."

As she had in the past, Rachel insisted that she was misled by Dan and knew nothing of the crimes he committed. When the host brought up her report that she'd seen
Sam with a man in a black baseball cap, she steered the
question back at Dr. Phil.

"You have a wife, right?" she asked him.

"I do. A beautiful wife. Thank you."

Attempting to draw a parallel between the TV host's
life and her current circumstances, Rachel continued, "If
your wife told you she just made a pot of coffee and it was
in the kitchen, then, you didn't see it, but later on, somehow,
it became really important, whether or not it was there,
and a cop asked you, 'Um, what was in your kitchen?' "
She moved her head theatrically from side to side and
peered down. " 'Oh, a spatula, fork, and' "—she looked
directly at Dr. Phil—" 'a pot of coffee.' I trusted him and I
trusted what he said was true. And, especially, before I
thought it really mattered, I didn't question him. And later
on in questioning, when the police asked me, 'Well, did
you actually see him?' And I said"—she looked down, as
if to ponder—" 'Well, no. I didn't.' "

In a voice filled with cynicism, McGraw told Rachel,
"I've got to tell you, that sounded like a really coached response. I want to know what *you* have to say about it, not
what you worked out in a conference room with your
lawyer to say about it. And it's my understanding you
didn't say you *inferred* that there was a third party, but you
told authorities that you *saw* a third party. Is that correct?"

Rachel shook her head from side to side. "I don't recall
telling that specifically to them."

Looking out into the studio audience, Dr. Phil asked a
member of the investigative team, "Did she say she saw a
third party? Is that in the record?"

"Yes, that's her statement."

Dr. Phil directed his attention back at his interview subject. "Your statement was that you saw a third party," he stated.

She nodded slightly. "Uh-hmm," she responded uncertainly.

Dr. Phil focused on an uncomfortable Rachel. "I'm watching you close because you're an actress."

She smiled nervously.

"You're a good one."

From the audience, her lawyer, Ajna Sharma-Wilson, piped in, "I have not coached my client at all. I have not told her anything other than, 'Tell the truth, Rachel.'"

Concentrating on Rachel again, Dr. Phil asked, "Did you say that you saw somebody, or did you just say there was a third party, and that was just an inference based on what Dan told you?"

"That's how I remember it."

Sharma-Wilson intervened. "Dan told her that that was accurate, and she implicitly believed the man that she was going to marry."

Dr. Phil looked back at Sharma-Wilson. "So I guess the interpretation could be that that could help, that maybe Dan wasn't the last person to see Sam alive—"

"In my mind," Rachel cut in, "I was thinking that it would help them find Sam, who I thought was just missing. And Dan wasn't under suspicion, as far as I knew, at that point."

Likewise, she contended that she told police that she'd gone to sleep after arriving home on the night that Juri was killed because that was what she normally did after a performance. "I was speaking in [general] . . . , trying to tell them probably what happened because I didn't remember at first," she explained.

But McGraw quoted authorities who said that Rachel

had sent Juri a Facebook message—perhaps to establish that she was unaware of Dan's plan—when she was supposed to be sleeping.

Despite the host's pessimism, Rachel reiterated that Dan never told her about his scheme. When she did find out, she stressed, she did nothing to help him cover up his alleged crimes. It was only at the Costa Mesa Police Department that Rachel grasped the full horror of the situation, she said, when Dan confessed to her in front of detectives.

"Did he tell you how" he executed the murders? McGraw asked.

"I don't recall if he told me how."

To Dr. Phil, it appeared inconceivable that Rachel would forget this kind of detail. "Wow," he said. "You don't recall?"

"At a certain point, you reach your shock level, and I think you just turn off your intake button because you can't handle any more."

But the producers were not about to accept these types of justifications. Steve Herr was invited onto the stage to sit beside Rachel and express the scorn that he'd grown to feel for the actress. "I absolutely believe she's guilty of what she's being tried for," he told the audience, reminding them how Sam was shot and dismembered. He turned toward Rachel. "For you to come on here, to go on the TV stations and 'poor me,' that offends me."

"Do you believe she belongs in prison?" McGraw asked.

Steve placed a finger over his chin and contemplated. "Yes," he retorted. His body suddenly jerked, and in a louder voice he declared, "Yes." He leaned back and nodded. "I do. And if she truly feels for the family, I would appreciate her stopping trying to get other . . ." He hesitated, reconfiguring the words in his head. "I appreciate if she doesn't give any more interviews until the [trial]. . . ."

Rachel looked forward, not meeting Steve's gaze but nodding as if she felt some form of solidarity with her accuser.

"In my estimation," he continued, "my belief is, 'You're lying and covering it up,' but we'll find out in court."

CHAPTER TWENTY-SEVEN

Even to people who wanted to believe Rachel Buffett, her decision to appear on *Dr. Phil* seemed to be a major public relations calamity. As practiced as she was at delivering lines, she was not prepared for Steve's wounded rage. Although her attorney had been close by, Ajna Sharma-Wilson was surrounded by members of law enforcement who'd been quick to point out any discrepancy in the actress' remarks. From the moment the show started, the host let the audience know his sympathies—and they certainly weren't with Rachel.

Already livid over their theater closing after the tragedy, the Hathcock family watched Rachel with the same attention they'd paid to performances on their stage, critiquing every head movement and deciphering every word.

While Nancy Hathcock had only met Rachel a few times, her reaction to Dan's fiancée was scathing and personal. "In every interview that I've caught of hers, she always lets you know"—Nancy contorted her face and affected a snooty tone—"*'I'm an act-or.'* And I just kind of go, 'Oh, give me a break.' It makes me want to throw up."

Having never seen the transcripts for Rachel's pretrial hearing, Jeff Hathcock was curious about how Rachel would explain her knowledge of Dan's actions. Within minutes of Rachel's introduction on *Dr. Phil,* Jeff concluded that she was obscuring the truth. "They were living together," he said. "She saw Dan leave with Sam and come back alone. Then, after they did their play that night, they went home and Dan disappears with a gun to kill Julie. She said she was sleeping, but I don't believe it. She had to know where the hell he was going."

According to the gossip Allyson had heard in the theater community, she found it difficult to believe that Rachel had blindly accepted Dan's explanations for his actions. "From what I heard, he was the one who enjoyed being led around and liked it that way," Allyson said. "Rachel wore the pants in that relationship."

Although the Kibuishi family decided not to appear on the program—allowing Steve to represent the voices of the victims—they posted a message on the show's Web site, focusing more on Juri's affable temperament than issues of guilt and innocence.

"Julie is one of the sweetest, brightest and most cheerful individuals," the Kibuishis said, choosing to discuss their daughter and sister in the present tense. "She snorts when she laughs too hard, and she's the one you'll hear singing from the top of her lungs at any concert. Julie is always there for her friends and family. She's the type of person who would drive up to LAX from Irvine just to pick you up from the airport. She's always had a passion for musical arts and dance. Our family appreciates the hard work the detectives and District Attorney's office have done thus far, and we rely on their expertise to bring this case to closure."

There was nobility in the way that the family portrayed itself, refusing to resort to name-calling or dignify either

Dan's or Rachel's defenses. Yet Juri's friends were most heartened by the recollections of the young woman they missed. While they shed tears—knowing that they'd never again hear Juri's laughter or experience her kindness— other readers of the show's Web site were venting their anger at Rachel Buffett.

Posted one viewer: "She is cold and fake. She had a blank look on her face and if anyone watched her carefully. . . . She's obviously acting."

A person identifying as a drama teacher and actor wrote that Rachel's appearance was worthy of an Academy Award: "I think the father had an absolute right to be angry that she took [her story] . . . to air before the trial to drum up support. I hope she rots in jail."

Commented another observer: "Frankly, she wasn't telling the truth. Too bad she didn't use this platform to tearfully confess that she was trying to save her [fiancé] . . . or at least was corroborating what he said. Instead, she chose to lie, furthering the degradation of the victims."

Emotions about Rachel also ran high among readers of local news outlets, who posted comments below articles about the case. On more than one occasion, she was compared to Jodi Arias, an equally attractive femme fatale from Arizona. On June 9, 2008, Travis Alexander, a motivational speaker and salesman, was discovered in the shower of his Mesa home by a group of friends. Travis had written a book that chronicled his troubled childhood—his parents were drug addicts—as well as the gratitude he felt toward his grandmother for introducing him, along with his three siblings, to the Mormon faith. Immersing himself in the principles of the Church of Latter-Day Saints, he said, enabled him to heal the scars of his upbringing.

Travis was thirty when his friends came upon his corpse. There was a gunshot wound to his face, as well as twenty-nine stab wounds all over his body, including a slit throat and a cut that penetrated his heart. While scouring the residence, the friends found a digital camera that had been run through the washing machine. Among the deleted images that police were able to recover were a series of sexual photos depicting Jodi and Travis from five days earlier— along with a picture of a man who appeared to be the victim bleeding on the bathroom floor.

The couple had met at a business conference in 2006 and moved in together the next year. Officially, they were a committed couple for five months. But they continued to maintain a sexual relationship after their breakup.

Jodi's initial story was that she had no connection to her lover's death. When forensic experts discovered that her DNA was mixed with Travis' blood, she revised her account to claim that two masked invaders—one male and one female—had entered the home, killing Travis and assaulting her. For reasons she couldn't explain, she said, the attackers had allowed her to live. Fearing retribution, she continued, she decided not to report the crime to authorities.

By the time of the trial, Jodi was telling another story. Now she insisted that Travis was abusive and attempted to hurt her after she dropped the camera in the bathroom. She'd only killed Travis, she explained, because she was trying to defend herself.

She admitted that her stories about the incident were inconsistent. "Lying isn't typically something I just do," she said. She'd distorted the truth both to protect her former boyfriend's reputation, she argued, and because she was "very ashamed" of her role in his death.

Three months after Rachel's appearance on *Dr. Phil,* Jodi Arias was convicted of first-degree murder. She'd be sentenced to life behind bars.

While the parallels between the two women came readily to Rachel's critics, other observers believed her narrative about being controlled and misled by Dan Wozniak and wrongfully targeted by the criminal justice system.

"There were so many things that bothered me about this 'inquisition,' " a viewer wrote on the *Dr. Phil* Web site. "I can't begin to imagine what this young lady's frame of mind was at the time—fiancé arrested, brother arrested, friends murdered, and she was being interrogated. . . . Her demeanor was controlled, yes. And if she had been tearful or hysterical, she would have been accused of overacting. She just couldn't win!"

Another commentator concurred that the authorities were hanging their case against Rachel on a few words that she uttered when she was at her most vulnerable: "So . . . she has a cold look to her. It doesn't make her guilty."

Even those who found her manner detached and curious urged authorities to consider the range of circumstances affecting Rachel's demeanor. "She's a weird one," opined a spectator in a lengthy post. "But weird doesn't mean guilty. . . . Her being awkward could be explained away by the fact that she's being accused of something she didn't do."

Remarkably, several viewers appeared less approving of Steve's appearance than of the young woman being charged. Rachel didn't cry, said one, because she was "in self-preservation mode." Steve, the viewer continued, expressed a lot of fury but, like Rachel, shed no tears.

"Sam's father . . . is just bitter," read a post, "and wants everyone in jail, even if they are innocent of killing his son. Sorry for his loss, but he is being ridiculous and vindictive."

Assented another viewer, "I do not feel she belongs in prison, and the father is taking his loss out on her. She was more respectful to the father than I would have been."

A person who claimed to feel compassion for the Herrs

sent a message directly to Steve: "If you ruin this girl's life . . . you will never forgive yourself."

In fact, numerous onlookers found Rachel relatable. "I have been in this girl's shoes, and know firsthand the shock and heartbreak that comes from learning that someone you care for . . . isn't who you thought they were," one post stated. "I really understood and sympathized with her when she made reference to her brain turning off. . . . I'm sure her fiancé didn't ask before he dragged her through the dirt."

Another observer maintained that Rachel did not deserve to be punished for Dan's sins: "I have no doubt at all that Dan is a terrible person. . . . But that's not what the show was about. . . . The show was about the young lady . . . trying to get [her] . . . side of the story out."

Meanwhile, Rachel's relatives were working hard to alter the public assessment of the actress. A poster appeared online featuring a photo of Rachel wearing a gown and holding a bouquet, her face framed by curled blond locks and illuminated by a smile. "FREE RACHEL BUFFETT!" the notice proclaimed. "She is 100 % Innocent!" This was followed by a quote from Hebrews 11:1 (Easy-to-Read Version): "Faith is what makes real the things we hope for. It is proof of what we cannot see."

On Facebook, there was a page supporting the actress' efforts to vindicate herself. Despite her photogenic appearance, there was only one picture included: the same one that graced the poster. The section marked "About" began: "Rachel Buffett is being wrongfully accused, humiliated, slandered and abused by the Costa Mesa PD and the media." This was followed by a longer appeal: "We Need Your Help! Post and comment on Rachel's behalf, and let the media and PD know that her friends and family are outraged at the treatment and slander she is receiving

[and] . . . that her name should be cleared and her reputation set straight! Rachel is a kind and tender-hearted girl. She is a hard worker and puts others before herself. She is intelligent, outgoing, ambitious and sensitive to others. She is a gentle and beautiful person inside and out, a great friend, daughter, sister, cousin, niece and granddaughter. Please post and comment on Rachel's behalf."

Over the course of the next three years, the page would receive just over 160 "Likes." "Thank you again for everyone's support and prayers!" read one post from 2014. "Rachel is still being wrongly accused and has been appearing at multiple court dates since her release from jail. . . . Please continue to pray for Rachel. . . . God knows the truth and we are constantly leaning on the Lord!"

"God knows I'm innocent," Rachel would tell the NBC show *Dateline*. "I never tried to help Dan Wozniak. I told the truth to the best of my capabilities to try to help the police get to the bottom of things. My heart was always in the right place."

Visitors to the page would come from as far away as South Africa and Sweden. Some admitted that they first learned about the case from watching *Dr. Phil*. Rachel's accusers were derided in one post as "nutcases." Readers were urged to flood Orange County District Attorney Tony Rackauckas' office with phone calls and plead that the charges be dropped.

On May 31, 2013, Rachel was in court again, hoping that the effort would wield results. Her lawyer, Ajna Sharma-Wilson, claimed prosecutors were playing a "shell game of dates" to create the impression that Rachel lied to authorities. The attorney argued that one date had been dropped from the original criminal complaint, but another was later added by prosecutors.

Citing the contention that Rachel had reported hearing about Sam's alleged family problems to police, Judge

James Stotler stated that there was reasonable cause to suspect that the actress was trying to divert attention away from her fiancé. The request to dismiss the three felony charges was denied.

For the Herrs and Kibuishis, the decision was a minor victory. With so many obstacles ahead, both families were still a long way from receiving anything close to justice.

CHAPTER TWENTY-EIGHT

As the authorities prepared for upcoming hearings, the absence of investigator Mike Delgadillo was apparent to everyone.

On March 5, 2013, Delgadillo, the father of four children between fourteen and twenty, was returning from a night out in his Mazda 626 LX. He'd reportedly been at Mi Casa Restaurant, then moved on to Skosh Monahan's, a bar and steakhouse owned by former Costa Mesa mayor Gary Monahan. At about 10:20 p.m., Delgadillo was on Newport Boulevard when he attempted to make a left turn at Bristol Street, jumped a curb, and collided with a concrete pillar. He was treated at the scene by his fellow officers and fire personnel, then loaded into an ambulance and rushed to the hospital. At Western Medical Center in Santa Ana—the same facility where Dan had been taken after his presumed suicide attempt—the thirty-two-year veteran was pronounced dead.

The unexpected loss of the fifty-seven-year-old detective had a dispiriting effect on the entire unit. After all, it had been Delgadillo who'd worked closely with Steve Herr at the beginning of the investigation and been in the room with Dan Wozniak when he confessed. Even more hurtful to the morale of the Costa Mesa Police Department were the results of the toxicology reports related to the accident.

After the crash, first responders had drawn blood from Delgadillo at the scene, as well as shortly before he died. There were small amounts of painkillers in his system, authorities determined, too minuscule to affect his driving. However, Delgadillo's blood alcohol level was 0.14 percent, according to the Orange County coroner, nearly twice California's legal limit of 0.08 percent. An investigation revealed that he was also texting and not wearing a seat belt.

If this weren't bad enough, another traffic accident two years later claimed the life of seventeen-year-old Crystal Morales, the daughter of lead investigator Jose Morales.

With so much personal tragedy impacting the people at the core of the Dan Wozniak case, there were questions over whether they still possessed the will to assist the loved ones of Sam Herr and Juri Kibuishi.

The intentions were certainly there. Still, over time, the department changed. Det. Sgt. Ed Everett was promoted to lieutenant. The lieutenant at the time of the murders, Paul Dondero, retired. Detectives Mike Cohen and Carlos Diaz were shifted to other units.

All insisted that they hadn't forgotten the families. Yet relatives wondered.

In 2013, Juri's mother, Junko, addressed the court during one of Dan's numerous pretrial hearings. "I can't die without seeing justice being served," she said. "I need to make sure I can tell my daughter in heaven that she can rest in peace."

Junko had good reason to consider her mortality. Both she and her husband, Masa, had been diagnosed with cancer. As they fought the disease, she beseeched the judge,

"Do we have to suffer any more? Please, please give us closure as soon as possible."

Investigators hoped they were moving in that direction when, one day in 2013, Dan contacted the Costa Mesa detectives and said that he wanted to talk.

They rushed over to the jail and set up a video camera in an interview room. Daniel entered and shook hands. Then, he looked around. "Where's my lawyer?" he asked.

"It's not our job to contact him," he was told.

"Well, I'm not going to talk if my lawyer isn't here."

Detectives tried calling Scott Sanders, but he was unreachable. They managed to find Tracy LeSage, the second public defender who'd been brought on specifically to handle the death penalty portion of the case. When Dan got on the phone, she advised him not to speak with authorities.

The suspect returned to his cell. Detectives never discovered what he intended to tell them.

Meanwhile, the process seemed to drag on indefinitely. "Julie's grandmother has passed away," Steve complained during a radio broadcast on KFI AM. "The longer the time goes, people forget. . . . Where are the rights for the victims? You kind of wish the justice system is for the victims, but it's not."

In a notebook, Steve kept a record of every hearing he attended, as well as a log of the excuses he heard for the delays. As of September 2014, he estimated that he'd attended forty separate proceedings for Dan. "Every delay hurts more." Steve said. "The anger builds."

He characterized the sluggish process as a "slap in the face" and told reporter Jeremiah Dobruck from the *Daily Pilot* that he was "starting to hate the justice system more than I hate Wozniak."

Raquel's sister, Miriam, usually joined the Herrs in court and contemplated shocking the authorities into speeding up the process by making poster-size images of the gory crime scene photos.

"We're forgetting what happened here, the gruesomeness of the murder," Miriam complained.

Added her husband, Mike Nortman, "We're the only ones speaking for Sam."

Before a typical hearing, the Kibuishis and the Herrs greeted one another warmly outside the ninth-floor elevators, near the courtroom. Junko had told detectives that, in some ways, she believed that the Herrs were hurting more than her own family. "They lost their only child," she said. "I am lucky. I still have three."

"That gives you an idea of the type of person she is," one of the detectives noted, "and the kind of daughter she raised." After dealing with malcontents, miscreants, and sociopaths on a day-to-day basis, authorities felt cleansed by the goodness that emanated from the Kibiushi family.

Steve paced anxiously in the hallway and rushed into the courtroom the moment that the doors opened, taking a seat near the front. Raquel, Miriam, and Mike sat beside him, along with Sam's cousin Leah Sussman. The Kibuishis sat down directly behind them.

Dressed casually but neatly, in dark blue slacks, a collared pullover, loafers, and white socks, Masa fidgeted nervously, repeatedly driving a finger into his palm, then the arm of his chair. Then, he removed his silver wristwatch and scrupulously examined it.

Despite her hardships, Junko maintained a youthful presence. Her dark hair was cut short, almost in Japanese schoolgirl style. When acquaintances made eye contact, she politely smiled. Still, her face betrayed signs of weariness.

Alone in her car, Junko listened to a CD of songs that Juri had compiled for her mother's birthday. It was a way to enjoy her daughter's thoughtfulness, even after the young woman's death. Around Junko's neck was a ring on a chain. It was one of Juri's few possessions that police returned to the Kibiushis—along with a pair of earrings and a blood-smeared hairpin.

Junko intended to wear the item for the remainder of her life.

After the families were situated, senior deputy district attorney Matt Murphy entered the room, took a seat in the gallery, and conferred with the Herrs and Kibiushis. Tall and photogenic, Murphy resembled a politician with state-wide aspirations, or an actor portraying a prosecutor. At one point, Steve moved his seat close to Murphy and asked him to clear up a number of questions. Then, Steve returned to his spot next to his wife.

The Orange County District Attorney's office also provided special victims' advocates, who greeted and kissed the families and handed out parking validation slips. Noted Leah, "They cushion the blow."

There were other cases on the docket, and Steve patiently sat through hearings for those defendants, rolling a pen between his palms. Raquel placed an arm around her husband while holding a copy of *Pursuit of His Presence,* a book billed as a guide to deepening one's personal relationship with God.

"I don't want anger," she'd tell the *Orange County Register.* "I want to go on with life, and I see him, how it's destroying him."

At one point, Miriam stood, walked over to the empty row behind Juri's parents, and placed a hand on each of their shoulders.

Meanwhile, a succession of defendants in orange jumpsuits paraded in and out of the courtroom—a woman from the Orange County Jail was clad in blue—the non-English speakers fitted with headsets. When Dan finally appeared, he was led to the defendants' table and uncuffed. While a deputy stood behind him, hands on hips, Dan listened as the judge extended the trial date yet another time. Then, just as soon as Dan had made his entrance, he was gone from the place that had become his new stage.

"What a freakin' waste," Miriam commented. "They get more rights than I do."

Junko Kibuishi released her clenched fist. Whenever Dan appeared, she'd ball up her hands and grit her teeth, holding in the tension for so long that, by the time the hearing was over, the cancer survivor was exhausted.

Until Dan was tried, the cases against Rachel Buffett and Tim Wozniak appeared to be on hold; the case against Tim's now-ex-girlfriend had been dismissed. In the interim, Steve continued attending their hearings, as well. He noticed that he never saw Dan's parents in court and wondered if they were torn over the fates of their sons. After one proceeding, as the Herrs were leaving the courtroom, Tim approached them and mouthed, *I'm sorry.*

Steve noticed that Dan's brother had tears in his eyes.

The two continued to run into each other in court, nodding but keeping their distance. At the end of another hearing, Steve suggested that they speak outside. Fearing violence, the detectives in the courtroom followed. But the two men simply wanted to have a conversation.

"Tim said he knew Sam and liked him," Steve said. "Dan and his brother went up to Sam's apartment one night for some kind of get-together, and Tim got really drunk. Sammy told him, 'Just stay here. Sleep it off. You can leave for work from my place tomorrow.' Tim thought that was really nice, and he wanted to let me know he felt bad about what happened."

Steve believed that the sentiments were genuine. But it did nothing to diminish his resolve about seeing Dan Wozniak strapped down in the death chamber.

CHAPTER TWENTY-NINE

The effort to sentence Dan to death would be curtailed by another murder and its unexpected repercussions on the criminal justice system in Orange County.

On October 12, 2011, Scott Evans Dekraai entered the Salon Meritage hair salon in Seal Beach—the town where Rachel Buffett had grown up. Dekraai, a forty-two-year-old former fishing boat captain with thinning hair and a salt-and-pepper goatee, had visited his ex-wife Michelle Fournier's place of work before—and friends warned her that he could be dangerous. Embroiled in a custody dispute over their eight-year-old son, Dekraai and Fournier each accused the other of making irrational threats. Dekraai claimed that his former spouse was a verbally abusive alcoholic. Fournier described Dekraai as "bipolar" and said that he'd pledged to kill her. After a fight with his stepfather in 2007, a restraining order had been issued, banning Dekraai from possessing firearms. By 2011, the restraining order had expired.

On this particular day, Dekraai was carrying a 9mm revolver, along with a .45-caliber handgun and a .44 Magnum. Clad in body armor, Dekraai appeared to be prepared for a shootout that he intended to survive.

There were approximately twenty people in the beauty parlor when Dekraai started firing, police said. Customers and employees tried racing into the street or hiding in adjoining businesses. In the course of two minutes, the gunman apparently managed to shoot eight people in the salon and another in the parking lot, pausing ever so briefly to reload.

Only one victim survived. The casualties included Michelle Fournier.

Police stopped Dekraai in his white pickup truck a half mile from the crime scene. He surrendered without incident and was charged with the worst mass murder in Orange County—eclipsing a 1976 massacre at Cal State Fullerton that claimed seven victims.

As with Daniel Wozniak, prosecutors announced that they were seeking the death penalty. They also planned to bring the case to trial quickly.

But Scott Sanders, the lawyer for both defendants, was determined that neither goal would be realized.

With his bookish bearing and wire-framed glasses, Sanders embodied the image of an activist attorney. A graduate of the University of Wisconsin and Emory University Law School, he'd been in the Orange County Public Defender's Office for some two decades, as devoted to his mission of exposing what he saw as injustice in law enforcement as death penalty proponents were to imposing the ultimate punishment.

The Chicago area native believed that he was fulfilling his goal of defending the underdog. The death penalty was uncivilized, he maintained—so much so that the totalitarian regime in Belarus was the last in Europe to enforce it—and rarely did it allow the victims' families to savor the relief that they wanted.

Generally, he reasoned, the fact that a murder suspect was sitting in the defendant's chair gave him or her an immediate disadvantage. Since many in that position were poor, they were assigned a lawyer from the public defender's office. While the popular assumption was that a free attorney wasn't as talented as a private one, Sanders tried dispelling the myth by spending time with his clients and learning who they were as human beings. If he could convey that humanity—in Dan's case, his sense of humor and taste for the arts—in court, jurors might be hesitant to sentence a defendant to death.

In 2004, Lynn Dean Johnson was about to be paroled after completing a sentence for the kidnapping and rape of an eleven-year-old girl when DNA evidence linked him to the unsolved rape and murder of a nineteen-year-old restaurant hostess in 1985. Prosecutors demanded the death penalty. But Sanders and his co-counsel, Lisa Kopelman, successfully argued that a better sentence was life without the possibility of parole.

Some believed that he'd saved an incorrigible with nothing to contribute to society. However, Sanders was proud that he'd managed to prevent the government from taking a life.

Another client, Jamie Balint, received the same penalty after he fatally stabbed his mother in December 2003. But Sanders did not consider this outcome a triumph. The lawyer had tried to convince jurors that Balint—who'd claimed that a prophet instructed him to slay his mother—was schizophrenic, delusional, and not guilty by reason of insanity.

While victims' families were quick to highlight the rights that accused killers seemed to enjoy, Sanders attacked every capital case with the assumption that the defendant was going to die from lethal injection—particularly in Orange County, where jurors were often upper-middle-class suburban retirees.

By Sanders' estimation, detectives and prosecutors were allowed unfair advantages. He believed that defense attorneys had the right to examine any evidence that prosecutors intended to introduce at trial. "There inevitably has to be trust in the system, that we can have access to everything they know," he stated. He also argued that it was necessary for some type of outside monitor to ensure that there were ramifications for misconduct from police agencies and prosecutors.

To Sanders, no one deserved a fair hearing more than the most maligned inmates in the criminal justice system. While he could never condone the actions of a person like Dan Wozniak, the attorney was convinced that there was a nobility in defending him. Sanders had seen too many cases of innocent people being manipulated into confessing to the most shocking crimes. They could only be exonerated, he deduced, if they were alive when the decisions were reversed.

Within the district attorney's office, though, the lawyer was seen as not a voice of the powerless but an obnoxious irritant whose attacks contained an element of personal venom.

When he was chosen as Orange County's public defender of the year in 2014, prosecutors were outraged. How could Sanders be celebrated for his courtroom achievements, they questioned, when he'd done everything to prevent the Dekraai and Wozniak cases from coming to trial?

After submitting a 505-page motion alleging prosecutorial misconduct in the Dekraai case, for instance, Sanders announced that he was too busy defending the accused mass murderer to concentrate on the motions vital for Dan Wozniak's upcoming trial.

"The situation is beyond awful," Judge James Stotler despaired. "It's beyond awful, awful. It's awful, awful, awful that we cannot get this case to trial."

Sensitive to how the relatives of the Seal Beach casualties felt, Steve Herr resented that the system allowed an attorney to cultivate feelings of resentment toward people anxious to see justice served for their loved ones first.

"They literally pit victims against victims," he said.

To senior deputy district attorney Matt Murphy, it was Sanders who was exploiting the flaws in the system. "These are dirty tactics," the prosecutor said in court, implying that the defense attorney was deliberately taking an excessive amount of time with his motions.

"If I could clone myself or find more hours in the day, I'd do it," Sanders shot back.

It took close to three years before Dekraai pleaded guilty to the murders of the six women and two men in the beauty parlor. But a judge ruled that the district attorney's office *had* engaged in misconduct and ordered that the California Attorney General's office now handle the penalty phase of the case—whether the defendant would receive life imprisonment or lethal injection. The circumstances of the Wozniak case were completely different, observers noted, and it appeared that the prosecution team would remain in place.

Although prosecutors and defense attorneys often maintained back-channel communication, Sanders and Murphy refused to even engage in small talk in the courtroom during Dan's hearings, forcing Tracy LeSage, the second public defender, to act as a liaison to the district attorney's office.

In front of Judge Stotler, Murphy regularly accused Sanders of procrastinating while the defense lawyer claimed that the senior deputy district attorney was trying to embarrass him. During one tense exchange, Murphy said that Sanders was smirking about the delays, triggering yet another confrontation.

"You want me to take a recess so you guys can cool off?" the judge queried.

At a hearing in August 2014, Stotler announced that he needed more time to read documents submitted by both the defense and the prosecution before setting a trial date. Suddenly Steve and Raquel began waving their arms and motioning at themselves. They wanted the judge to know that they had something to say, too.

With his jaw clenched, Steve told the judge about the effort he made to ensure that Sam's head was sewn back on to his torso, allowing the war veteran the dignity of being buried in his Army uniform. Steve had made these types of statements before to the press. But now he wanted it in the official record.

"How much longer do we have to sit here and listen to this crap?" he demanded.

Outside the courtroom, Raquel pleaded for the adjournments to end. "You never forget your child," she told the *Daily Pilot*. "But I would like as much as possible to go on with my life."

Ironically, the Herrs would have been able to enjoy that option if they were willing to agree to a single condition. Sanders had offered to persuade Dan to plead guilty and immediately begin serving a life sentence without the possibility of parole, as long as the prosecution no longer sought the death penalty. Steve flatly refused to acquiesce.

It didn't matter that Dan was willing to publicly admit his guilt, Steve reasoned. Neither the defendant nor his attorney deserved any kind of special consideration.

"People can adapt," Steve told KFI AM radio. "I don't want [Dan] adapting to prison. I don't want him getting a job there. . . . I want him dead."

* * *

The first official execution in the state of California occurred in 1878, when four Native Americans in San Diego were placed in front of a firing squad for conspiracy to commit murder. Over the next ninety-four years, the state would impose the death penalty on 709 inmates until both the California and U.S. Supreme Courts concluded that the practice violated, respectively, the state and national constitutions.

With the advent of electricity, Thomas Edison argued that his method of direct current (DC) electrification was safer than the alternating current (AC) favored by the Westinghouse Electric Company. To demonstrate this, the Edison Company began using AC to electrocute animals. The displays had an unintended impact on law enforcement. If electricity could kill animals, it was deduced, why not use it to neutralize the most reprehensible criminals in society? In 1890, after New York State dismantled its gallows, William Kemmler, a convicted hatchet murderer, became the first American to die in the electric chair at upstate Auburn Prison.

In California, though, authorities were partial to the gas chamber. Between 1937 and 1967, 190 men and 4 women were killed by lethal gas in San Quentin's execution room.

But after the Supreme Court ruling in 1972, 107 California death sentences—including those of notorious inmates such as death cult leader Charles Manson and Sirhan Sirhan, the assassin of presidential candidate Robert Kennedy—were commuted to life imprisonment. The ban lasted four years before the Supreme Court reinstated the death penalty. At San Quentin, the execution chamber would be redesigned so inmates could be administered lethal injections.

As a rule, Californians supported this system. In 1978, more than 70 percent of voters in the Golden State approved a new death penalty law. Nonetheless, very few convicts would receive the fatal punishment—just thirteen by 2015. Appeals—it was noted by both sides—frequently hampered the process by decades.

In 2012, the state's longest-serving death row inmate, Douglas Stankewitz—twice sentenced to die for kidnapping and shooting a twenty-two-year-old woman in 1978—had his sentence converted when a federal judge ruled that jurors should have been told about his mental health problems, as well as his abusive childhood.

By that point, executions in the state had been on hold for close to seven years, as death penalty opponents challenged lethal injection methods.

Steve followed the controversy closely, particularly a 2012 ballot initiative that would have repealed California's death penalty. The punishment had been banned in other states by this point, and this was the first chance Californians had to vote on the issue in more than three decades.

With 727 inmates on death row in California—nearly a quarter of the more than 3,100 awaiting the death penalty around the United States—a repeal would have had national implications. Law enforcement officials, three former governors, and victims' rights groups loudly campaigned for the state's citizens to block Proposition 34, the plan to convert all lethal injection sentences in the Golden State to life without parole.

Steve had only seen a portion of the crime scene photos from the Liberty Theater. But he'd walked through the attic and had an acute sense of what Sam had suffered in the final moments of his life. Plus, Steve had been the one who'd first found Juri's blood-soaked corpse in his son's apartment. As debate swirled over Proposition 34, the ex-Marine fantasized about going into the police evidence folder, removing the pictures, and traveling the state, showing voters the graphic images as a means of convincing his fellow citizens—one by one—that the death penalty should never be abolished.

"I don't care what anybody says," he said. "Look what that bastard did in Colorado." He was talking about James Eagan Holmes, who'd opened fire during a midnight showing of *The Dark Knight Rises* in Aurora, Colorado, slaughtering two dozen and wounding seventy filmgoers. "Come on! Does he deserve to live when he took the lives of so many other people, and permanently injured so many others? There's just bad people out there. Why mess around?"

In the end, Proposition 34 lost by about six percentage points, muting the aspirations of death penalty foes. But the battle continued. In 2014, a federal judge in Orange County ruled that the sentence violated constitutional prohibitions of cruel and unusual punishment.

Most sentences only led to "an inordinate and unpredictable period of delay preceding [the] actual execution," said U.S. District Judge Cormac J. Carney, in response to a petition filed by convicted killer Ernest Dewayne Jones, sentenced to death in 1995 for the rape and murder of his girlfriend's grandmother. Those who are executed, Carney added, "will have languished for so long on death row that their execution will serve no retributive or deterrent purpose and will be arbitrary."

By this point, Steve's primary goal was simply seeing Dan—and whichever accomplices he might have had—brought to trial. Still, Steve wasn't going to be pacified until a judge pronounced a death sentence.

The entire extended family supported Steve's intransigence. "[Dan] doesn't deserve to live," said Steve's brother-in-law Mike Nortman. "That's the most frustrating thing, that he's still living and breathing and watching TV."

As a gay woman with progressive leanings, Sam's cousin Leah Sussman had been opposed to capital punishment before the murders. As the family grieved, her opinions changed. "If you'd been in our family's situation," she said, "you would understand. I can't imagine if something like this ever happened to my daughter."

Even if Dan was sentenced to death, she imagined his attorneys extending the appeals process for decades. But she vowed that, in the event that Steve and Raquel didn't live long enough for the execution of the man accused of killing their son, she'd continue the fight for them.

CHAPTER THIRTY

In court, defense attorney Scott Sanders continually came up with reasons to postpone the trial while the court deliberated over what he termed prosecutorial misconduct. For instance, the lawyer alleged, the interview that Dan agreed to do for the MSNBC show *Lockup* violated his constitutional rights.

According to Sanders, Orange County Sheriff's Department deputies deliberately set Dan up by facilitating the interview, hoping that the defendant would make the type of incriminating statements that would hurt him at trial.

The charge was vehemently denied. The producer repeated her claim that she chose Dan because the charismatic actor had caught her eye; she knew nothing about his case beforehand.

Witnesses claimed that deputies were not even present when Dan was asked to appear on the program. But even if they had been, attorneys for both NBC and 44 Blue—the company that produced the *Lockup* series—said that the show actually provided Dan with a forum to make his case to the public.

"Wozniak denies that he committed the murders," the producers stated in court papers, recounting Dan's on-air appearance, "describes his surprise when he was arrested during his bachelor party, explains how he attempted suicide after his arrest, and professes his love for the Bible."

Indeed, senior deputy district attorney Matt Murphy insisted that he knew nothing about the interview beforehand. When he did learn about what transpired in the jail, he said, he extended the professional courtesy of informing Sanders about the interview. With a confession from Wozniak, Murphy continued, he was uninterested in using an excerpt from the program to convince jurors of the defendant's guilt.

Once again, the prosecutor blamed Sanders for creating a scandal where none existed. But the lawyer was unconvinced that his adversary was being truthful. "A lot of coincidences seem to happen in that jail," Sanders told City News Service.

The lawyer was even more vehement about an "unchecked and lawless custodial informant program" that he claimed was institutionalized in the Orange County jail system. On January 31, 2014, Sanders and fellow public defender Lisa Kopelman filed a 505-page motion asserting that the district attorney office's informant system prevented their client Scott Dekraai—the accused Seal Beach salon shooter—from receiving a fair trial.

Shortly after Dekraai's arrest, he was placed in a cell next to a fellow prisoner at the Central Jail Complex in Santa Ana, a gang member facing charges in two separate cases. After speaking to Dekraai, the inmate allegedly told deputies that the suspect had provided him with details about the 2011 killing spree. In response, prosecutors had a recording device installed in Dekraai's cell and recorded him continuously for 132 hours, the motion maintained.

The county's informant system had also been utilized,

Sanders argued, to entrap Dan. In the Wozniak case, his defense attorney said, a paid informant was used to elicit a jailhouse confession. But Murphy countered that he generally avoided using data provided by jailhouse "snitches" and did not plan to include the man's statements at Dan's trial.

The use of informants by American law enforcement predates the founding of the United States. The first documented wrongful conviction in the newly formed country centered on a forger, Silas Merrill, who was placed in a cell with Jesse Boorn in Manchester, Vermont, in 1819 after his brother-in-law, Russell Colvin, disappeared. Merrill testified that Boorn confessed that he and his brother, Stephen, had murdered Colvin. The siblings were convicted of the killing and sentenced to death—while Merrill was set free. But before the Boorns could be sent to the gallows, Colvin was located in New Jersey.

According to the Center on Wrongful Convictions at the Northwestern University School of Law, prosecutors had used informant testimony to convict close to 50 percent of all inmates exonerated from death row. This meant that erroneous testimony from informants was responsible for the greatest number of wrongful convictions in the United States—hence the slogan "If you can't do the time, drop a dime."

After Sanders filed his motion in the Dekraai case, Superior Court Judge Thomas Goethals ruled that prosecutors had improperly used informants and didn't turn over necessary evidence. However, the judge added, the actions were "negligent rather than malicious."

Sanders vowed to continue the pressure. "Unless there is a fear created . . . that there are ramifications when you commit misconduct," he told the Davis Vanguard, a watchdog and news reporting organization for the city of Davis, California, "it's going to happen."

But while these platitudes were being discussed, prosecutors were so preoccupied with defending *themselves* that bringing an actual case to trial seemed like an afterthought. And that meant that the agonizing wait to see Dan Wozniak face a jury would continue a lot longer.

CHAPTER THIRTY-ONE

Up until this point, public sentiment had been largely sensitive to the struggles of the victims' families and disparaging of the accused murderer. Even Rachel's supporters had reviled Dan for pulling his fiancée's name into the plot. Then, in January 2015, a blogger began writing about her fondness for Dan and, at times, questioning whether he truly was guilty of his crimes. Eventually, she would name her page *Daniel Wozniak Is My Friend*.

"I have a new friend," she began her first post. "Actually, I met him for the first time in 2010, but he really only became my actual friend . . . a few months ago when I first wrote him a letter. He is in jail. He is 'awaiting trial.' He's been waiting a long time, too—four years and seven months so far. . . . It's especially a long time if you sit inside a cell 22 hours a day . . . and the prosecutor is asking for the death penalty."

Initially, the blogger used a pseudonym to describe Dan. But anyone who'd been following the case could immediately identify him. The woman wrote about meeting the suspect in 2010 when she was working at the Hunger Artists Theatre and he was appearing in *Nine*. Although she wasn't particularly impressed with his acting abilities, she said, she liked him personally, and he was a consistent crowd pleaser. "He seemed like a nice guy. He was good-looking and personable. He was funny and polite. He was even engaged to one of the actresses in the show. . . . He seemed like he had his life pretty organized."

Because Dan was the only man in the play, he used the theater's office as a dressing room. A curtain separated him from the blogger, who was selling snacks at the front end of the office. Whenever he heard someone order a soda, he'd produce the item by extending his hand through the curtain.

"He made me laugh," the blogger said. Then, several days after the play closed, Daniel Wozniak was arrested.

If, like so many others who knew Dan, the blogger was attempting to mine her memories to come up with a sign of the imminent violence, the passages would not have stood out. But in subsequent posts, the writer elaborated on her fascination with both Dan and his crimes. Her bookcase was peppered with true-crime books, she said, including biographies of "Son of Sam" killer David Berkowitz, Milwaukee "cannibal murderer" Jeffrey Dahmer, and the LA "Night Stalker" Richard Ramirez. "So I have this (possibly unhealthy) obsession with crimes and killers," she explained, "and *bam*, here is a possible killer who I've already met!!"

After reading about the crime, she believed that Dan was "probably guilty" and admitted that she was "enthralled" by her short-lived tie to notoriety. Her children were no longer young, she said, and she found herself with time on her hands. Among the hobbies that she'd decided to pursue was writing. Because of her interest in serial killers, she contemplated a true-crime book. "It was close friends who kept telling me that it would be more interesting to write about my own involvement with Daniel. Anyone could report, but I had a connection."

As tenuous as that was, she sent a letter to Dan, hoping "our brief meeting years earlier would entice him to write me back."

The first letter arrived at the Orange County Jail in August 2014. The blogger reminded Dan of their interactions but said nothing about her intended project. In fact, five months later, she'd reveal, he'd yet to learn about the blog devoted to him.

"When I began writing to this man who is in jail, I had one goal in mind," she said. "I saw him only [for his crimes] . . . , and I saw myself as the next Truman Capote." However, as they continued to correspond, she said, an actual friendship developed. "There are probably tons of people who would think I'm 'nucking futz' for calling an accused murderer my friend. I wonder about it myself, so I don't blame them."

The difference, she pointed out, was that she knew Dan.

"I think I do," she added. "I sure as hell hope I do. I really want to believe I do."

In his first letter, she said, Dan talked about his sadness over the recent death of Robin Williams and about his appetite for theater. "He talked about depression and suicide attempts. . . . He wrote about his fiancé [sic]. Now, she was his ex-fiancé [sic]." In Dan's version of his life, the blogger claimed, Rachel had been his only friend.

"His life revolved around her," the post continued. "He was devastated when, after he'd been in jail for three months, she cut off all communication with him."

Recently, he claimed, he'd helped his cellmate earn a GED. This was consistent with Dan's life philosophy that centered on "making a difference, and doing what you can to make things better, no matter your circumstances," the blog read. Dan also mentioned his faith in God, asking the blogger not to judge him by the details of the crimes. "He hopes that I can see that he is not an evil man."

At the time of the murders, Dan allegedly told the blogger, he was consuming drugs and he had only "foggy" recollections about the period. When she brought up their conversations at the theater, Dan admitted that he wasn't sure if he remembered her. He urged her to send a photo to jar his memory.

"I immediately went looking for pictures of me where I look cute."

Since she couldn't recall the color of her hair at the time she met Dan, the blogger sent out three separate photos. "I wanted him to recognize me," she said. She also mentioned that she "thought it was cool to get mail from an inmate."

Dan replied with musings about his lack of freedom. "Your life is what you make it," he apparently said, "and if you philosophically break it down, everyone is confined and limited in some aspect."

But he appeared to place his captivity in context, writing that, although he was incapable of driving to a fast food restaurant to order a meal from the drive-through window, she couldn't "fly to the moon to get some cheese."

In response, the blogger said that she still felt more liberated than her new pen pal, since she *could* go to the supermarket to purchase cheese, if she craved it.

As the blogger studied the letters, Dan's "crazy, neat printing" stood out. She claimed to have asked the accused murderer if he'd always had such perfect penmanship and he replied that incarceration had helped him perfect his talents.

Eventually, she said, she informed him about her blog, noting that the average person—upon reading reports about the deaths of Sam and Juri—would automatically assume that Dan was "a monster." Yet she believed that people who didn't look beyond the surface were missing important details. "The man I met four years ago did not appear to be a monster," she wrote the inmate, "and these well-written and thoughtful letters you've sent me have only made me even more aware of your humanity. . . . Who is this man accused of such heinous acts, and how is he the same creative, funny and seemingly kind person who is writing to me about helping a fellow inmate get his GED?"

Over time, she began to question whether Dan was a murderer at all. She speculated that he might have been manipulated by detectives during his interview, since no lawyer was present and Dan was likely drunk after his bachelor party. She also wondered if police had threatened to imprison Rachel if he didn't confess.

Nonetheless, she also conceded that Dan "was young and cocky, and believes he is smarter than anyone else." Did that mean that he tried to outwit detectives, even though he was guilty of the double homicide? Or did they exploit his talkative nature to get him to say things that indicated culpability?

During a jailhouse visit with Dan, the blogger learned that Steve Herr had also come to the facility to speak with the suspect. Surprised, the writer asked about the grieving father's motive.

"He really wants to know the truth," Dan reportedly answered, "and I don't think he trusts the justice system because of what happened in Sam's own murder case."

It was then that Dan told his companion about Sam's arrest and acquittal. "Daniel went on to surmise that possibly Steve Herr was worried that Daniel would 'walk free,'" she wrote, "just as his son did years earlier."

More than any defense attorney had done so far, the blogger was impugning the victim's character.

Still, she insisted that she wasn't becoming brainwashed. "On Facebook, I was accused of being a 'Manson girl,' " she said. "For the record, that comparison is not entirely accurate, since it was actually the 'Manson girls' . . . and two male followers of Manson who committed the murders. I am just writing about a murder case. I didn't murder anyone."

While she kept her identity hidden online, her fixation with Dan took a conspicuous turn when she turned up at a court hearing and exchanged smiles with the defendant. "I didn't want my friend to smile at me, or to smile period," she wrote. "I want him to look serious and contrite or something that doesn't resemble happy. I feel that's the way to go when you're being accused of murder.

When she overheard two reporters in the courtroom conversing about Dan's upbeat demeanor, she became worried that his smile would be misinterpreted as a "smirk." She said that deputies warned Dan about looking at people in the gallery. "I don't think Scott Sanders was pleased, either. Daniel didn't mean anything by it, but that doesn't matter, does it?"

As problematic as her presence may have been for the defendant, the blogger was gratified when a producer from the TV show *20/20* noticed Daniel mouthing, *Thank you,* to his follower and invited her to lunch. "This was exciting," the blogger wrote. "I love *20/20*!

". . . She told me that any program they might do on Daniel's story will try to give a complete picture of him. I would hope so. I guess that includes talking to his friends and maybe even reading their blogs."

Beyond the exhilaration, though, the blogger claimed to feel sympathy for the victims' families. "I'm guessing they wouldn't like me very much," she contemplated. "Not that I would blame them. I am his friend." Her goal, she stated, was not to hurt them, but look into Dan's soul and see the goodness that she knew was there. But she also harbored doubts about the way law enforcement was addressing the case.

"Does that make me crazy, naïve?" she wrote.

"No matter what Daniel Wozniak may have done, I don't believe he should die for it.

"I understand why the families of the victims do, though."

During one hearing, she worked up the nerve to speak with Steve after he held a door open for her. "I thanked him," she said, "and could swear he smelled like Old Spice, a scent that reminds me of my father and of loss. Maybe it was just my imagination."

It turned out that Steve was aware of the blog and had been reading it to see if Dan had uttered anything that shed additional light on the crimes. After the initial exchange, Steve occasionally communicated with the blogger on Facebook. Unlike some of her readers, she noted, Steve did not make any value judgments about her decision to befriend Wozniak and write about it. "If I were asked to come up with an adjective to describe Steve's tone, it would be 'frustrated.'"

In reality, Steve's behavior toward the woman reflected his genuine attitude. He viewed her as a courtroom buff who may have been misguided in the character she chose to follow. But he also understood that she spoke to Dan and was thus in a position to pass on a message to him. So he made a simple request to the blogger.

"Ask Dan one question," Steve wrote. "Did he murder Sam and Julie? Then, post his answer. Everything you have posted is conjecture, which is your right. However, just ask him that one question. His response, whatever he says, should make great reading!"

CHAPTER THIRTY-TWO

In early 2015, the Orange County District Attorney's office heard that Scott Sanders planned to file a 500-page motion backed by 20,000 pages of exhibits on behalf of his client. At a pretrial hearing in January, Matt Murphy, the senior deputy district attorney, blasted the defense lawyer in front of Superior Court Judge James A. Stotler, claiming that the document would exceed—by fourteen thousand words—the cumulative text of the U.S. Constitution, the Koran, the New King James Bible, *Moby-Dick*, *War and Peace*, *Mein Kampf*, *The Communist Manifesto*, *A Brief History of Time* by Stephen Hawking, Martin Luther King's Letter from Birmingham Jail, the *Iliad*, the *Odyssey*, and the Gettysburg Address. This effort to delay the start of the trial, Murphy argued, was nothing less than "unconscionable."

As in the past, Sanders countered that the prosecution was belittling him and his attempts to find fault with the judicial system.

Almost unnoticed during the testy exchange was the

defendant, whom writer R. Scott Moxley of the *OC Weekly* characterized as "merely a smiling, upbeat observer at today's hearing."

"I was pissed," Steve Herr said. "Every time they argue like this, Sam Herr and Julie Kibuishi become secondary. Sometimes, they don't even mention their names."

So irritated was Steve by the slow process that he couldn't even muster the fury that most in his position would feel when Dan nodded at him. The defendant did not appear to be self-satisfied or taunting. "He just acts like nothing happened," Raquel said, "nothing at all."

Yet the Herrs sensed that Dan was having a good day. "After being in that jail, he comes out, the courtroom is sunny, there are people there," Steve said. "He can sit back and watch these guys argue with each other. For him, it's a show. It's entertainment. I'm sure his demeanor will be a lot different once we get this damn thing going."

But it appeared that the trial would not occur for a while. Because so many judges were former prosecutors, Sanders indicated that he was on the verge of filing another motion seeking to disqualify the entire bench of Orange County Superior Court.

Then, on January 27, Judge Stotler announced that after days of "soul-searching" he'd made a painful decision.

The previous Friday, as Sanders lobbed "vociferous invectives" at prosecutors, the judge wondered whether people in the gallery were questioning why he didn't halt the defense attorney.

"I was actually thinking that," Judge Stotler said. Yet he allowed Sanders to continue, he explained, so he could "dig his own grave."

In other words, Judge Stotler had grown to dislike the lawyer so much that he wanted Sanders to sabotage himself. "That's not proper judicial thinking," Stotler concluded.

As a result, he said, he had no choice but to recuse himself from the case.

Steve was stunned. "It's just not fair, sir," he shouted in court.

"This is a travesty of our justice system," he told the *Daily Pilot*. "What [the judge] . . . did was add another year or two to the case."

What infuriated Steve the most was that he'd been promised that the trial would start within a month. Stotler "despised the public defender, but that didn't help us out," Steve said. "Sanders doesn't want this case to go to trial unless we drop the death penalty. He's dragging it out, and it's working for him. Now, we have to start again with a different judge."

Within weeks, Superior Court Judge John D. Conley had been assigned the case. Sanders immediately filed a motion asking him to step down, as well. Between 1972 and 2001, Sanders pointed out, Conley had worked for the district attorney's office. During Conley's time as a homicide prosecutor, the lawyer claimed, he relied upon at least four questionable informants—including a man called "Orange County's most used informant," a habitual criminal who answered to a plethora of aliases and was convicted of felonies in both California and Utah. Since Sanders intended to call Conley as a witness during hearings about law enforcement misconduct in Orange County, the attorney insisted that the judge was not suited to preside over Dan's case.

Murphy claimed that he'd never seen a judge challenged so close to the start of a murder trial. "This is all new territory for us," he said.

Conley maintained that he hadn't used a jailhouse informant in more than thirty years and asked if Murphy and

Sanders could decide on another local judge to consider whether he was biased. "I think it's unlikely we're going to agree," Sanders replied.

In March, a judge in neighboring Los Angeles County denied Sanders' motion. It would take months for Conley to catch up on the motions and filings related to Dan's case.

"Remember, I'm coming in the middle of a movie," he said.

With the focus off of his capability at being a fair arbiter, Conley attempted to assert his authority by scolding both the prosecutor and defense lawyer for bickering in court. "Both of you say the exact same thing—'My opponent is a jerk. He keeps accusing me of untrue things. I don't like him and I don't trust him,' " the judge said at one hearing. He termed the confrontations "child's play."

"Your own personal dislikes for each other have taken over your cool detachment," Conley said. "You have gotten wrapped up in this, and you are angry at each other and you are striking out."

The therapeutic lecture did nothing to ease tensions.

After one hearing, Steve and Sanders were standing outside the courtroom and briefly exchanged greetings. Now that the attorney had failed in his effort to replace Judge Conley, Steve said, it was time "to get this trial going."

He claimed that Sanders replied, "Get the death penalty off the table and we're done."

"I can't do that."

According to Steve, Sanders said, "Then, expect a lot of motions."

Steve viewed the comment as akin to extortion. He wrote a complaint to the California Bar Association, hoping to bar Sanders from the case. Not surprisingly, the effort was denied.

* * *

In August, Sanders filed another motion—this one 754 pages long—along with thousands of exhibits, once again accusing law enforcement of decades of improperly utilizing informants, withholding evidence, and general misconduct.

In a letter to his blogging friend, Dan contended that the lengthy motion was part of a remedy to an engrained virus that affected more than just him. "You can't cure any sickness without finding the CAUSE and removing it," Dan wrote. "People are angry and confused as to why this has taken so long. Well, how about looking then to the REAL CAUSE? This motion is the cure to MANY individual ILLNESSES because it's targeted towards what's truly damaging our justice system: CORRUPTION!"

Murphy had heard every argument of this nature before and remained unmoved. "These are the same allegations Mr. Sanders made in February of 2014, and again, in January of this year," the prosecutor said. "He has added nothing new. These claims were false then and they are false now."

In an interview with the *Orange County Register,* Sanders agreed that the victims' families "have suffered terrible losses, and we empathize completely with what they have been through. However, this case was never delayed for the sake of delay. We continue to believe that the motion was meritorious and was needed to be brought in Mr. Wozniak's case."

Yet for Junko Kibiushi—still wracked with guilt because she had been too busy cooking to give Juri a final hug—Sanders would never understand the taxing effect that the delays were having: "If he were in the same shoes as we were, and if he is a parent, if this happened to his child, I don't know if he would do the same thing

as he is right now. He said in court, 'I'm not a bad person.'
Well, I don't think he is, but understand how *we* feel."

But her frustration would soon come to an end. On October 27, Judge Conley denied Sanders' request to recuse the Orange County District Attorney's office from the case. Three days later, Conley also ruled that—despite what may have occurred during previous investigations—there was no evidence of prosecutorial misconduct in Dan's case and the district attorney's office would be allowed to argue for the death penalty.

"This case cannot be used as a vehicle to right any wrongs there might have been in the past, or to express disapproval of them," Conley wrote. "Mr. Wozniak's potential sentence should not be reduced based on what law enforcement did or did not do in other cases. His case must stand on its own."

After attending more than one hundred hearings over the past five years, Steve sounded both relieved and optimistic.

"We're now moving closer toward a trial," he told KABC in Los Angeles, "which is all we've ever asked for."

Nobody in law enforcement doubted that the defense would file other motions that might further slow the process. But it looked like Daniel Wozniak was running out of options and, sometime in the very near future, he'd face justice.

Or so they hoped.

CHAPTER THIRTY-THREE

Five years after the murders, Leah Sussman still flared when she looked at her daughter, Sonia, and realized that Sam would never be part of the child's life.

"He was such a beautiful man," Leah said. "So kind. When you're with my uncle Steve, and you get past the grief and anger, you see the giving side, the silly side— the man he really is. Sammy was all that and more. It's just sad."

Oddly, one of her most enduring memories of Sam involved another loss that the family suffered: "When my mom died, Sammy was just beside himself. He couldn't even talk to *me* about it. I brought it up a few weeks before he was killed, and he was still so emotional about the loss. That's how much he loved her. That's how much he cared. And that's the way we'll always feel about him."

There were times when she thought about how Sam would have reacted if she'd been the one who'd died early. But she already knew the answer: "Even though he was my little cousin, he'd want to protect me. He had the sweetness of my aunt and the macho, teddy-bear nature of my uncle. I know the way he'd grieve.

"He'd never forget."

On the most somber day of the Jewish calendar, Yom Kippur, Leah went to synagogue, grasping a Velcro patch bearing the name "Herr"—a remnant of Sammy's Army uniform—as she prayed. During visits to her aunt and uncle's home, Leah and her daughter, Sonia, slept in her cousin's old room. "The whole experience alters your beliefs," she said. "It smells like him. You feel like there's actually someone watching you. I have a sense of comfort when I'm in his room. I like it there."

A few miles away, Juri's friend Jessica Wolf moved on with her life but was regularly reminded of the fun-loving girl with the bright makeup and indelible laugh. At times, Jessica would go on Facebook and see a post from Juri's mother, Junko, and just stare at the computer screen. "It stops me dead in my tracks every time," she said. "I just sit there and think about that missing piece of her parents' life. I want to write something back to her that will make her feel better, but there's nothing I can say. It's just"— She paused to find the right word, then settled for "heartbreaking."

After Jessica became a mother, Junko messaged her several times and asked to see the baby. Junko explained that seeing Juri's friends filled her with memories, and a window into how her daughter's life might have turned out.

"I want to go over the house," Jessica said. "I want her mother to meet my baby. But I haven't had the courage to do it yet."

She sat quietly for a moment as a tear slid down her face.

In El Cholo, the Mexican restaurant where Steve and his wife had looked at photos of their son's grave on the anniversary of his death, the parents speculated about how the legal proceedings might play out. Steve mentioned that he wanted Rachel to have a separate trial from Dan, so whatever role each played would be clearly delineated. He feared the prosecution using her as a witness and granting her immunity in return.

"Let them each be tried on their own merits," he said. "And if Rachel is found not guilty, she'll walk. At least, we'll know what happened. At least, we'll know what she did or didn't do."

Steve claimed that he was looking forward to seeing an aggressive Scott Sanders in court. "I want him to be good at his job, and I want him to attack. I want him to grill every one of the witnesses. When I'm testifying, I want him to grill me. I want him to grill Wesley. I want him to grill everybody there. Because then, we can come to an educated conclusion. Then, we can find out some truths."

By this point, Steve had visited Dan a total of three times in jail and was considering going again. "The first time I went, when I told him, 'I know you had help with this,' he said, 'I can't tell you.' The second and third time, he said, 'I did it alone. Nobody helped me.' I didn't believe him, and I told him that I knew he was lying to me. And he said, 'I can talk to you more after the trial.' "

But Steve wondered if he'd ever know the entire story. And, in a bizarre way, he believed that both he and Dan were using the same coping mechanisms. "I try to live my life day to day," he said. "But every day, it bothers me—especially at night, when I'm trying to go to sleep and I can't stop thinking about it. But most of the time, I try not to think about it. I need to keep my sanity. And Dan probably does the same thing."

Yet for Steve it would always be worse. If Dan was

sentenced to death, it would be over. Long after the execution, Steve would have to live with the knowledge that his son's life had been stolen just as it was starting to bloom.

"It's always there," Steve said. "The hurt, the anger, the angst. It doesn't come out all the time. Most of the time, it doesn't come out. But it's always there."

CHAPTER THIRTY-FOUR

In a pressed button-down shirt, his hair and beard neatly trimmed, Dan Wozniak leaned back in a darkened court-room, watching a video of himself projected on a screen for the benefit of the jurors.

The prosecution wanted the court to see the actor performing in *Nine* after Juri Kibuishi was murdered.

"This is not a great moment in my life," Dan's character, Guido Contini, was heard saying with a believable Italian accent. "I have a great many things on my mind."

By contrast, the real-life Dan Wozniak, now thirty-one, appeared carefree, smiling and scratching his beard and occasionally leaning in to exchange a comment with his lawyer Scott Sanders. After five and a half years of delays, Dan was finally on trial, seated at the far end of a long table, facing Superior Court Judge John D. Conley.

At the opposite side of the table, senior deputy district attorney Matt Murphy stood, his hair noticeably grayer than when the proceedings began, leaning on a podium, his eyes transfixed on the image of Dan—bathed in a spotlight on a small stage at the now-defunct Hunger Artists Theatre, singing for the appreciative crowd.

Certainly, the notion of Dan performing in a play after committing a murder was jarring. The videographer testified that Dan—normally a "perfect actor"—seemed "a little bit off" that night, hesitating to the point that some feared he might drop, or miss, a line. Nonetheless, the man onstage exuded so much life, joy, and creativity, it seemed odd that this was the footage that Murphy had chosen to help convince a jury to sentence Dan to death.

But this was not the only video that Murphy planned to show at the trial. And what would follow would be far more damning.

The trial began on December 9, 2015, after prosecutors overcame one final obstacle. On November 13, Conley ruled that Costa Mesa police did not violate Dan's Miranda rights during his interviews when he mentioned the possibility of speaking to a lawyer before quickly changing his mind and continuing to talk. As a result, Sanders' request to have the confession thrown out was denied.

Although Dan was pleading not guilty to the two murder counts, the attorney who'd spent so much time focusing on minutiae offered nothing resembling a vigorous defense at the trial, waiving an opening statement and not calling a single witness. Rather, the defense strategy appeared to be saving its efforts for the penalty phase after the inevitable verdict was rendered.

Still, this didn't deter Murphy from methodically building his case for the jurors.

"It was all about the money," the prosecutor said in his opening statement. "That was it."

On the same screen he'd later use to show Dan performing in *Nine,* Murphy projected a chart outlining the defendant's plan to acquire the funds he desperately needed:

1. Don't get a job.
2. Figure out Sam's PIN, kill him and take his ATM card.
3. Find someone else to withdraw money.
4. Use Sam's phone to lure a woman (any woman) to Sam's apartment.
5. Murder her as a decoy for police.
6. Stage the scene to make it look like Sam did it in the midst of a sexual assault.
7. If questioned, use charm and acting skills to make sure police spend all their time looking for Sam.

The evidence against Dan was overpowering, Murphy said. An invitation for Dan's wedding was found in Sam's apartment, for example. The handwriting on the envelope matched the scrawl on Juri Kibuishi's body. And there'd be more: crime scene photos that illustrated just what the handsome actor was willing to do to other human beings, incriminating Internet searches, and video of Dan initially attempting to outsmart detectives and, finally, describing the homicides, as well as Sam's decapitation, in detail.

By the time that jurors broke for lunch, Murphy was finished with his opening statement. At this pace, it appeared that the trial would end relatively quickly.

With Miles Foltz, Sam's friend from Camp Keating, holding Raquel's hand—and occasionally warning overeager reporters to keep a respectable distance—alongside her sister, Miriam, and her husband, Mike Nortman, Steve took the stand and described the way that he found Juri's body—stripped and adorned with graffiti—in Sam's apartment.

Across the aisle, Juri's parents and other relatives tensed

and listened. By now, they'd heard the story so many times. But it never got easier.

Dan didn't look at the Kibuishis. Throughout the trial, though, he occasionally made eye contact with his blogger, a rainbow-haired woman who sat writing with pencil on to a notepad, several rows behind Sam's relatives. With the exception of Dan's attorneys, she was the only person in the courtroom even remotely supportive of the defendant.

In fact, people who'd once meant a great deal to Dan were lining up against him.

Now a young adult who'd developed interests in photography and film, Wesley Freilich was called to the stand to talk about how he met Dan at age ten while performing in a play at the Liberty Theater. Six years later, Wesley said, Dan phoned him "out of the blue" and offered to pay him a small fee to withdraw money with someone else's ATM card.

Dan's brother Tim also appeared in court. Like Dan, Tim was tall, broad chested, and ruddy skinned, but with a goatee and wavy sandy-blond hair. Before his testimony, Tim made an effort to look over at Steve—now seated with his wife in the front row—tighten his face, and give the grieving father a purposeful nod.

As Dan gave his sibling a wide-eyed gaze—periodically making subtle head gestures—a visibly uncomfortable Tim admitted to battling alcohol addiction, which resulted in a number of arrests and clouded his memory. He also acknowledged that accessory after the fact charges were still pending against him. However, his lawyer had pointed out that, as long as Tim cooperated with authorities, he was unlikely to serve any time.

Shortly after the murders, Tim said, he met Dan at a 7-Eleven near the Camden Martinique apartments, where the actor had promised his sibling a few dollars for gas money. It was there that Dan handed his brother a crate and asked him to transfer it to his vehicle. A few days later, Tim said, he and his brother were at Rachel's brother Noah's home, where Dan removed the tools used in the dismemberment from the crate.

A backpack inside the box contained a gun that Tim believed had been taken from their father—as well as Dan's bloody crime scene clothes, Sam's wallet, and spent shell casings. According to Tim, Dan claimed that the items were tied to a murder that "someone else" had committed.

Within hours of Dan's arrest, Tim told the court, he ran into Rachel outside his parents' house. "She said Danny was in trouble, and he needs an attorney," Tim said. "He's in big trouble."

Too frightened to approach authorities himself, Tim said, he handed the gun to a friend, who turned it in to the Long Beach Police Department—providing authorities with a key piece of evidence against Dan.

When he completed his testimony, Tim fleetingly looked over at his brother. Appearing more amused than angry, Dan stared back at Tim, who quickly averted his gaze and walked briskly out of the courtroom.

In addition to the testimony of the people he once trusted, Dan was being sabotaged by his online searches. These included "quick ways to kill people," "making sure a body is not found," "head gunshot wound," "how far away to hear a gunshot," "how loud is a gunshot," and "how to make a fake thumb print." But the groom-to-be apparently also had his mind on his honeymoon. Among the other items typed during this same time frame were "Mariner of the Seas cruise deals" and "Puerta Vallarta all-inclusive day rates."

In the Internet age, online communication had become such a factor that the judge even incorporated it into the jury instructions. Before being discharged at the end of each day, jurors were warned not to have any discussions "or do any kind of research" about the case.

The one person conspicuously absent from the courtroom was Rachel, still facing her own accessory charges the next month. But her presence was very much felt. In fact, at one point it appeared that Sanders was trying to lessen Dan's culpability by suggesting—like Steve Herr and certain members of law enforcement had suspected—that Rachel had played a larger role than she admitted.

When former detective sergeant Ed Everett—now a lieutenant—testified, Sanders seized on an opinion he'd expressed indicating that Rachel belonged next to Dan at the defense table. Pressing the investigator, Sanders managed to get Everett to say that if a person helps a killer plan a murder that cohort is responsible. The lieutenant immediately qualified the statement by saying that he couldn't prove that Rachel had anything to do with plotting either of the homicides.

"She was being untruthful to us," he explained. "I don't know why."

In particular, he noted that both Rachel and Dan deliberately avoided telling detectives about Chris Williams, the visitor to their apartment who saw Dan and Sam leave together.

Lieutenant Everett also expressed his judgment that Rachel appeared "cold and callous" shortly after Dan's arrest, trying—in Everett's view—to distance herself from her fiancé. In fact, Rachel had told detectives that Dan had a small penis and was an inadequate lover—strange, self-serving behavior, investigators concluded, when they expected more concern about two dead acquaintances. Although she claimed to love Dan and hoped that the marriage would work, she also apparently said that, if it didn't, at least she'd get a nice honeymoon out of the arrangement.

While Murphy may have shared some of the detective's cynicism about Rachel, now was not the time to articulate it. The goal was to prove Dan's guilt. And so, after Sanders was finished with his query, the prosecutor had the lieutenant admit to three factors that suggested that Dan alone was blameworthy. Rachel spoke about the case to her fiancé on the telephone after his arrest—even though she knew that the call was being recorded and could implicate her if she was involved. She also told police about the backpack containing evidence. And shortly before Juri was killed Rachel was scanning the Internet for topless dancer jobs—a sideline she likely would not have considered if she knew that a windfall was on the way.

During breaks from the proceedings, Dan was handcuffed and taken to a holding cell. When the trial resumed, he'd be marched back into the courtroom, bouncing from leg to leg with a grin on his face, seemingly oblivious to the fact that the jury's findings could send him to the death chamber.

Relieved that the case had finally come to trial, the Kibuishis and the Herrs were generally relaxed outside the courtroom. After so many years of exchanging information and attending the same hearings, the parents interacted as friends, sometimes exchanging jokes. One afternoon, Masa Kibuishi returned from lunch with a visible stain on his shirt. As his wife urged him to button his jacket, Steve intervened. "Wear it proudly," he proclaimed as both couples laughed.

After Everett's testimony, Raquel's sister, Miriam, chatted outside the courtroom with Allyson Hathcock, who'd come to court to try to make sense of the man who'd obliterated her family's dream by committing a murder in their theater. Meanwhile, Steve admitted that this was the first time that he'd ever heard the story about Rachel telling detectives about her fiancé's small penis.

Steve's face lit up with a grin. "I hope Raquel doesn't say that about me if I ever get into trouble," he said, chuckling.

It was the kind of line he knew that Sammy would have appreciated.

Whatever levity there was at the courthouse, however, ended the moment that prosecutors decided to play the tapes surrounding Dan's confession. Although the family knew many of the details of what had been recorded, this was the first time that anyone outside of law enforcement received the opportunity to see and hear Dan describing what he did to Sam Herr and Juri Kibuishi.

On the first tape, Dan—dressed in a Hawaiian shirt and khakis after being picked up by police at his bachelor party—was seen attempting to engage in a genial exchange with Detectives Mike Delgadillo and Mike Cohen. At first, the investigators maintained a cordial, nonjudgmental tone, ensuring that Dan remained calm and conversational.

Hoping to explain away his circumstances, Dan admitted to engaging in a credit card scam with Sam—a plot hatched, he said, while the two were drinking. "I was getting married," Dan said. "I definitely needed some money, so I fell victim to that." He sighed for effect.

Why Sam would participate in a scheme that involved tapping money from his own account was bewildering. But

Dan spoke with the earnest tenor of a very convincing salesman.

Dan claimed that he told Sam to wait on the Los Alamitos Joint Forces Training Base and use his cell phone there—in order to create a record verifying that he was nowhere near the spot where the money was withdrawn. But Dan said that he was close by in Long Beach when his former theater student Wesley went to the bank machine. "I said, 'What you're going to do is grab your skateboard, go over there, enter the PIN number, take out four hundred dollars.'"

Once Dan had the cash, he said, he drove to the base to pick up Sam. But if police were wondering why there was video of Dan departing the grounds alone, he offered this account: "As we were leaving, I said, 'Oh, shit. There's a camera. Duck down.' So he cuddled up into a little ball in the corner, and we drove off the base."

That night couldn't have gone better for Dan, he remembered. He performed in *Nine* with Rachel and returned to their apartment. "I took a shower," he said. "We had sex and then, we went to sleep." The next morning, on Saturday, May 22, 2010, Dan asserted that he received a knock on his door. "It was Sam. 'Hey, man, what's going on? Is everything okay?' He's like, 'Not good. We're in trouble.' 'What do you mean, we're in trouble? What happened?' He's like, 'I can't talk about it here. We need to get the fuck out of here. . . . Please, can you get me out of here?'"

Furtively, Sam allegedly handed his neighbor a laptop. "It's sitting in my apartment right now," Dan told the detectives in a voice that suggested that he really wanted to assist them, "on the top shelf of the bookcase with the power cord. . . . It's at my apartment, D110."

The two left the building to go for a ride, Dan said. For

some convoluted reason, Dan claimed, they decided that he should drive his friend's car. They were on the freeway, Dan continued, when Sam disclosed that there was a dead body in his apartment. "Literally, I pulled off to the side of the road." Dan seemed to draw into himself, expressing his dismay in physical terms for the investigators. "I was, at that point, on the 405 going southbound." He shook his head from side to side. "I don't even remember what exit it was. But I pulled off the freeway and I'm like, 'What the fuck? What have you gotten me into . . . I don't feel comfortable with this at all. This is not me. What did you do?'"

According to Dan, Sam needed to be taken someplace where he couldn't be found. Dan agreed to assist, he said, because he realized that he was a "partial accessory" by virtue of being in the same car as a murderer.

Once again, Dan said, they returned to the base at Los Alamitos, this time with two six-packs of beer, to talk privately. According to Dan, Sam had been looking at photos of Juri on the Internet. High and drunk, the veteran became "just emotionally upset," Dan said, and invited her to his apartment. "He asked her for sex. He was pretty fucked up. She said no, and he just shot her twice in the head."

If Dan ever told anyone about the murder, he said, Sam threatened, "I know where you live. . . . I'm going to kill you. And better yet, I'm going to start with your wife."

Listening to the tale in the courtroom, Juri's mother, Junko, shook her head. Across the aisle, Miriam raised her eyebrows and looked at Raquel with disbelief. At the defense table, Dan took on an officious demeanor, slowly turning the pages of the interview transcript while glancing at the screen.

Continuing his story, Dan said that he drove Sam to the Los Altos Shopping Center in Long Beach, where he'd previously worked in the Verizon store. That's where Dan said Sam exited and disappeared into the Southern California landscape. Then, Dan claimed, he found a nondescript street and ditched the vehicle. "His car is a white Pontiac. . . . It's on the corner, not on the corner. It's on a little inlet street." He looked across at detectives, making exaggerated hand gestures. "If you go down Baker, it's the second street in on the left-hand side. That's where I parked it." He asked for permission to stand. "Where Camden is, it's here." He moved sideways toward the door of the interview room. "You have Harbor running this way." He stepped forward. "If you take Harbor up, you get to Baker." He held his hands apart, then shifted his body to the right. "Turn right on Baker." He gestured forward. "You go two streets in. . . ." He sat. "I parked it along the curb."

Like the laptop, the keys were in Dan's apartment. "You can get those, by all means. Absolutely. They're fully at your disposal."

When police came to question Dan, he said, he was anxious to distance himself from the crime. So he made up the story of Sam's mysterious companion with the black baseball cap. Sounding sad, Dan lamented that he lied about the incident to Rachel and his friends. Lowering his voice to an even more contrite tone, Dan added, "I lied to you. . . . I feel like a miserable piece of shit right now."

The goal for detectives at this point was to keep Dan talking. When Delgadillo left the room, Dan turned to Cohen. "I'm so sorry," Dan said. "I'm *so* sorry."

Delgadillo returned with a drink for the suspect and asked to take a DNA swab to "eliminate" Dan from any involvement in Juri's death.

"Eliminate?" Dan asked. Detectives thought that he seemed a bit nervous.

Dan opened his mouth, and detectives quickly inserted a Q-tip into his mouth. "That's it," Cohen said.

"Oh," Dan replied, forcing out a laugh.

It appeared that Dan believed that the police were accepting his tale. Even after the DNA test, he seemed confident and loose. Maybe he really *would* get away with this. When investigators asked him for the spelling of his name for a form they needed to send along with the DNA swab, Dan joked, "I'm changing it to 'Smith' next week."

Then, the mood abruptly changed. "There's more to this than you're telling us," Delgadillo stated. "There's a whole lot more."

But Dan maintained that all he wanted to do from this point forward was cooperate: "I'm done playing games. No bullshit."

Asked if he'd seen Juri's body, Dan countered, "I did not see Julie dead in the apartment. I didn't."

"Were you there when she was shot?"

"No, I wasn't."

"Are you sure about that?"

"I don't even know *when* she was shot."

Delgadillo offered his own theory, "For all we know, you capped Sam after you capped Julie?"

"Excuse me?" an apparently piqued Dan shot back.

At this stage, detectives were sure that Dan had played a direct role in at least one of the murders. "You're telling us this story about taking Sam here, there, and everywhere else," Cohen said. "And it doesn't jive."

". . . Because why?"

"Why do you think?"

"I don't know, Officer," Dan replied, indignantly raising his voice.

"You're an actor," Delgadillo cut in. "But you're not that good of an actor."

Dan contemplated the words, rubbing his beard. Eventually, he repeated his contention that he only had assisted Sam out of fear.

"How was your life in danger?" Delgadillo asked.

"He *threatened* it," Dan shouted.

Time dragged. At one point, Dan was given a lie detector test and failed. But he still seemed convinced that he was going to be able to talk his way out of police headquarters—until investigators told him otherwise.

"So I'm staying here?" he asked in disbelief.

"Absolutely," Cohen said. "You're arrested for murder, okay?" He clarified the charge. "Accessory to murder. That's what you're being arrested for."

No longer composed, Dan frantically tried cutting a deal. "I will talk to you about anything if it gets me to my wedding on Friday. That's what I will promise." He jerked his head, shifting his gaze from Delgadillo to Cohen. "Anything you want."

"The truth?" Delgadillo challenged.

Dan scratched the back of his head. "Oh my God," he muttered, bringing down his arm and slapping his thigh.

In the midst of the turbulence, Detective Sergeant Everett entered the room and joined the conversation. "This is your chance to clear the air," he flatly told Dan.

"For what? If I'm not going to be there on Friday, my life is over."

The detectives appeared unmoved. "Where is Sam?" Everett demanded.

"Not without a bargain that I am out on Friday."

"We're not in a position to bargain. . . . There aren't any bargaining chips at this point."

Dan rested his head against his hands. "Here's what I'm saying," he declared. "I'm saying that each one of you and Sam has killed my chance of happiness."

Ultimately, Dan conceded, "Yes, I saw the goddamn body. Is that what you want to hear?"

Detectives were uncertain whether their suspect was being honest or sarcastic.

"We want to hear the truth," Everett answered.

"That is the truth."

"Then, tell us what happened." The sergeant decided to take some creative liberty and pretend that he already had the results of Dan's DNA test. "How'd your DNA get on her?"

"'Cause I was right over her body."

". . . DNA doesn't just fall off."

"I don't know."

According to Dan, Sam had led him into the apartment and pointed out what he'd done to Juri. Dan said that he noticed two bullet wounds.

Everett quickly noted that even the detectives would not have been able to tell how many times the victim had been shot; all they would have seen was bloody, matted hair.

Yet Dan was thinking quickly. He'd noticed two shell cases, he pointed out, and advised Sam to dispose of them.

Over the course of several hours, Dan entered and left the interview room numerous times. Jurors watched the drama unfold on the screen in the courtroom, taking particular interest in an exchange between Dan and his fiancée.

Police had brought Rachel there, hoping that she might encourage Dan to speak. But because of her monotone delivery and dramatic background, it was unclear whether the pair was engaged in a genuine interaction or theatrical performance.

"We're not getting married," a dismayed Dan told Rachel.

"Yeah, obviously," she responded.

In a soft voice, Dan reiterated that he and Sam were involved in a fraud scheme. "Sam came down and knocked on our door Saturday morning," he said, "took me upstairs, and I saw Julie and her body and everything."

Everett cut in, informing Rachel that police suspected that her fiancé might have caused Juri's death. "It's not a production," the sergeant stressed. "It's not a play. It's real life. There's a twenty-three-year-old girl dead, and I don't know if he's responsible for it." Rachel had been brought into the interview room, Everett said, "as a courtesy," to hear the facts directly from Dan.

"Thank you," Rachel told the investigator in a measured voice.

The conversation seemed to go nowhere. Rachel accused Dan of lying to her, and Dan did not elaborate on anything he previously told detectives. "Is there anything else you want to say to me?" Rachel asked Dan.

"Don't hate me," he whispered.

Rachel looked at the investigators. "There's nothing he can do at this point to make it better?"

"Absolutely," Everett responded. "He can be truthful with us and truthful with you and truthful with everyone."

All Dan was willing to divulge was, "I fucked up."

"Yeah, you did," Rachel concurred. She again focused on the investigators. "What if, I mean, if he does everything that you guys want . . . ?"

"It doesn't change anything," Everett answered. "I can explain to Julie's parents what happened. I can explain to Sam's parents what happened. I can explain to Wesley's mom what happened. I can explain to whoever, his parents, what happened. He doesn't care."

"This is a dream," Rachel said softly.

"It's not a dream," Dan pointed out.

When the conversation ended, Rachel left police headquarters while Dan was escorted back to his cell.

A short time later, Dan called her cell phone from jail. In court, jurors listened to the audiotape. At times, it sounded as if Rachel was cognizant that the conversation was being recorded, particularly when she lectured Dan that people were more important than money— "We never need money," was her exact line. "We need to be good people and just have each other"—and he never should have gotten involved in a credit card scheme with Sam.

"What did you do?" Rachel pointedly asked.

"I helped Sam cover up some stuff and get some drugs. I didn't murder anybody."

But Dan appeared to become unglued when Rachel mentioned that she was going to tell detectives about a recent discussion with Tim Wozniak.

"Tim says that he had evidence with him, or he knew where it was or something."

"Then, I'm doomed," Dan replied, almost whispering.

"What?"

"Tim said that?"

"Yeah. Do you know that Tim has some evidence?"

"Yeah." There was silence for a moment. "Oh God, oh God, oh God."

If the items were turned over, Dan said, "I'm dead. I'm really dead."

"Babe," Rachel replied, "you're already dead."

Once again, Rachel asked Dan to tell her exactly what he had done.

"I think you know what I did. . . . Babe, listen to me. I'm going to do something, and you're not going to see me for the rest of my life. Do you understand that?"

"No, no."

Dan told Rachel that when she found out the truth she was going to hate him. "I'm not a good person."

She promised to return to the jail to see Dan another time. Before hanging up, she told him, "I love you."

*   *   *

Jurors next saw footage of Daniel in the interview room again. He was still wearing his Hawaiian shirt and khakis, but the clothes were wrinkled and he appeared disheveled and disheartened.

When detectives had picked Dan up at his cell, he was staring through the bars with his blanket slung over his head. "I want to talk to you guys," he promised, "and tell you guys everything."

By now, Delgadillo seemed weary of the suspect and anxious to finally learn what had occurred. "Pull yourself together," the detective demanded. "Pull yourself together right now."

Once again, he read Dan his rights.

"I'm crazy and I did it," Dan said.

"You did what?" he was asked.

"I killed Julie and I killed Sam."

"Okay. All right,"

"I killed them both."

No longer double-talking, Dan systematically explained the way he shot Sam with Daryl Wozniak's .38. "Sam is decapitated. He's at the military base. In the theater."

"In the theater," Cohen repeated.

"If you go up the ladder from the theater, his head and hands have been decapitated, as well as his arm that had a tattoo."

"And you did it?" Delgadillo questioned.

"Yes."

"Okay. Are the body parts there?"

"No.

"Where are they?"

"The Nature Center in El Dorado Park, in various locations . . . I decapitated the body so it wouldn't be found."

Sam had been killed, Dan said, while bending to help Dan lift an object. "I shot him once, and then, he was still alive. . . . He was still talking, saying, 'I need help.' "

Instead, Dan admitted, he fired a second time. "He started bleeding. He wasn't moving. He wasn't talking. He was in a pool of blood, started to form."

On the screen, Dan's head dropped and he appeared to weep. But it seemed that no one in the courtroom felt sorry for him. The victims' families watched the confession with a mixture of melancholy for their loved ones, hatred for the killer, and resentment that the whole process had taken this long.

"I'm sorry," Dan told the police. "The truth is I've been slowly going crazy and becoming a pathological liar, and I find it hard to tell the truth."

Dan recalled meeting Juri outside Sam's front door, where they each expressed concern for their friend. Once they went inside, Dan asked her to enter the bedroom. "Did you see this in Sam's bed?" he asked the unsuspecting victim. "He was really freaking out over it?"

When Juri leaned forward to contemplate the imaginary item, Dan said, "I put two bullets in the back of her head."

He noted that Juri "was wearing like a crown tiara" when she died.

Listening to the recitation of the manner in which her daughter was killed, Junko Kibuishi quietly cried in her seat as a relative rubbed her shoulders.

Bizarrely, Dan told detectives that he smiled and laughed when he returned to the base and cut off Sammy's head. Asked why, he responded, "I don't know. I reached a point where I couldn't even believe I was doing this."

In another era, men like Delgadillo and Cohen might have grabbed the suspect and thrown him against the wall, administering a minuscule dose of justice of behalf of the Herrs, who had had to endure the suspicion of authorities when their son was simply guilty of helping the wrong person move some items, and the Kibuishis, whose pure-hearted daughter was sacrificed in the most evil manner possible. But this was 2010, and everything was video-taped. So on camera, Cohen awkwardly attempted to give Dan some sort of positive reinforcement for admitting his crimes. "For once in your life, you can say you told the truth and feel good about it," the detective said.

Before elaborating on how he obtained plastic bags from a café to transport Sam's body parts, the killer released a squeal that sounded like a blend of a laugh and a sob.

When the confession tape ended, the families and jurors poured out of the courtroom. Miriam went around a corner and buried her head in another woman's shoulder, crying loudly. Jurors gingerly passed her on the way to the bathroom.

Several reporters had tears in their eyes. One stared straight ahead and mumbled, "I don't believe in the death penalty, but he should fry."

Steve paced the hallway with flushed skin. "This is what we had to wait for?" he raged. "This trial should have happened three years ago. Look at the tape. It's all there. And we had to wait."

He took a breath. "When this is over, I want to talk to Sanders, let him know *personally* what he did to us."

On December 16, a week after the trial started, the verdict came in. As the victims' relatives held one another and cried, Dan stared straight ahead, betraying no emotion when the courtroom clerk announced that he was guilty on all counts.

Matt Murphy said that he was looking forward to the penalty phase, when he could describe the victims "as people" to the jurors considering whether to sentence Dan to death. As Murphy stressed in his closing arguments, "There's nothing wrong with his head. It's what's wrong with Daniel Wozniak's heart."

Tracy LeSage, the lawyer who'd try to convince the court to spare Dan's life, pledged to place the emphasis on subtleties. "Everything is more complicated than it is," she said. "Nothing is cut and dry."

As Dan was led out of the courtroom—with no sign of his parents in court, and his brother, fiancée, and even the kid who once idolized him as a theater teacher firmly in the enemy camp—Steve returned home and posted the following Facebook message: "Raquel and I want to thank all Sam's Buddies for their support these past five and one half years. . . . What can we say, guys? Raquel and I love you all! Great big hugs!"

CHAPTER THIRTY-FIVE

The penalty phase began on the first workday of 2016, after jurors had been able to distract themselves with Christmas and New Year's. With the merriment of the holiday season behind them, they were once again confronted by the gory, disturbing details of the double homicide.

While the purpose of the trial had been analyzing the evidence and determining guilt, the penalty phase would consider the circumstances of the crimes, Dan's frame of mind at the time of the killings, and the sense of loss suffered by the families of Sam Herr and Juri Kibuishi.

"We spent a lot of time talking about Daniel Wozniak," senior deputy district attorney Matt Murphy told jurors in his opening statement. "Now in the penalty phase, you get to think about those people."

Although jurors would vote on whether Dan received life imprisonment or the death penalty, the final decision was ultimately made by Judge John Conley. However, the process was largely a formality. The likelihood of a California judge rejecting a jury's recommendation in a capital case was next to impossible.

From the moment Dan's attorney Tracy LeSage stood to make her opening statement, it was clear that the defense had no intention of diminishing the atrociousness of the crimes. Rather, LeSage stressed that it was important to "keep an open mind." Dan's once-promising life "took a tragic detour," she said, urging the jury to "be fair to both sides."

But viewing the case objectively was going to be a challenge. While the families may have questioned the authorities' behavior earlier in the case, Murphy now emphatically spoke on their behalf. Dan's actions were "as cold as it gets," he insisted, reminding jurors that they'd seen the tape of Dan describing how he'd laughed while cutting off Sam's head. Juri, according to the prosecutor, had been used as "a ruse . . . a stage prop." All because Dan needed funds for his upcoming wedding. "That is the most base, vile motive of all. It's money."

The fact that Sam was killed simply so Dan could drain the veteran's combat pay was "enough to come back with the death penalty," Murphy said. But he stressed that jurors should also remember that the killer sang and danced alongside his fiancée in *Nine* while planning Juri's demise. "Folks," Murphy said, "that is disgusting."

If the facts weren't strong enough, Murphy called friends and relatives of the deceased to underscore the prosecution's position. Miles Foltz choked up while recalling how, while serving in the U.S. military together, he and Sam each pledged to be the best man at their respective weddings. It was Sam who introduced Miles to his wife—at the pool of the Camden Martinique complex where the killer and victim both lived. When Sam's murder precluded him from making good on his pledge, Miles said, Steve stood in for his son.

Wistfully, Miles spoke about the way Sam always dressed up wherever they traveled—to the point that their

Army friends nicknamed him Suit. Because of Dan Wozniak's actions, Miles claimed, he could no longer slip on a jacket and tie. "I don't wear them anymore," he testified. "The only thing I think of when I put them on is how much I miss him."

There could have been more testimony about Sam's loyalty, humor, and bravery in Afghanistan. But prosecutors were cautious. Before the trial, Scott Sanders had submitted a list of witnesses related to Sam's 2002 murder case. Judge Conley had struck down the effort; this was about Dan Wozniak's guilt, not a series of proceedings in which Sam was acquitted. But the threat loomed. If there was too much emphasis on Sam's attributes, the defense might again attempt to attack Sam's character by invoking the death of Byron Benito.

Still, Miles was allowed to speak. As a veteran himself, the judge appreciated the bonds formed in combat and believed that Miles was entitled to express his bereavement over a comrade taken prematurely. While observers could sympathize with Miles' longing for his friend, the testimonies of Sam's and Juri's families unfettered a storm of wrath, along with sorrow.

Steve described viewing his son's body in the mortuary. Although parts of the dismembered corpse were stitched together, one of the arms was still missing. Sam's head was wrapped to hide his mangled, unrecognizable features.

"Animals got to my son's body parts in El Dorado Park," Steve said. "They found him. They ate his flesh off him. They urinated on my son."

While people in the gallery cried, Steve spoke about his need to remember what Dan Wozniak did after Sammy was already dead: "In my mind, I see him whacking away at my son's head. I see him sawing my son's arm off. I have trouble sleeping at night because when I turn off the TV, that's what I see. I don't want to forget the heinousness of this."

Murphy prodded Steve along. "As time goes on," the prosecutor asked, "the pain and anger, does it go away?"

"No, I visit my son's grave every week. The one thing I get out of this is that my anger and my hate has grown exponentially."

Juri's brother Taka admitted to struggling with guilt for allowing his sister to leave his side to go to Sam's apartment—where she was shot between the right ear and the tiara that her brother had given her. "I had so many chances to stop her," he said, crying. "I protected and helped her her whole life, and she was with me [before she was killed]."

Like Murphy, Taka was revolted over Dan's admission that he slaughtered two people in order to secure the money that Sam had saved while serving his country. "We lost Sam and Julie for something so simple," Taka said. "It's pathetic."

The best character witness the defense could produce was a fellow inmate, convicted gun burglar Daniel Munoz, who recounted that Wozniak was "generous" in the way that he shared soup in jail, and "talked about God."

According to Scott Sanders, Munoz's testimony showed "what a person can become after they do something terrible. Is he redeemable? Is it a life that has value?"

Murphy appeared unimpressed by Munoz. "I'm surprised that guy didn't get arrested again going out of the courthouse," he cracked.

Like at the trial, Sanders mentioned Rachel's possible involvement in the crime, but this time he presented four witnesses—including one of the former Disney princess' ex-boyfriends—who described her as "manipulative" and controlling."

Mentioning the disdainful view certain detectives had

toward Dan's fiancée, Sanders characterized Rachel as the mastermind of the relationship—and, possibly, her boyfriend's offenses. "She's the smarter of the two by far."

During college, an acquaintance told the court, Rachel had engineered a scheme to embarrass a friend in a love triangle. "It's this weird thrill about putting people in dangerous situations," Sanders said.

In another instance, jurors heard a story about Rachel encouraging an associate to steal. "She does get off on stuff she shouldn't get off on," the attorney said. "I say Rachel Buffett is relevant to the circumstances of the crime."

Argued Sanders, "The circumstances of the case include who you're with and what these effects are on your life. Think about who's in the household and who he's marrying."

But Murphy was dismissive of the strategy. "They need a villain," he said, "someone to point a finger at to distract you from what Daniel Wozniak did." Even if Rachel was involved, the prosecutor stated, it wouldn't lessen Dan's blame.

"That man made a series of decisions that brought us all together," Murphy said, motioning at Dan, "and Rachel is not responsible for what he did. Each one of us is responsible for our own decisions."

Even so, Sanders told jurors in his closing arguments, there was enough uncertainty about the nature of the relationship that Dan should be spared the death penalty. "There are no words to describe the horrific nature of the crimes," Sanders conceded. But a sentence of life without the possibility of parole, he continued, would still honor the lives of Dan's victims.

Despite his acumen for filing motions, Sanders' words did nothing to persuade jurors. On January 11, 2016, after slightly more than an hour of deliberation, the jury recommended that Dan Wozniak be put to death.

Orange County District Attorney Tony Rackauckas had never seen a jury return a swifter decision on capital punishment.

For the first time during the proceedings, the condemned looked concerned. He glanced down for a moment, blinked several times, and gazed over at the jurors. When he looked down again, he appeared completely on his own. No one rubbed his back or whispered reassuring words in his ear. Although they were seated beside Dan, both Tracy LeSage and Scott Sanders appeared to be thinking about other things.

"The lies, the dismemberment, the murder for money—it was all terrible," one juror told the *Orange County Register.* "Sam was a veteran who served in dangerous places and then, he comes to Orange County, the safest place you would expect, and he's killed. It was so unnecessary."

Upon hearing the jury's recommendation, the Kibuishis grasped one another and cried. Junko reached for the chain around her neck and held on to the ring that Juri was wearing on the night she died.

"Now, it's over," Junko said.

Taka stood back and watched the media swarm his grieving parents, along with the Herrs, as they spilled from the courtroom into the hall, marveling at the way both families had managed the press while remaining focused on the details of the case.

"It was so, so, so, so long overdue," Steve told the cameras. "But I can start healing."

The normally reticent Raquel spoke, too. "It's a closure," she said in her Argentinean accent. "I feel like a ton off my shoulders."

Junko described the recommendation as "closure to our nightmare chapter." She'd later say that she wished there was an even stronger penalty than lethal injection.

While there was no joy in knowing Wozniak's fate, hearing the word "death" uttered in the courtroom filled the mother with "relief and thankfulness to the jurors for understanding our pain."

Noted Steve, "It was very therapeutic to know that twelve people from different cultures, genders, and beliefs found that certain crimes can be so heinous, so terrible, that death is the only justifiable option." He laughed to himself. "And in just over an hour. I was expecting days of deliberation. I mean, this is a guy's life. But it only took them an hour to see what we'd been seeing the whole time."

In fact, the decision had not been an easy one. Several jurors privately cried over their conclusion that a man deserved to have his life taken away. But two images persuaded them: the photo of a grief-stricken Steve and Raquel at their son's funeral and a picture of a younger Juri engrossed in a dance performance.

Jury forewoman Jenny Wong made it a point to hug both families. She told the media that the jurors never thought that Rachel Buffett's influence had any effect on Dan's guilt. "We felt that was just smoke and mirrors," she said. In fact, there was an "utter lack" of mitigating factors in the murders.

The families left the Superior Court building determined to continue their relationship away from lawyers and detectives and court officers. Junko told the Herrs that she remembered Juri describing Sam's kindness and realized that he'd inherited his goodness from his parents. Steve spoke about Juri's "golden heart."

One day in court, Steve had brought the Kibuishis a present: hundreds of flash cards that Juri had made to prepare Sam for an anthropology exam. "And he got an A, by the way," Steve said.

Over the course of five years and seven months, he'd

come to know a lot about Juri's family. When they weren't discussing the case, Junko was frequently expressing admiration for the Los Angeles Lakers. To Steve, the immigrant's dedication to a team that, at the time, was battling the Philadelphia 76ers for the worst record in the NBA was thoroughly charming.

In fact, it was reminiscent of the "hopeless romantic" description often attributed to Juri.

"This tremendous tragedy," he said, "brought love between two families."

Despite the sentence, Steve was aware that he was going to continue to see Daniel Wozniak in court for years to come. In California, all death sentences are automatically appealed. Of the nine hundred people sentenced to die in California since 1978, only thirteen had actually been executed, as of this writing. In fact, no one had been put to death in the state since 2006, when a judge ruled that a three-drug lethal injection combination was "inhumane."

Authorities now advocated for a one-drug injection that could restart the process. Nonetheless, on average there was a twenty-five-year gap between death sentences being imposed in California and carried out.

"I'm very realistic," Steve said. "The years of appeals are to be expected. I've always known this, just as I know that I probably won't be around if and when Daniel Wozniak is actually put to sleep. I'll be at all those hearings. But, right now, I'm grateful that I got the best that I could get."

Although he'd fantasized about confronting Scott Sanders during the trial, Steve now wanted to shift his attention to other matters. After all, Sam would have wanted his parents to pursue activities that relaxed and enriched them. Steve continued working out and played golf once a week. Since childhood, Raquel had been playing accordion, guitar, keyboards, and flute—all by ear. Now she wanted to take formal lessons.

As two former teachers, the Herrs spoke about volunteering their time to help children. Despite everything that they'd endured, they were grateful for the years that Sam had been in their lives and for the people who had come to comfort them since his death.

They still wanted to give something back.

"This has taken a huge load off our backs," Steve reflected. "Before this happened, we were very private people. But we didn't hide our feelings with each other. Sam was a big lug. But we'd always hug him and kiss him. We still feel like doing that. But now, it's in our hearts."

EPILOGUE

Even today, after a number of newsmagazine shows have done in-depth programs on the Dan Wozniak case and everyone from jurors to former associates to psychologists has weighed in on what motivated him to kill, the story continues to confound. Although the specifics of the slaughter are relatively clear, there's still the question about how Dan went from a perspiring goofball who bought too many drinks for strangers—and whose fiancée mocked his manhood to investigators—to a pitiless executioner who laughed as he decapitated a friend.

In 2012, after hearing so many theories and characterizations from others, I decided to visit Dan myself and see if he could tell me something that everyone else was leaving out.

I arrived at the Orange County Jail on a Saturday afternoon, as the case was snaking its way through the court system. Once inside, I was instructed to leave my cell phone, tape recorder, notepad, and pen downstairs. After passing through security, I was escorted to the same room where Steve had his conversations with Dan. Like so many others, I immediately noticed Dan's open face and smile.

Dan hadn't been expecting me. He'd been waiting for his parents, he explained. When I arrived, he pointed out, "they probably got bumped." Yet he betrayed neither anger nor disappointment, acting as if I'd dropped in at his apartment on a busy day.

I explained that I was trying to make sense of his situation. How does a seemingly sensitive actor—well regarded by friends and the parents of children in his theater classes—end up facing the death penalty for the murders of two people? Dan nodded and smiled as I raised these topics, then responded apologetically.

He couldn't speak, he told me, unless I went through Scott Sanders. The attorney was apparently unhappy that Dan had chosen to appear on *Lockup* and didn't want the suspect granting any new interviews without a consultation. Once Sanders approved a meeting, Dan said, he'd be happy to talk. Maybe we could even speak in a room downstairs, he suggested, where there was more space and we wouldn't have a Plexiglas barrier between us.

Dan appeared relaxed and detached from his drab environment. He couldn't possibly be this enthusiastic, given his circumstances. His manner reminded me of a waiter in an upscale restaurant—maybe a handsome guy like Dan, with some theatrical training—exuding false gusto while chirping out the dessert specials.

He said that he was "flattered" that I'd come to the jail to work on a book about his case. He'd like to cooperate, he said, because, as an actor, he respected writing as an "art."

As I uttered my good-bye, he cheerfully stood and waved.

Sanders declined my request to formally talk to Dan and opted not to be interviewed for the book. But I sent Dan a letter, reemphasizing my desire to hear his side of the story.

I received one reply, written neatly in pencil on lined paper:

Thank you for the kind letter. It found me well. I remember you vividly and, as I said before, I have a great deal of respect for artistic individuals including authors, such as yourself. . . . Are you writing a book just about myself or is there going to be multiple individuals? What are your overall aspects of the book (positive or negative)? . . . If you do plan to visit me again, I . . . ask that you extend me the courtesy of prearranging your visit also through my lawyer. Due to the nature of my alleged charges, I hope you understand my extreme caution in talking . . . or disclosing anything about my past or present conditions.

I wrote Dan one more letter, attempting to answer his concerns. It was returned to me with a red stamp just above the address: "CONTENTS NOT ACCEPTED."

Yet even if we had engaged in a lengthy letter-writing exchange, I'm dubious that he would have provided that one nugget of truth that helped me understand him.

Does he ever think of Sam Herr and Juri Kibuishi as people who lived and loved and meant something to others? Surrounded by inmates incarcerated for the most malignant of acts, does he believe that he's in his element or project an artist's superiority toward his fellow killers? Has he confessed his sins to the God he purportedly worships, or does his self-flagellation end after he chastens himself for getting caught?

There are so many questions I still have for the storefront-theater actor. But I'm not sure he'll ever remove his stage makeup.